FORGIVE US OUR PRESS PASSES

A Society Editor's Prayer

by

Majie Alford Failey

Guild Press of Indiana, Inc.
6000 Sunset Lane   Indianapolis   Indiana   46208

Library of Congress
Catalog Card Number: 92054441
© Copyright 1992 by Majie Failey
All rights reserved, which includes the right to reproduce this book or portions thereof in any form whatsover.
Hardcover Edition   ISBN 1-878208-13-6

Thanks...

To all of the newsmen and women of the staff of *The Indianapolis News* who made it "The Great Hoosier Daily" that it was in "my day" and to their standards: excellence in every part of news reporting.

PREFACE

"Stories happen to people who can tell them," said the novelist Thomas Hardy. And, if I may paraphrase, adventures happen to those who can share them. In the journey of this book, Majie Alford Failey shares stories and adventures which you will remember after you relive them with her. I do not know if Majie has a gift for being in the right place at the right time—or a special gift for making any place where she is turn into the right place. In either case, she is going to take us with her in vivid memory to some interesting places, inhabited by some unforgettable people.

Majie has lived a spacious life, at home in many roles—writer, journalist, citizen, wife and mother. Blue eyes sparkling with energy, vision, humor, determination, she has made herself at home in many worlds. She makes others feel at home, too. You will feel at home in this book, as Majie shares with disarming candor and vivid details vignettes of the worlds she inhabits, and some of the worlds she has covered as a journalist. You will find familiar faces in the world of this book—Carl Sandburg and Kurt Vonnegut chief among them—and you will discover new faces and voices, thanks to Majie's chronicles as a journalist, a keen observer and a thoughtful friend.

"Wherever you are, it is your friends who make your world," Henry James observed. Majie helped brighten Carl Sandburg's world during a difficult time in his personal life. She is too modest to tell you that, but as a biographer of Carl Sandburg, I can testify that she gave him hospitality and understanding. He felt at home in her house, with her family. He took special delight in the company of her children, during a time when he felt estranged from his own grandchildren. He and his family welcomed Majie to Connemara, their home in the Blue Ridge Mountains of North Carolina.

It was our mutual friend Peter Sterling who introduced Majie and me. He knew of her friendship with Sandburg and of my work on the Sandburg biography. I often thank Sterling and Sandburg for leading me to Majie, who has enriched my life and sustained my work. Friend to friend and writer to writer, Majie and I have shared our personal and professional journeys. Much of the time the telephone is the lifeline of our friendship; writers are usually not the best correspondents, for writing is what they *do* all day. Majie and I also have that special radar that good friends share—somehow knowing just when there is a crisis or celebration in the personal landscape. Geography has nothing to do with it. Majie has the gift for friendship which Harry Golden described in Carl Sandburg:

> *Carl was all-out for friendship. If Carl was your friend and your son was sick, Carl worried as much as you. If you were depressed, Carl wanted to share your depression as he wanted to share your exhilaration when you were happy. Carl, as a friend, accepted your entire universe, every star, jungle, and person in it.*

Substitute *Majie* for *Carl*, and you have some idea of the kind of person she is.

Better yet, step into her universe and see for yourself. Read, listen and enjoy as Majie Alford Failey shares adventures, escapades, joy, disappointments, insights, wisdom—Life.

Penelope Niven

FOREWORD

Carl Sandburg said to me, "Oh my God, girl, don't get into writing, it's a lousy racket." That was in 1944. Kurt Vonnegut said to me, "Hey, have you finished your book?" He was waiting for it. That was October 9, 1991. Now, as I finish this, I wonder which one was right.

What do I know about writing a book? Well, I was a journalist. My job was to write stories, mostly society stories, for *The Indianapolis News* in the "Golden Years" when it was one of the ten top evening papers in the nation.

I wrote about social events, meetings and weddings. Boring! Then I slipped into columns, not so boring! Ironically, I always loved writing anything that wasn't society, and I loved just being on a newspaper. Seeing my own name under a headline was like having my name in neon lights blinking on a theater marquis.

But there was more. Being a newspaper writer gave me a full education in people. Hadn't I learned this in college? Absolutely not. I learned it by being a newspaper writer and a team member whose duty it was to report accurately and honestly.

Later, that background and the fact that I was a special correspondent for a good many years kept my oar in the waters of writing. I kept clippings of my stories, old letters and files of articles by other writers, columns by some of my favorite colleagues, now gone, some by young writers of today, and these all went into my storage tank of subjects to write about when I was gone from the paper and had taken up motherhood and community service.

Causes were good for me and helped me take my education even further. My favorite "cause" was abused children. It was easy for me to relate to that. A champion of the underdog? Yes, you could call me that. There were a lot of things that *were* unfair, *are* unfair and always *will be* unfair. We are all related to "unfair" somewhere in our lives. I was good on that subject.

So my files are popping out of every drawer in the house, and my "experience file" is ever larger now, forty-four years after I left *The News*. "Why don't you write a book?" they asked, and I guess it was natural.

"They" was anyone who cared about my subjects. I have a good team of "theys" too, because my life has been enriched by scores, hundreds of famous and not-so-famous people. Carl Sandburg is one of the famous ones. When I was a junior at Indiana University, I spent a weekend at the home of my roommate while Sandburg was a guest there. Her parents had brought him to their small town of Union City to speak at the high school. I heard him speak and I heard him sing his ballads in that deep, non-melodic voice, so rough and raw that it was beautiful. Then I got to know him in his various attitudes and moods by just standing around the kitchen talking and drinking coffee; by sitting at the family dinner table with him while he tossed his white mane from side to side; by seeing him working in his bedroom in the morning when he polished his "program." You could not help but watch how he approached strangers who had been invited in to meet him after his talk and note that he was very interested in whomever he spoke to. His theme through life was always people. "The people, yes."

Another "they" is lifelong friend Kurt Vonnegut, for whom I have deep affection and regard. The last time he came to our house I found myself, as usual, going to get groceries and pushing some clothes over in the closet in his room so he could hang up his suit. My children and their children were having a case of the sweats over "What should I say to him, Mom?" I told them, "Just say hi, or hello, or hocus pocus."

The wonderful part of these "famous" friendships that have somehow come into my life is that they seemed so normal. That's the way those friends wanted it. We learned this when Carl Sandburg was coming to our house in 1956 and my husband went out and bought the Lincoln volumes. "Why in the world did you do that?" I queried.

"I have to bone up on Lincoln so we'll have something to talk about when he comes!" he responded.

Talk about being on the wrong track! It wasn't that kind of visit at all.

Another of the famous, but everyday "theys" are my cousins, by marriage—the great grandchildren of General Lew Wallace who was the author of *Ben Hur*. Actually, they are my husband's first cousins, and their whole lives have proven that they have inherited some things from Lew Wallace—his love of adventure, his jewels from the days he served as minister to Turkey, his writing genes.

There are many more "theys" in Indianapolis and beyond who wanted me to tell about my experiences, especially as a working newspaperwoman. There's a lot to say about the press these days. When I started *Forgive Us* . . . I had many more benign feelings about the press than I have now. During the past year I have been insulted by the hearings of Clarence Thomas and Anita Hill and enraged by the lack of ethics our governing cast of chararacters showed in those hearings. I am also angry at media people who dig up whatever dirt they can to hurt public figures. And since there is plenty of rage to go around, I have been outraged at the press for ridiculing Dan Quayle and at the entertainment industry for using him as a target for their "sicko" wit. Writers who use unfair and untrue ridicule to entertain are not worth the name of journalist, and the nit-wits who laugh at them are worse.

In the late 1940s and '50s I was very proud of being a member of the working press. Today, I am not so sure about being proud. I don't think we intended to set any standards. We were, after World War II, a vast sea of young people who had to try to put our worlds back together to get over our losses of husbands and friends and fathers and brothers. It happened to be a very opportune time to be on a newspaper staff—all who were left back on the home front did what they could to keep things going as normally as possible. We had a job to do, no matter who or what we were.

But beyond that, there was purpose and hope in newspapering in the U.S. then. Great American dailies were looked up to as trend-setters and opinion makers. To write for a newspaper then, it was paramount to be accurate and report the news honestly and fairly. What has happened to our honorable profession? I think we have, in the words of that old Hoosier saying, dropped our pants in front of the outhouse, and the flash bulbs are flashing. And we deserve what we get.

Perhaps it's the whole society that has dropped its pants—or at least its standards. Kurt Vonnegut and I talked about our youth and our high school days and the behavior patterns of young and older people alike in the society of the late '30s and '40s. We may have been naughty, perhaps mischievous, but not cruel. We did not shoot an innocent person out of the driver's seat of the car for getting in our way, or for giving someone a dirty look, as is happening on our freeways today. We didn't shoot our parents for not giving us the car. And we would never even believe a kid would throw a huge rock off an overpass and hit a windshield, blowing it to bits and killing someone.

I do not want to be considered a nostalgic old fogey, because I'm not one, but some things need to be said. We seem to be on automatic pilot to destruction as we approach the turn of the century, and nobody is willing to say much about it. People of my generation can't understand all the senseless violence. We didn't even talk back to our parents because they wouldn't give us the car. In fact, we did not talk back to our parents, period! Even if we had a car! There's a perspective here that needs to be looked at. Something is wrong, and it needs to be fixed.

We may not have liked our rules but we obeyed them. We accepted what our parents dictated, since they were the mainspring of our security framework. We said a prayer in assembly in the mornings in school, and if someone did not agree to that, he could put his head down on the desk and count to one hundred and backwards, who cared? We were following the rules in a principled society that knew where it had been and where it was going, and saying a prayer in school was a good way to start the day.

We are now known as "Mid America," conservative, secure in our values, middle-of-the-road thinkers, anti "way-out" and pro just good old Midwestern practicality and good sense. So be it!

The press itself today panders to the unprincipled violence, materialism and disrespect that has become an epidemic in our society. Maybe my look back at Indianapolis, the Hoosier State in general and some of its people, and the press in particular may help us get a little focus. So hold onto your hats—and your press passes—and press, you'd better look out! It's my hope you'll have to change your ways!

Dedication

To my children,

Bill, Cathy, and Gaye

who put the music in our Sandburg saga.

1

GETTING STARTED

Anderson, Indiana was the family home of the Alfords, and I guess it was a fine enough town to get started in. Historically, my mother's ancestors, the Heatons, are an integral part of Henry County, pioneers who came by covered wagon from Springfield, Ohio. The National Road was at that time a rough trail beset by roots and fallen trees. Later it became a brick road going from the East through Ohio to Richmond and Cumberland and Greenfield and Indianapolis and westward.

I have a souvenir brick from that national road. Mother's Heaton family ancestors founded and settled Knightstown, Indiana. When my mother died, the papers kept calling me for details of the Knightstown connection, and I realized I had in my possession a complete genealogy of the Heaton family. It turned out to be a historical bonanza of facts and memorabilia—letters from the original settlers of Knightstown. They belong to that town, and I have promised to send the old papers one of these days to Thomas Mayhill, the Editor of the *Tri Town Banner*.

Mother's parents came eventually to Anderson, where Mother's father was a dentist, and they lived in Anderson until Mother was sixteen. Then they moved to Indianapolis.

My father's family, on the other hand, were latecomers to the Anderson area, arriving in the 1890s. My grandfather, William John Alford, was from Beaver Falls, Pennsylvania. Grandmother Nellie Crane had been from Hacketstown, New Jersey. These two had met at a Presbyterian youth conference in Atlantic City.

When they married, my grandfather set about analyzing the country to see what section would be best to settle down in, raise a family and provide him resources for financial success. He settled on Madison County, Indiana, because a gas boom had just gotten under way there. One of the new industries that was developing was the glass business. Cut glass—I can give you cut glass in all shapes and sizes. My grandmother's house had one wall full of it!

True to his nature, my grandfather made it in Anderson and became one of its industrial pioneers. He was a determined man, and he valued a college education above all things. I'm sure that this was because Grandfather, William John Alford, was himself one of seven children and the son of a very poor Presbyterian minister of the old school. On Sunday the family walked six miles to church and back, because nobody, including horses, could work on Sunday as far as they were concerned.

When Grandfather was working in the summers, planning to continue his job after high school graduation, his own father had said, "I can't leave you any money when I die, but I can give you a college education. Quit your job." Grandfather was a real success, and he was convinced his college education was responsible for that.

He had a scholarship to Geneva College, and he made sure that all of us, his grandchildren, had a college degree. He was even more insistent about our graduating from college because only one of his own three children had ever made it through.

My grandfather Alford went to work for the Anderson Shovel Company, which was finally bought out by the Ames Shovel and Tool Company. Eventually, though, the invention of the steam shovel affected the business and he decided to push on.

Early on, then, in 1902, my grandfather, ever looking for wider opportunities, returned to the East to establish a paper company in New Jersey. Grandmother could not bring herself to leave, and remained in Anderson for the best part of her life. Why? My cousin says it was because she was unable to part with the past, her children's growing-up time, and particularly the grave of her youngest child, little Eddie. He had died at three years of age in Grandfather's arms and was buried nearby, in a grave she thought was too near the river and might flood. Grandmother never quite recovered from the shock of losing her baby, and so she stayed near where he had lived and died.* "I'll buy you the finest house in Greenwich, Connecticut, if you will only come east," Grandfather is supposed to have said at one time. Grandmother would not leave, though, and spent her days in the big, comfortable house we loved to visit, and where the only car she ever learned to drive was an electric one.

So Grandfather moved to the East, and my uncle William J. Alford, Jr., and eventually my father went to the Hill School in Pottstown Pennsylvania. Grandfather planned to take the boys in on the new and successful paper box board business he was running.

Soon a new business in New Jersey was not enough for Grandfather, and he decided to expand by buying with two partners a board mill in England, on the Thames River. It was necessary, I suppose, for him to be there in England, and he stayed there much of the rest of his life, returning often to supervise the other family enterprises.

He probably should have been supervising his boys more. My uncle Will, older by some years than Daddy, was having to regulate his wild little brother "Chap," who was getting into trouble already with the more sophisticated lifestyle of the East—the parties, the trips, the fast cars.

Uncle Will graduated from Hill School and then Yale; in the case of my father, though, the administration at Hill recommended that he seek education elsewhere. Eventually Chap was taken into the New Jersey business, the Continental Paper Company. At some point my father returned to Anderson to marry my mother, whom he had known since elementary school, and he brought her east after the wedding.

I was born in New York City while my father was working for Continental Paper. My parents lived in the Roaring Twenties, and their own lives mirrored to a degree those of F. Scott Fitzgerald and Zelda and Ernest Hemingway in all their glory. That glamorous era meant grand times, wild abandon, short dresses and cloche hats and dancing the Charleston. Money flowed and so did booze. Prohibition only made drinking more adventuresome. Stutz Bearcat was symbolic of the sporty, classic cars; raccoon coats and silver flasks were the flashy emblems of the abandonment of Victorian values.

Could the materialistic yuppies of today be a replay of those days? Oh, what a carefree prelude to the end of the world that was coming. These wild days and this "go-to-hell" attitude could not last, at least for my

---

*Many years later, there would be another little Eddie. A namesake was born to my father and his wife in the '50s. My half brother and my children are contemporaries. "What shall we call him?" they queried. He became "Little Uncle Eddie" and belongs to all of us.

parents. My father, already beginning to drink too much, impressed his father as ready to "fall" in the more sophisticated East, and he sent Herbert back to Anderson, where it was hoped a more serious attitude towards life would prevail for the young husband and father. Soon after that our small family moved to Indianapolis to stay.

My first real memory in our new home in the Hoosier state involved a party with much singing and laughing and piano playing. My father came to the back part of our house and fetched me, sound asleep and protesting, from my little bed, carried me down the long hall to the living room and held me up to see what was going on. A man was playing the piano. I rubbed my sleepy eyes and wondered what this was about at two o'clock in the morning. Daddy said, "I want you to listen to this man play the piano. He's going to be famous some day."

Does a four-year-old give a hoot if she is listening to Hoagy Carmichael playing the piano at some ungodly hour? At her house when she wanted to be in her warm bed? Talk about putting Hoagy on the spot! And now, each summer in Harbor Springs, Michigan, a man named Randy Carmichael plays the piano and sings some of his father's songs in one of the clubs. He's a familiar sight there, a favorite, riding around on his bicycle and waving at everyone.

When I first heard him perform up there, I told him I had something for him. I had just opened the mail and found that an Indiana University alumni magazine had arrived with a soft disk recording of "Chimes of Indiana" in it. I put it in my purse as I went to the club for dinner, and when Randy was about to play, I handed him the disk. He had never heard of the song, which his father had been commissioned to write for Indiana University. And I told him briefly that I had heard his father play as a sleepy-time gal in Indianapolis long ago.

To return to the Roaring Twenties. My grandmother, then, was heading the Indiana branch of the Alford household. She was not alone, because she lived with her daughter and her granddaughter, my cousin Barbara. We lived with them, too, in Anderson for a while, as my father was trying to decide what to do with his life before moving to the state capitol.

His father, then fully aware that my dad was an alcholic, gave him suggestions about how to succeed and sent him a ticket to come over to England, alone. "It is not a good idea to take small children on a boat," Grandfather said, so my dad crossed the ocean on a liner without Mother and me to see if he could learn the operations of the British company.

Apparently not, because with my parents' move to Indianapolis, he became involved in the new automotive sales business that was flourishing there. Many fortunes were being made—the Marmons were marketing new cars, taking them as far as Pike's Peak to test. Donald Test and Ralph Boozer and many others were in the automotive parts business. It was my father's opinion that Indianapolis could have been Detroit and manufactured cars in a permanent and lucrative way. The Franklin, the Cole, the Stutz, the Packard, the Deusenberg—they were all here. If Indianapolis had been on a waterway, it might have been a "Detroit."

Daddy bought a new car every year, because he wanted to experience what was novel. He was very talented in engine mechanics; he should have been allowed to follow his own bent instead of his father's plan. The Indianapolis schemes failed too, and by the time my sister was five, my mother had decided the marriage would not work.

Mother stayed in the home at 3311 North Meridian. We never fully left Anderson in our hearts, I guess, though, and every Sunday we would return to Grandmother's house as we always did, the four of us. My choice childhood memories have always been the time I spent there, and once each summer, my aunt and uncle, the W. J. Alford Jr.'s and their four boys, my cousins, and their Finnish nanny Mary Matilla came from New Jersey to be with us. My cousin Barbara Hill, who lived with her mother and our grandmother, and my sister Joan and I had one fine time with one and all. We delighted in the fact that Barbara called her mother "Mama" and our grandmother, "More Mama."

My grandmother's house was pure delight. She raised chickens in the far back of the property where no one would notice. After Sunday school and church I would notice, though. My grandmother's hired "man for all seasons" would pick out two or three chickens and wring their necks. My fascination was watching those chickens jump around with their heads off until they flopped on the ground once and for all!

The scene to follow every Sunday included wonderful fried chicken dinners, prepared to perfection by the cook who never saw what I saw on the "back forty," (or did she?). It did not dampen my taste for fried chicken and the biscuits that went with fresh apple butter and all the other trimmings, served always on Sunday.

There were nice, simple things to do. We could take wooden clothespins and make hollyhock dolls, using the spreading flower blossoms as the dresses and buds for the heads. We also tried stealing flowers from neighbors' gardens and making little bouquets which we then sold to them! And we pulled up every green onion from the plot of a neighboring uncle who was short and plump. When he chased us, three little girls dropped spring onions in a telltale path all the way from his house to Grandmother's.

The house at Anderson was happy and comfortable. Behind the garage was a big playroom that intrigued my little sister and me. My cousin Barbara, though, always thought of mischievous things to do, and I always caught the blame from my aunt. One thing she could not control was the giggling. If Barbara and I sat next to each other, we would look at each other and giggle. If we were moved to opposite ends of the table, we could look at each other from far away and giggle more. If I was blamed for the laughing, it fell on deaf ears.

Childhood memories stay bright and fresh in your mind, liked dried flowers in a bouquet. In the distance were railroad tracks that went up a steep grade near our grandmother's house. My cousin John still recalls lying in bed in Grandmother's house. "Till I die," he says, "I will remember waking up about three a.m. and hearing those freight cars on the old Nickel Plate, or was it the B&0, chug, chug, chugging up that hill and wondering if it would make it. An eerie sound in the still of the night at Grandmother's." And so it goes. The roots climb and wind around and grow down and grow out, and then they seem to reach back to where they started.

My mother's family's hometown of Knightstown, Indiana, had its bright spots too, and we kept returning there for visits after we had moved to Indianapolis.

I can remember my great-grandparents in the home where Mother was born. It was the homestead for several generations, and it had a two-story barn and a big grape arbor which produced years and years of jars of grape jelly. Unlike Grandmother Alford's big house, which was solid and traditional, this old house rambled over uneven floors. It had a musty smell. The whole house seemed to spill into the big back yard where a child could wander around and peek into an old cinder alley, where there was a barn with a real upstairs.

In addition to the musty smell, the house had a faint odor of natural gas, which Grandma used to heat and cook with. That place had the feel of a venerated landmark, which it was. No matter what went on, though, each thing that happened was always accompanied by a feeling of love, even adoration for the petite, charming only child who had grown up there and for her two daughters when they came. Every relative Mother had doted on her, and we always left Knightstown feeling loved, appreciated, and vociferously thanked for taking the time to make a visit.

I do not remember ever passing a night in Knightstown. Nor did I ever realize that these Heaton people and their forebears were responsible for Knightstown's being there in the first place. I knew very little about it until 1978, when my mother died. She had tried to give me her family's history, but I was always too busy to go into it in depth. I suppose mothers in their wisdom know that sooner or later, whether they are around or not, their children will discover, and then finally be consumed by, the history they once shunned, usually after it's too late to ask any of the principles for their impressions in person.

Mother was left with the rearing of two daughters in the Indianapolis of the late twenties and thirties. She was an artist, tiny, really adorable, with a size three shoe, very talented and versatile, and she did a good job as a single parent in an age when that was an unusual state of affairs. She made her own clothing because she could not be fit—no one made size four in those days. She went into the French Room at Ayres and copied the styles to make patterns for herself, making swish dresses of gold lamé and suits and coats of lovely fabric.

Grandmother Alford and my aunt and cousin made frequent trips in from Anderson to go with us to the great store with the corner clock, which through the guidance of the Ayres family had become a great pleasure for all of us, and a tradition for the town. Before going to Ayres, which was the good part, my relatives and Mother and I would have to do the bad part, which was go to the Hume Mansur building for doctor's appointments of one sort or another.

It was *the* office address for a majority of the doctors and dentists, the place in which my grandfather, Dr. Heaton, had his practice. As cars drove up to deposit their patients for the orthodontists or the pediatricians or the internists, the same wonderfully friendly doorman in his brown uniform would help us out and we would head for our favorite elevator operator. We would disembark, walking across black and white tile floors to the smell of disinfectant. All that courteous service helped take the sting out of what was ahead behind the frosted glass doors.

Many out-of-towners came to Hume Mansur to make a day out of it. When I was a small child they could ride on the interurban, which had little stands looking like guard booths all along the roads in and out of Indianapolis and its environs, or drive the spiffy Ford cars into the big city. After the unpleasantries came the pleasantries at the tea room. There would be a long line, a delicious luncheon of chicken velvet soup and frozen fruit salad with celery seed dressing or the Ayres special huge sandwich plate.

It was an experience to remember for children. A gracious waitress leaned down to take your order from a special menu—things like "Peter Rabbit Luncheon," "Donald Duck's Favorite," "Piggy Wiggy Luncheon," or "Little Miss Muffin's Bowl." Then, a child could pull a toy out of the treasure chest while doting Grandma and Mama, wearing their white gloves, looked on.

L.S. Ayres Downtown was closed after the May Company bought the department store landmark, and I think those people who closed the store and its wonderful tearoom didn't know what they were doing. It doesn't surprise me—how could a high-tech, computer-oriented corporation feel what real gentility was like? There was a huge public outcry when the institution died. Kids and adults who had loved the pleasure of downtown Ayres didn't care anything about a printout that showed loss instead of profit. The kids would have grown up to be good customers, and public relations would have been at an all-time high.

When we were little kids and had finished our trip to the tearoom treasure chest, it would be on to the fourth floor, where children's clothes were waiting, and delightful Mrs. Yeager would wait on us.

On the women's floor my grandmother would pick out pretty frocks and coats and call for her favorite dressmaker alteration person to give her a fitting. It was a profitable day for us; Grandmother always treated her granddaughters to new shoes.

The house at 3311 North Meridian Street—the Woodsmall house we had moved into—was a huge, red brick duplex, now torn down. It was a convenient, wonderful location within walking distance of almost everything. It was one block from Tudor Hall, right around the corner from School Sixty, my beloved grade school, a block from Shortridge, and next door to our church, the Trinity Episcopal Church (then the Church of the Advent).

When I was a young child that wonderful "New Northside" neighborhood went all the way to 38th Street on the north, east to Fall Creek and the neighborhood just south of the Fairgrounds and west to Crown Hill. It was part of a very set pattern of neighborhoods I came to recognize little by little as Indianapolis.

Indianapolis had started at White River in the early 1820s, then soon became centered around the Circle, which in early days was just a round village green in the middle of what was a field of golden wheat, bowing to the breezes. Near the Circle were a few houses and pigs and a church or two. By the Civil War the town had spread a mile square and beyond and had a population of approximately 19,000. By the 1890s, it occupied what is now the Lockerbie and Old Central Neighborhoods, College Corners around Thirteenth and College, where Northwestern Christian University (now Butler University) and the "Old Northside" south of Sixteenth Street.

By the turn of the century fashionable houses had moved (along with Butler) east into Woodruff Place and Irvington and north along Meridian and nearby streets. Working class people moved into the near eastside, in places like Brightwood and Spades Park and west of White River and in a new factory district just south of Washington Street.

The Southside, a few streets further out, was the home of up-and-coming immigrant groups—the Italians, with names like Mascari, Catalano and Caito, and the Germans. George Theodore Probst's book *The Germans in Indianapolis* lists names like Henry Severin, Herman Lieber, Nicholaus Jose, William Kothe, Clemens Vonnegut and Henry Schnull among the early arrivals. Making money in fast-rising firms like Vonnegut Hardware, Schnull & Company and Chas. Mayer Co., the Germans who originally clustered just north and especially south of Washington Street spread out into all the neighborhoods.

German families intermarried. Mrs. Franklin Vonnegut was Emma Schaal. Mrs. George Vonnegut was Lillie Goeller. ("Receives Tuesday," as the Blue Book of the twenties said.) Mrs. Kurt Vonnegut was Edith Lieber.

Kurt Vonnegut's grandfather Bernard Vonnegut was a well-known architect to the German community (and beyond). The Schnull House, now a landmark on Meridian Street, was designed by Bernard Vonnegut, and so was the Athenaeum, also known as the German House, one of several German institutions (the Turnverein was another) where fine German food and activites bound the community closer together. Kurt Vonnegut's father Kurt, Sr., was also a leading architect in the city, designing such buildings of note as Indiana Bell Telephone.

Coming close in numbers to the Vonneguts were the Frenzel family, whose most prominent men went into the banking business. My mother went with Otto N. Frenzel to Shortridge High School, and I went to Tudor Hall with his daughter, Eleanor ("Dickie"). Otto Frenzel seems to me to be typical of a good generation of civic leaders—bastions of integrity and business acumen. He was one of the builders of Indianapolis society, one of a generation which has faded from the scene today.

Second generation German families and other "old families" of various types from Indianapolis had come together on North Meridian near Shortridge when we lived there; they became our friends. The Glossbrenners, the Brant family, the Coffin family, were in this neighborhood. Mr. and Mrs. Walt Hiser lived across the street from us when they were first married. The Geupels and the Jewetts and the Freihoffers lived down on 36th Street. The Binfords' home was at 34th and Central in a block of lovely homes with large, manicured lawns.

But though our neighborhood was the most "well located" for everything, it wasn't really the most elegant neighborhood. In fact, this "New Northside" addition to the old original town, the area around Shortridge, was just finishing its period of fine living, and many families were already choosing houses further out from the city. Broad Ripple had been annexed to the city in 1922, and brand new houses were scattered all the way out to White River there and beyond. Developments with such names as Meridian Highlands, Shooters' Hill, Spring Hill, Crow's Nest, Woodstock, Golden Hill and High Woods developed in the mid-1930s, and lovely homes spread out along roads leading north, particularly along Kessler Boulevard and the streets around it, Meridian and College Avenue, and the avenues to the east of it. In the thirties, also, many fine new residences began clustering around the new Butler University, which had just made another move from Irvington to Fairview Park on the canal at 4600 Sunset.

The Shortridge neighborhood was a grand place to grow up. School Sixty was considered a fine school, along with Sixty-Six and Seventy a little further north. People would pay tuition to have their children come to School Sixty. The Glossbrenner girls, for example, lived far from hub of things out at Oaklandon. Their father brought them into the "good school" every morning, and when school was over, Mary and Caty came to their grandmother's house at 32nd and Meridian, now the site of Winona Hospital.

How comfortable it was for a child along those tree-shaded boulevards! I could walk or ride my bike anyplace freely. It was a nice, wholesome life. Those were the days of live-in help, and we kids became acquainted with the help at the homes of our friends too. They were a part of the households. We had a maid who did everything including cook for us for five dollars a week.

My mother was busying herself in the "horsy" life of the city. A great group rode horses at Arlington Stables—the Metzgers, the Moggs, the Bohlens, and the Hamiltons were involved with her, going to horse shows, showing horses, going to Lexington to horse sales. I have always said some others of that generation and I grew up in a barn. Madeline Pugh (who wrote for the "I Love Lucy" show) had a sister who taught us all to ride. Audrey Pugh was a wonderful equestrian at Arlington Stables. She always seemed to be the hub of the activity.

I began to be aware of clubs in Indianapolis about this time. We belonged to Woodstock Club and earlier to Highland Country Club. What Mother was really interested in, though, were art clubs, and she loved art history. She wrote and edited the *Hoosier Equestrian*, the Indiana horse magazine, doing all this out of necessity when, after the divorce, my father stopped sending rent money. She remained single. For years she was a popular guest at parties and events, and her painting and her horses and her writing and work kept her busy and independent.

School Sixty I attended twice. The first time was in the first and second grades. Mrs. Ray, the principal was so regal, looking as if she were Queen Elizabeth's mother. But Grandfather Alford returned from England after second grade and was unhappy to find I was in "public school." He insisted I be put in Tudor Hall, and off I went for third and fourth grades.

It was supposed to be a girls' school, but to my amusement I found boys there. Today some of the movers and shakers in Indianapolis don't like to be reminded that in early days Tudor had boys to the fourth grade and they went to a girls' school, but they did. Tom Binford was there then, along with Bill Elder and Bob McGill.

But by fifth grade I returned to School Sixty and rejoined a group that was well formed by then. Bud Gillespie and I would ride our bikes all around that wonderful neighborhood. Our friends included Weir Cook's daughter Susannah. My father knew Charles Cox and Eddie Rickenbacker and other World War I flying heroes, some of whom were also now in the automotive business. We would go out to the airport as children, when it was just a few, bare fields, and fly in the little light planes.

Louise McNutt, daughter of Paul V. McNutt, the governor, attended School Sixty, along with John Jewett, whose father was once mayor. What was good about Indianapolis public schools in the twenties and thirties? Exceptional teachers, good sound values, solid families which sent hard-working students to school in the first place. Strict but loving discipline. Psalms, poems, lots of history, and prayer. I thought, and still think it is very important to start the day at school with a prayer, and I think taking it out of the schools was a loss. We were taught right and wrong as strong qualities, and we were afraid to do wrong.

Finally, Grandfather came in again and asked his inevitable question, "Where are the children in school?" Mary Jane was happily ensconced in School Sixty again, thank you. But that was not good enough for the man who valued "getting ahead through education" above all else, and I found myself again at Tudor Hall for the eighth grade.

Tudor Hall Grade School was a very difficult, a very different place from the comfortable friendly place I had just left. It was fun to me only when we went out for kickball or some other sport; otherwise it was an ordeal.

In the first place, the student body was mostly made up of not-too-friendly young ladies. One should never change schools in the eighth grade if it can be avoided. Eighth graders, it seems to me, are usually snobbish and unfriendly, and the Tudor girls had an exaggerated case of eighth-grade-itis. These tomboy-types were well able to take advantage of the excellent athletic program, and I wasn't particularly good at this. There are always cliques formed, with strong bonds, by that age. It is hard enough to come in as a freshman, but it is a better starting point. If my parents understood this social barrier, they were powerless to convince my grandfather that "fitting in" is important, and so is belonging. The only word I can think of to describe the girls in my class was snobbish. Typical, early teen, self-oriented people!

I recall that in that eighth grade at Tudor Hall I had fallen in the halls and sprained my ankle, and many girls just passed by, hardly looking at me as I lay there in pain. One good Samaritan, Selena Alig, helped me up and went to call the teachers. I have never forgotten that good deed.

My situation at Tudor Hall was complicated by the fact that by the eighth grade I had turned into a shy, sensitive girl definitely affected by my father's problems. My father would turn up unexpectedly and not always in very good form and embarrass me in front of my friends. It seemed to me that he was constantly getting married and divorced, and that confused my sister and me. He did not contribute to our support all the time. I could not concentrate on school work, and I hung my head down to avoid people, and I developed colitis. I was emotionally injured.

I missed my old friends and the comfortable atmosphere and personal support of the public schools terribly, and one day in the middle of my sophomore year, I went on strike against Tudor Hall. I said I was not going back to Tudor Hall, no matter what, and I went to my room and stayed there, crying. Mother knew I didn't get emotional very much, so she took it seriously, and went to see Fred Hadley, the vice-principal at Shortridge.

I went to Shortridge in the second semester of 1938, and there were the genuine people of School Sixty plus many new friends to welcome me. I had actually been taken into a social club while I was still at Tudor Hall, and so I knew the girls, the PD Club, and this became an important part of my life from the moment I joined it, and still is. Some of those girls were Marge Geupel, whose father was a busy contractor in Indianapolis, Barbara

Masters, whose father was a leading opthamologist in town, Mary Jo Albright, later Mrs. C. Harvey Bradley, and Helen Marie Madden.

Time was passing. In the ten years since we first moved into the area around Shortridge, the "best neighborhoods" had definitely moved north (and farther out in all the sections as a matter of fact, but I lived in the Northside). By 1939 most of my friends lived in the area from 52nd and Meridian, Washington Boulevard, and Pennslylvania and Illinois north to the canal. Williams Creek and Meridian Hills at about 8000 north were beginning to develop even beyond that, and houses stretched to Road 100 (8600) in some cases.

The Geupels, for instance, had built one of the early homes in Williams Creek. Because Mr. Geupel was a builder, the home he built for himself and for other members of his family had floors of reinforced poured concrete. He was a preminum builder of exacting standards. The Geupels started a trend, and people began to take lots around them in Williams Creek.

But Shortridge High School was still the mecca for the Northside teenager. The school, which was built at 34th and Meridian in 1927 and occupied in 1928, was in my time a living legend, and all of us there knew and believed that it was one of the three top high schools in the country (*New Trier* and Cincinnati Withrow being the other two.) Teachers were outstanding role models, as well as giving us a fine education. My favorites were Mrs. Browning in math and Mrs. Martin in Latin. After school almost everyone's special hobby or interest could be served by Mythology, German, Radio, Spanish, Equestrienne, Fencing or a score of other clubs.

Over 130 social clubs met outside of school in the boys' and girls' houses. The SUBDEB Club and EUVOLA were, of course, the "top two" of those sorts of clubs. They had "legacies" which were passed from mother to daughter or sister to sister. Many of the girls' clubs were junior sororities—operating with elaborate rush teas and pledging and formal and informal initiations. CORPSE was the male equivalent of the "big two" girls' clubs.

I did not feel that we were snobbish; our periphery of friends was wide. Maybe others felt different, but to me everyone was interested in everyone else, everyone felt part of the pride which was Shortridge in the heyday.

But the center of my friendship and life was the group of "Precious Darlings." The letters PD in the beginning had stood for "Pixilated Debutantes," and I guess you would have had to have lived as a young person in the late 1930s to understand that. It smacks of the sort of devil-may-care, bratty sarcasm that many of us teased each other with. It sounds odd today, so for years we have referred to ourselves as "Precious Darlings."

Marjorie Ann Geupel was the first president, and the weekly dues were a dime. We were typical congenial adolescents of the time, wearing white canvas jackets called beer jackets. They fastened with gripper snap fasteners, and they carried as many friends' autographs as was possible, embroidered, finally by our mothers. I don't think we were drinking much beer at the time, so the name didn't really suit. We were pledged never to tell another soul about what the name PD meant, so we were shrouded in a mystique that only teenagers could appreciate. Finally the *Shortridge Echo* revealed the forbidden news, causing a minor uproar.

Running around in our Spaulding saddle oxfords and bobby socks we believed ourselves not only chic, but also enormously innovative, respected and admired. Popularity was gauged by how many dates we had and how many boys from the stag line cut in at the ever-present dances, and how many of these "boys" we counted as "really keen." That made it hard to ever decide just whom we really liked, and being fickle was just what drove them crazy.

We drooled over the big band leaders and played "Moon River" till our parents blew the whistle and put out the porch light. If we spent Friday and Saturday nights in our own homes, we were either being punished or sick!

There was a certain sense of security about operating in the PDs. Our parents called a meeting early on and made up a set of rules to keep us in line and on the same track. We knew they cared about us in a positive way and it made us feel united and gave us a feeling of equality and fairness. One of us surely has a copy of those rules, and President Marge still has her beer jacket. Through all of these years this remarkable group has stayed in close touch, and we all still call Marge by her rightful name—"Prez."

Each of us went to college, we all got married, at least once, and we all have grandchildren now. Since we lived through World War II we prayed fervently that our children and theirs would never see a war. Throughout forty-five years we have kept in touch with a news and caring network as strong as a chain link fence. We are fiercely loyal to each other.

The first of the Precious Darlings to die has just "crossed the bar"— Barbara Masters Laird, wife of the former Secretary of Defense, who showed the Precious Darlings all around Washington a while back. Her death was an enormous blow to those of us who had remained close. And hard to accept—even though, as we youth-loving "golden girls" know, one of us had to be the first.

I think other groups in Indianapolis have had the same experience with high school friends of that era—whether it was at Howe or Tech or Broad Ripple, friendship born in the thirties and forties was deep and good. Indianapolis is that kind of town.

I marvel at all we found to do in those days before TV and long activities after school. We went to each others' houses constantly and listened to the big bands, Artie Shaw, Tommy Dorsey, Glen Miller on the "platters" we bought at downtown record stores.

Our high school crowd, boys and girls, lived under a value system that is probably as different from the present one for young people as the sun is from the moon. Kurt Vonnegut, Skip Failey, and the girls I've mentioned, really all of us, grew up with Victorian-bred parents. It was a bit painful, because as a spinoff of the Victorian mores, parents did not really talk to children in close ways. Respect was the foremost quality and unspoken love the token.

If someone was close to you, there was a lot of understanding, not a lot of verbalizing. My children say, "Bye, Mom. I love you." They say it so easily, and I think it's good they say it. Still, Victorian value systems had good points: true respect, courtesy, a sense of right and wrong and the notion that one existed to contribute something to society. We picked that up even at the age of sixteen, along with the fact that fun had better be wholesome.

How easily we all moved about in Indianapolis in those days. Every Saturday we would get on the bus and go downtown to Ayres and have lunch and then go to a movie—at the Circle or Lyric or Loews or the Indiana Theatre. Wow! That was fun, browsing around the Circle, gawking at people, "messing around," as we called it, dropping in at the dimestores or Craig's Candy Store for a Persian Nut sundae.

In the early teens our parents would take us to Riverside Roller Skating Rink and we would roller skate to the music. There was a big rotating, mirrored silver ball there too, and we began to notice boys as we whizzed around the circle, watching the reflections rotate on the floor.

Riverside Amusement Park was also a place to go to when you were too young to date yet. There the "Thriller" and "The Flash" zooped us up and down the steep, but rickety old hills. Once I got my tailbone loosened on one of those roller coasters, and it never was the same. There were the dodge-'em cars, the fine ferris wheel and the fun house, where sailors used to take girls across the front to have the fun-house operator blow their dresses high with hot air from whatever secret place he controlled it. "Don't wear a full skirt to Riverside," mothers used to warn their daughters. Then at the Mill Chute you rode in the dark through a tunnel, hopefully with a boy, and then plunged down a roller coaster hill to water below, with a big "whoosh."

And when we got our drivers' licenses we went out to eat—to Eaton's. Eaton's was at 38th and College Avenue. Eaton's, along with the Hawthorne Room, the Tee Pee, Hollyhock Hill and the Mandarin Inn, were the great Northside eating places. We drove in our convertibles or junkers to the Pole at 56th and Illinois, which was supposed to have sold more Coca Cola than almost anyplace in the country. We cruised, and that was one of our real hangouts.

We were outdoorsy, too, learning to play tennis and swimming in the summer, at the country clubs but more popularly at the Riviera Club, where seas of girls and some boys lay flat on the boards drenched with iodine and baby oil in the hopes of creating a glorious tan, and eating frosted malts and fifteen-cent hamburgers at noon.

Not many of the "crowd" worked in the summer. We loved to visit Lake Maxinkuckee at Culver, swimming and having hot dog roasts at the cottage of Mary Jo Albright, for instance. The Academy! Culver Military Academy. Summer school with sailing, woodcraft camp, riding camp, uniformed cadets. Dances once a week—all every girl's dream of heaven. Mothers sitting above it all in the balcony, watching all the happy faces below. And the behavior, sometimes not heaven.

The dances were all "dreamy," romantic and fun. There were marvelous evening dances for young people starting at about the eighth grade at the Athletic Club Ballroom, and the Indiana Roof, with its whirling ball of glass bits that caught the light and spun it around the room, and the Riviera Club. Some daring souls went out to Westlake, where the really big bands played, while cool breezes blew the long pageboy hairdos and the tails of the boys' zoot-suit coats.

Delightful tea dances occupied Friday or Saturday afternoons sometimes. We had pretty silk party dresses, and the hours were from three or four p.m. till six or seven. Punch, tea or later on sherry would be served and everyone practiced formal manners learned at Mrs. Gates' Dancing Class at the Propylaeum.

Indianapolis has always been a town where entertaining was done mostly in the home. There were lovely dinner parties, and teenagers learned the art of party-giving by having, or observing formal dinners with candlelight and several-course meals. I have a scrapbook of invitations for events from high school and college. It is loaded with invitations to all sorts of parties and open houses, and its faded corsages and dance programs show the place formality played in most occasions. "Mr. and Mrs. Frederick Appel request the pleasure of your company at a tea dance on Monday, the 22nd of December from 4 to 6 o'clock at Woodstock Club." Even boys kept albums.

On the invitations are many of the same names you see now, the Aligs, the Hollidays, the Elders, the Johnsons, the Tests. They speak of a time of the last of the dance cards, and carnations tied to wrists with pink bows and fragrant gardenias in the girls' hair and slow, dreamy dancing to "Stardust."

In the late forties and fifties, debutantes were presented in families such as the Ayres and Ruckelshauses, who hired the Athletic Club or Columbia Club and arranged for big-name bands to play, while champagne flowed from the fountains and the stag line gawked at beautiful young women being introduced to society. Indianapolis wasn't always New York, though, and there was sometimes something a little self-conscious about these affairs.

During the Shortridge era, at about the same time we PDs were enjoying life, the Farragut Literary Society—a small but special group of young men—organized themselves. The Farragut Literary Society (FLS) considered themselves to be the intellectual elite of the school—more brains than brawn. They were not your usual macho jocks; even in high school they had well-planned aspirations to become lawyers, bankers and writers, which they did do, and today still maintain wry, weird senses of humor and great imaginations.

Kurt Vonnegut was probably only one of the high school "intellectuals" who was scorned and ridiculed by the sports' stars—the lettermen in Shortridge of those days. The Shortridge football squad were City Champs in '39 and so ruled the world. You "had to be a football hero to be in love with the beautiful girls"—and lacking that you weren't good for anything else, either, so they thought. One day one of the lettermen pushed Kurt into a locker. Kurt got even, not mad by helping found the Farragut Literary Society, which has taken its place in the halls of fame for high school madcap adventure in Indianapolis.

I have been told that during the basketball tournament one year, the huge event for which Hoosiers are famous and which always created a monumental traffic jam, certain members of the Society "borrowed" a few purple funeral procession flags from a local prominent mortuary, stuck them on their cars, turned on their headlights and headed for Butler Fieldhouse. They had no problems with traffic, getting to the tournament with plenty of time to spare. This is just a little example of how clever these quiz kids were.

How did the club get organized? I pleaded with George Jeffrey, who is a clever writer and gifted Thurber-like poet, to try hard to remember the founding of the Farragut Literary Society. Here's what he finally said.

> *You might say that membership in the Farragut was an honorary thing. On the other hand you might not want to say this. The original motto, "Damn the torpedoes, full speed ahead," was taken directly from Admiral Farragut's battle cry at Mobile Bay. But after Skip Failey got off the troop transport in England he changed it to, "People are our most valuable asset."*
>
> *Unlike its companion organization, Societe Nationale Francais, membership in the Farragut was divided into classes. Gold Seal membership was the highest class. Red Seal was the lowest. So that nobody would get a big head, membership classifications were determined in inverse order, according to one's literary ability. As a consequence Skip and I have always been full Gold Seal Members.*
>
> *Kurt Vonnegut was originally a Gold Seal member, but I think he slid down to Blue Seal after he was published. Ben Hitz was Red Seal, although he could easily have gone Blue Seal had he not gone into banking and usury.*
>
> *Most of the records were destroyed in a tragic fire in the archives, but I did find the following which appears to have been presented at one of the meetings in honor of our mentor:*
>
> > *An old salt who fought at Manilla*
> > *Liked ice cream, especially vanilla*
> > *But after the battle*
> > *He moved to Seattle*
> > *And married a girl named Priscilla.*
>
> *While all nuances of this pitful verse are not readily apparent, it is obvious that the author has confused the Civil War with the Spanish American War and the reference to Priscilla indicates that he might also have gotten Admiral Farragut mixed up with John Alden. It has been suggested that this whole thing was devised by Skip so that he could irritate certain people by*

making them Green Seal members (which was the same thing as having Herpes) and then never promoting them no matter how hard they worked or how deserving they became. And this scurrilous accusation can be easily disposed of by simply asking yourself . . . Would Skip ever do anything like that?

Who is the Skip mentioned, anyway, from the old Shortridge days? William Henry Comingore Failey. He managed to live that name down, better yet, to make lemonade out of it. It sounds just like the name of a person belonging to the Farragut Literary Society. He learned to play ping pong at an early age and eventually became City Table Tennis Champ. When asked by a stranger if he knew anything about ping pong, he would say "not much," and then proceed to beat the pants off the totally baffled opponent.

Skip and Kurt Vonnegut probably learned a lot about life and friendship and what it was like to be young in that more easy-going time in the Farragut Literary Society and at the Shortridge of the Golden Age. Kurt, who received one of the student body's highest "popularity" award—being a candidate for Uglyman—refers to Shortridge in his books, in his conversations, and in his heart, and he is not the only one.

I had a ball at Shortridge High. What was wonderful about it was that I was happy there, not being constantly hounded about the academic world and my obligations to it—"to graduate from a four-year college." The truth was I hated school, but I loved the people and the projects and the extra-curricular activities. Certainly I was in one of the best schools in the Midwest for college preparation, and of course it was too good to last. My grandfather came back on his annual visit and found me, again, in the public school. He made Mother and my aunt go east to find "appropriate young women's schools" for me and my cousin Barbara Hill.

My mother felt Dana Hall would be a good place for me. She visited and liked the feel and style of the place and the town of Wellesley, Massachusetts itself. What I didn't know was that it was ranked the third highest academic school in the nation for girls at that time. My aunt picked Abbot Academy, near Andover, so Barbara would be near our grandmother's sister.

I tried to resist, but the club over my head was the pot of gold at the end of the rainbow if I completed the four-year-college. I went!

I left for Dana Hall in 1938 around the eye of a hurricane, a horrible one which knocked age-old trees all over lawns and fields and countryside.

Transportation to Boston was cut off from all directions. I woke up one morning in a Pullman car in New York City thinking I was in Back Bay Station in Boston, where I was supposed to be. My roommate, I later found out, was from Rhinelander, Wisconsin. She was sidetracked, too, in New York. Girls who are not yet sixteen aren't usually very adept at adapting. She lost her wallet sometime in the night in the Pullman berth, thus finding herself in the wrong city, for an unknown length of time without any money. All she could do was call home, collect, and cry, "I want to come home." She wasn't the only one. From Penn Station to Long Island there were long distance calls to schools and homes, and finally the missing students were found and the apprehensive parents reassured.

Luckily for me, my mother had brought me to school, and although she was pretty confused, she took charge. We were fortunate to have Alford relatives in Hackensack, New Jersey, and so for ten glorious days I did not have to go to school! What a bonanza. I was overjoyed. I didn't want to go anyway.

Finally we were able to get an overnight boat that went up the coast. While it was not very luxurious, it was fun to see the coastline by boat. It was on the boat, though, that we began to comprehend the fury and devastation of the hurricane. There were students aboard who had been in the eye of the hurricane and who had lost family members in it.

Here in the Midwest it is hard to imagine a hurricane and the whirling dervish of a monster it becomes as it lashes at whatever is in its path. A relative of mine brought it home with his description, "Trees and shrubs were writhing in tremendous turmoil. This awful thing had charged down on our peaceful little home and our pines and oaks were fighting back fiercely. The wind would sweep down in tremendous surges. Every moment it seemed that this tree or that must go down, but still they stood, bending far over to evade the full fury of the blast. Blanketing all this was the hideous howl of the hurricane, a universal roar, in which no individual sound was distinguishable. . . lights went out, no telephone, no radio."

And after the storm? Everything beautiful and peaceful once again. But the victimized areas we saw as we arrived lay in desolate tangles of uprooted trees and broken limbs and debris, things that before had been a home or a car or someone's refrigerator, mangled into a mockery of their former shapes.

We spoke to people, and everyone talked of the natural disaster. Since we were from the heartland, we could not even imagine being in a cottage in Cape Cod, listening to raging waters and racing up to the third floor or roof top to pray the water would recede before everybody drowned.

(When I graduated from Pine Manor Junior College in 1943, the Wellesley Campus nearby was still not totally cleared, and fallen trees still crossed the paths all over town. There are people still in this world who won't forget the Hurricane of 1938.)

February 11, 1940, greetings came, not from Uncle Sam but from my grandfather, and it found me, resigned and plugging along as he had commanded:

Dear Mary Jane:

I have been trying to write you for some time, but I dislike only by-hand letters. I haven't heard from you or about you but I have been told you are doing well and keeping up with your classes. I am backing and betting on you to pull out on top and make us all proud of you. This is a great world and the greater education you get the better you will be able to understand, enjoy and appreciate it. I know it will add much to your life.

After the BIG message the writing becomes illegible and then

With lots of love,
Pop

And then,

Let me know how you are getting along.

How was I getting along? Hah. I was coping, but basically miserable. He was unwittingly being perpetrator to a classic case of emotional abuse. He was putting his pride and his vanity into one big basket and pushing me on with my studies in a place I didn't want to be.

Looking back I have realized that if it hadn't been so academically demanding, I would probably have been as happy as a clam at Dana Hall. There were good times, lasting friendships, and the wonderful joys of the Boston area. In some ways I was in hog heaven.

It was a rather prim, prescribed sort of fun though. The "rules" for the Dana Hall Senior Prom of 1941 show the social structure in the East at the time (though we avoided it when we could).

Each senior may have ONE meal in the village with her prom guest. . . . Any girl not attending the class picnic who wishes special permission to have tea at Seilers must apply for special permission in writing to Mrs. Johnston before Friday noon.

Mrs. Johnston has offered her house as place where six boys may change. If you wish your guest to be one of the six, notify Mrs. Williams at once, or as soon as you know.

There is to be no riding in cars, no sitting in cars, no entering cars.

Seniors are not to accompany their guests to the villages except when they take their one dinner permission.

And so on, through eleven more regulations as to where to park your car (though you couldn't be in it) how drinking wasn't EVER to even be thought of, and when "lights out" was.

It wasn't that all this wasn't fun; it was that the rigorous, constant studying stifled me. And the fact that I had been forced to go to "improve" myself academically.

There was more humiliation ahead. At the end of my stay at Dana Hall, it was time for me to prepare to go to college, and I needed to take the college entrance exams. I signed up for the test at Dana and paid my registration fee. At the last minute the headmistress at Dana Hall thought it would be just as easy for me to take the test in my home town, at Tudor Hall.

I returned for the summer, and the Saturday of the exams arrived. I went to check in and the headmistress, I. Hilda Stewart, accosted me. "What are you doing here?" she asked, her ominous black eyes flashing sparks and terrifying me the way they used to when I was a student.

I told her.

She all but screamed at me, "You have no business whatsoever taking college boards. You are not college material." With that she flounced back into her office, tripped over the door stop and headed for the floor. It was disappointing, I must admit, to see her land on her feet. She was so angry. Then she screeched, "And besides your fee was paid to Dana Hall and not to us."

What a wonderful way to start the day. I sat in study hall, the exam in front of me. As the seconds ticked by, I could hear, "You must not let me down. I am counting on you." And then, "What are you doing here? You are not college material." But then, there was also, "There will be a pot of gold at the end of the rainbow. . ." Everything in the room seemed to scream, "How dare you come back here! You'll never go to college."

My heart pounded, my stomach hurt, my brain could not conjugate a French verb or remember a French idiom. "Oh, Grandpere, I will fail."

And I did. Smith College, the choice of the "Wise One" for me, would never see me. I was tortured for years with that sense of failure, and needless to say, bitter. I still awaken in the night hearing, "You failed, you failed, you will never go to college. You are stupid, stupid, stupid." All was not lost, of course. I applied to, and was accepted by Pine Manor in Massachusetts.

Now of course it is true that I received benefits from my grandfather, and I should not pass over those lightly. For one thing, he taught me the value of money, and how to take care of my own financial affairs. He also made me strongly realize the value of the saying, "Neither a borrower or a lender be." But a tyrannical parent or grandparent who never takes the time to know a child's life or school and then dares to make demands that are impossible to fulfill without ever thinking of the child's wishes is guilty of a form of child abuse just as surely as an alcoholic parent is guilty of inflicting child abuse.

I had been so traumatized by my school experiences that I was still paralyzed by the administrators when my own children were students. Now that I have grandchildren, I am finally able to see education as a bridge to future success and not as a monster dragon that caused me to have ulcers as a child. Of course I did go to college and I did graduate, but when I was urged to go on to a master's program, I laughed in the department head's face. Would anyone ask for more punishment than my so-called trip "over the rainbow?"

Pine Manor was, as it turned out, a lovely school for me. I had a fine time, especially the second year, when I was invited to live in the French House. This was a special privilege, and the epitome of the experience was being served breakfast in bed every morning. A petite French maid with a little white apron over her black uniform would bring a tray and put it beside my bed. First she would knock on the door and say *"Bon jour, Mesdemoiselles, Il est sept heures et demi* (7:30 a.m.)" And we could leisurely, or hurriedly, have our juice, roll, and coffee.

We were from that time on, all day each and every day, not allowed to speak English (until we were out of earshot of our housemother). One of our favorite pranks was to go through a closet and into the unfinished attic by sliding through a small opening. There we would puff away at our Philip Morris or Camel cigarettes. Mademoiselle Stewart, our beloved housemother, could never find the source of the smoke she smelled. The door to the attic was made for trolls. So Mademoiselle could only sniff, look around and exclaim, *"Qui fume, qui fume?"*

While I was at Pine Manor, I travelled around a lot to see sights like Salem and Concord and to go to concerts and plays. The Boston Pops, with Arthur Fiedler conducting, was a favorite treat. Some of the boys I knew were at Harvard. As a matter of fact, it seemed I knew people in schools all over New England, and they invited us to a round of parties and events.

I had not gone on to college from the comfortable old neighborhood around Shortridge, because in 1939 mother moved us out north. She designed and built a charming, little gray-clapboard cottage just off Meridian Street, on an acre that had been given to my parents as a wedding gift from my grandfather. The house abounded in pine paneling and country charm and was darling, but it was a mistake, because something was soon to happen that would change all our lives. It was World War II and, like many other people in that time of confusion, she would soon find her personal and financial picture changing. She was lonely out there, and I was busy leading the somewhat sophisticated life of a college girl in the East, enjoying matinees, going to the Ritz Carleton for tea dancing, revelling in concerts, parties, trips into New York, visits to Dartmouth and Harvard and Brown. But in the summer I returned to Indianapolis. That was, after all, my home.

Something really rewarding during those years for some of us in college were the College Boards of the department stores. Ayres, Blocks and Wassons had a promotional program and hired young college girls who seemed to them attractive and or had some clothes and style sense to work during the summers. Their function was to get the stores' young female customers ready to go to college, to have fashion shows for them, where we members of the College Board walked around casually showing classy clothes, as if we were in a little Miss America contest. The girls of the board had their pictures on the wall, and if a young woman came in wanting to get clothes suitable for college, the clerks would urge her to talk to someone on the College Board.

It was loads of fun and there was a percentage off on the clothing we bought at the store we represented. I met Franny Julian that way; we became fast friends at that time; together we modelled the clothing with heavy shoulder pads, the bobby sox and saddle shoes that were a part of the fashion picture of the day for teens.

Franny's family—the Blochs—are typical of the families of substance who helped make Indianapolis what it is today. Her father Joseph Bloch helped keep our symphony alive. Others who served on the College Board with me were Mary Lou Westfall and Beth Anderson. Helene Sternberger was our resident boss.

Girls, of course, did not have the amount of clothing that young people do today. Closets simply weren't made large enough to hold vast wardrobes even if girls had wanted them; most parents had just lived through the Great Depression and couldn't, or didn't want to flaunt affluence. I like the tone that was about then among both girls and boys.

After summer at home, I returned to Pine Manor for my last year, immersing myself in studies and fun.

The war closed in on us while I was at Pine Manor. On December 7, 1941, my roommate and I from Pine Manor and two Princeton boys went to a beach party at Revere Beach. We thought it would be an adventure to get some hot dogs and potato chips and have a winter picnic. We took the radio and our blankets and were getting ready to build a fire when the radio came on, "We interrupt this program to announce that the Japanese have bombed Pearl Harbor." We were just struck dumb and we stood there a moment and the boys said, "OK, Let's go." We didn't have any picnic, didn't even eat. We just got in the car and the boys drove us out of there to Wellesley. Then they were gone. I never will forget their stricken faces.

On Monday we were back in Pine Manor, and everyone was crying in the bathrooms between classes. It was a frantic time, with a terrible feeling that everything we knew was closing down. Relationships accelerated or fell apart. Some girls I knew went out for flings and got pregnant, some hurriedly got married with boys who would be shipped out in a week or two, some just did what they had been doing. But we knew that everything was changed, changed completely and for always.

Mother was unhappy in her new house and upset by the war. I came home, and it turned out that Indiana University was (luckily) a "certified four-year college." I hadn't really wanted to come home; by then I loved the East. When I came to IU most of the men were gone into the army or navy and the University and town seemed backwards, boring. I found the place a barren cornfield into which I had been parachuted and left to die. It was a miserable transition. Then I went through rush and pledged Kappa Alpha Theta.

It didn't hit me until I was in rush week that I had become part of a unique social institution. As an older girl, with two years of college in the very intelligent East, I found pledge week stupid. Walk on only the wood part of the floors at the edge of the carpet, stay in the clothes all week that you had on when they announced "hell week." I wore a beige suit and a drooping orchid for a week, and then I almost said, "This isn't for me," but I did stick it out. As I eventually came to see, the Theta House was a house of beautiful people and achievers, and I came to love it.

But at first I was bewildered, deflated with the flatness both geographically and culturally that I found in Indiana. During this low period of adjustment, good fortune came. My roomate, also a transfer from another college and a fellow graduate of an eastern boarding school, was Margaret Keck—"Maggie." We were compatible and became good friends. She lived in a very small town that divided that part of Indiana from Ohio—Union City, population 2,000.

One October day Margaret's Mother Stella Keck called with an important message. Carl Sandburg was coming to lecture at the local high school on Thursday night. His talk would be sponsored by the Woman's Club at the Union City High School, and because there was no hotel in Union City, Sandburg was going to be staying at their house for the whole weekend. Margaret should come home for this, her mother urged, and she could also invite her roommate, Majie, to come with her.

Would I like to come? Holy unbelievability! I was stunned out of my socks. I had read this man! I knew "Chicago, hog butcher of the world," and "Fog." (Probably that's all.) If I had been faced with a final exam in a major course at IU, I would have left anyway and flunked it by default. That's how excited I was to meet this man and be with him, and it was the prelude to my wonderful friendship with the great poet and my "far off uncle," Carl Sandburg.

During those three sublime days it was marvelous to listen to his evening lecture, hear his rough-hewn voice singing to the guitar he was playing. It was almost unbearably exciting to be at the family dining table with him; to take a walk through the golden October leaves at his side; to see him vie with a competitive contemporary; and to have him actually take me aside in the big kitchen and discuss my future plans. Writing, of course. "No, no," he said. "Lousy racket, writing."

I immediately felt a great rapport with this man. My roomate remembers very little about that long weekend. To Maggie, he was Carl

Sandburg, author, poet, Lincoln biographer—meet him, over and done with. But to me he was near holy. I was so struck by the dynamic quality of his being that I could hardly bear to go out of the house for errands or visits. I might miss his words! I observed him in all of his mightiness: in his quiet hours of preparation and in his conversations about his life and family at home on the dunes of Lake Michigan. I saw him in humility and as a prima donna; he was a myriad of moods and undulating tones of voice and gentleness. Teasingly, he coined a name for me—his little "Creole heartbreaker."

Stella Keck, his hostess, made an impact on me, too. I think she impressed Carl Sandburg also. Effortlessly she played the role of the totally natural and unassuming hostess in that large house with ample guest bedrooms. She was gracious without being overly solicitous. He was, of course, notoriously casual in his personal appearance. If at one moment Sandburg's hair needed combing, she told him, with tact. If his coat needed brushing, she did it. She took charge of him in her house, and let me tell you he was in good hands. That was a gift to him. Attention he liked!

Bringing Carl Sandburg to a town of two thousand was no small event. Maggy Keck's grandfather was also a resident of the Keck household; he was in his own right a dynamic and witty person. He was also very German and slightly overbearing. *He* was used to being center stage, and there were a few times at the dinner table and later that I thought Mr. Schemmel as host might have been a little more gracious to the guest.

When it was over, and I was back at school, I turned my experiences with Carl Sandburg into writing, which led to a debacle involving my creative writing professor. The old Sandburg saying, "I never spit before noon" was absolutely true. He was up all hours writing or socializing and then observed a policy of DO NOT DISTURB in the a.m. Even so, the two college juniors had been allowed to come into his sanctuary to meet him for the first time. He was propped up in bed in his famous attire: white sweater, moth-eaten and weathered, paisley silk ascot tied dramatically at the neck, and in a general state of interesting disarray. He was working on the upcoming lecture. We literally met him in bed.

So, the title of my first article on Carl Sandburg, which I wrote for the *Atlantic* annual college competition, was entitled, "I Met Him in Bed." The story was a good first-hand impression, and I held out for the truth in that title. My creative writing professor was being difficult and held out for propriety and discretion. He was very insistent; I suppose he was dazzled by the idea of *The Atlantic Monthly* and didn't want to jeopardize his chances for a little reflected glory. I nearly flunked the course, and then the *Atlantic* turned *me* down.

I was humiliated beyond tears. How could this happen to me? I had written my new friend and told him about the article and asked him to read it. He kindly wrote back that, busy as he was, "I think that I shall take the time to read it." And now it was rejected. Oh! The little "Creole heartbreaker" was shaken, her face crimson, hurt beyond reason!

I recovered, of course, and that was only the beginning of the relationship, the most wonderful of my life which I'll cover in a later chapter.

Indiana University had its own feeling, like any institution I suppose. When you were on the campus nothing outside mattered. Indianapolis or Cincinnati could blow up and nobody at the Book Nook would know it. IU was a universe, and only the people and events there existed. Even after they graduate, Indiana University people are very loyal, very political and very enthusiastic. This spirit sticks with IU grads through all of life and keeps them young—and very supportive.

Still, by the time I left, I knew I belonged back in Indiana. And if I hadn't stayed here, I never would have worked on *The Indianapolis News*, which was the most exciting phase of my life.

The impoverished minister's son, my paternal grandfather William John Alford, who obediently got his college degree and rose to be Chairman of the Board (far right, back). A rather serious, if not intimidating group.

"Sa" and "Pop," Mr. and Mrs. William J. Alford of Anderson, with Majie on Pop's lap (the one and only picture of the two of us). Grandchildren pictured are (l to r.) William J. Alford III, Robertson F. Alford, Majie Alford, Barbara Alford Hill, and John Crane Alford.

Portrait of William John Alford, Chairman, Thames Board Mills, Purfleet, Essex, England, done for dedication of new building.

The electric car and the *only* car our grandmother, Nellie Alford, ever drove. We grandchildren loved to play in it.

My loving maternal great-grandparents, Susan and Waitsell Heaton, Knightstown, Indiana, in the early 1920s.

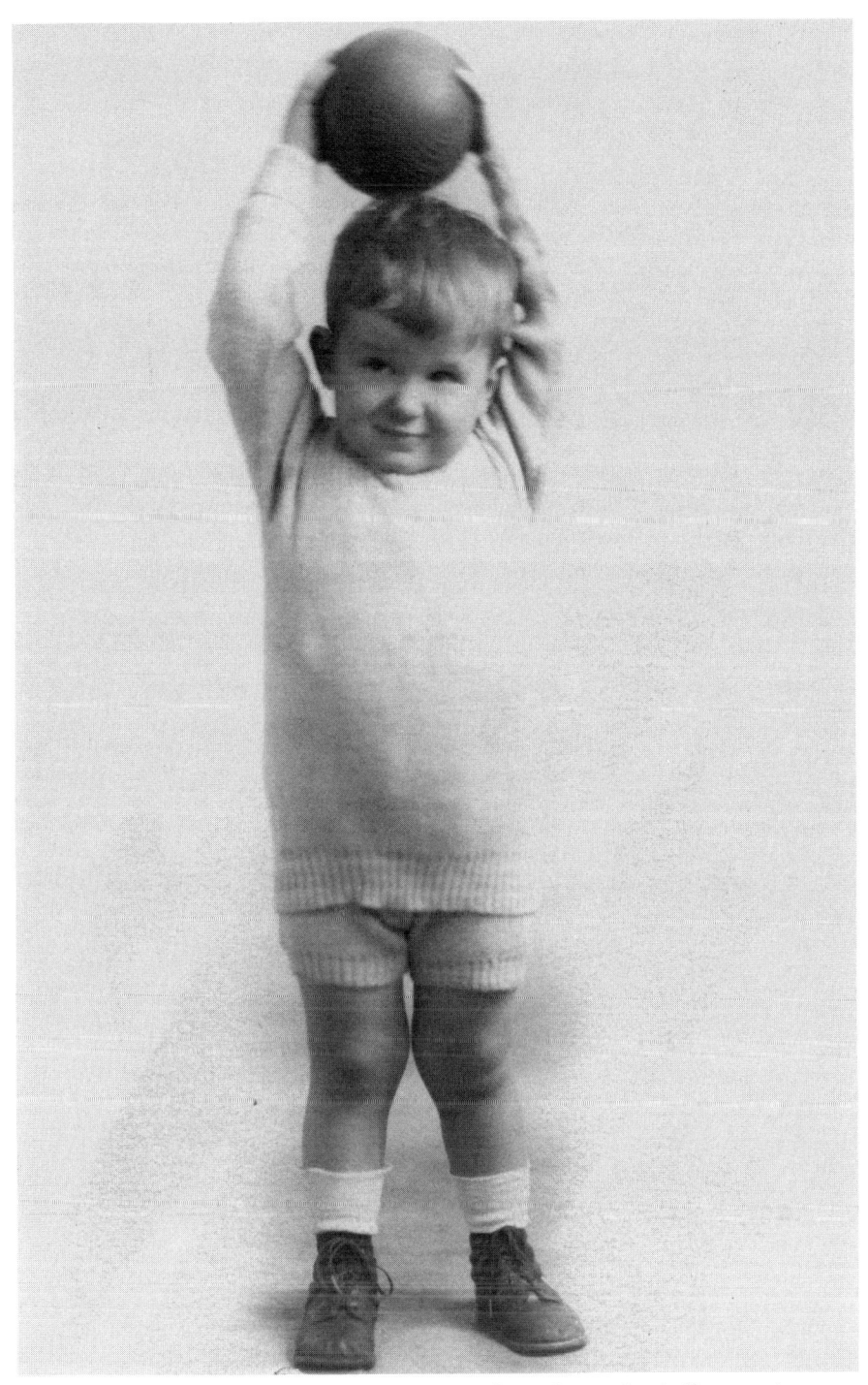

William Henry Comingore Failey (age 3) ready to throw this ball at a prize porcelain figurine and then run.

Shortridge Freshman football team, 1937. Among them are Freihofer, VanTassel, Kothe, Claycombe, Craycraft, Maynard, Jose, Goldsmith.

Candidates for the coveted "Uglyman" at Shortridge High School. Included are (far right) Kurt Vonnegut, who became a famous contemporary author, Joe Shedron, who became a croupier at Las Vegas gambling tables and Fred Maynard, Vice President and General Counsel for Traveler's Insurance.

PD dance at Christmas time, 1938. Majie is third from left, front row. Barbara Masters Laird (fifth from left, front row) and Kurt Vonnegut, (far right, back row) are also included.

Dorothy Heaton Alford, my mother. She is typically "of the times," with serious pose, in a dress our father brought her from Paris, mid-twenties.

HORSE FEATHERS

Looking them over
By Nick

VOL. I   APRIL 1934   No. 2

HOOSIER EQUESTRIAN

Life changed for Mother in the thirties. Now on her own, she was an artist, photographer, editor and columnist for *Hoosier Equestrian*.

The way we were at Dana Hall, Wellesley, Mass. in 1939. Recreation in cold New England winters included class sleigh rides.

Ayres Tearoom, an institution, a tradition and a joy in eating, was closed in 1991 to the horror of all who had shared it. The entire store was closed. So endeth another nostalgic historic landmark.

2

PRESS

I received my college degree on a warm Sunday afternoon in April of 1945, perfect for a graduation. College was over. The last eight years had been academically gruelling for me. The cap and gown gave me warmth, strength and pride, and above all—relief. For eight years I believed that if I could just make it through college and get my degree, I had it made! For life!

I was ready for the world now. No more finals, no more worry about hard courses, no more lectures, no more studying. Whoopie!

THE WORLD suddenly loomed ahead in big black letters. What was the world anyway? I had a feeling that it meant reality, a frightening word. Oh God! The World War II years were terrible years for the young college crowd. Many of us, the young men and women who should have been venturing out into a beautiful world of golden opportunity had ventured instead into a black night of grief and horror.

Hadn't it been lovely and protected in the sorority house, a haven of beautiful people? Suddenly it was over. There I was, carrying all those happy times, along with my old textbooks and bedspreads, out the doors and into the car. I felt the heavy sinking feeling of an ending, the Omega. And the pressure of going out into the world, the Alpha.

Little did I know I was about to begin one of the two most important, happy and stimulating periods of my life, the most productive times and the best of times. The immediate years following my graduation would have impact and dynamic influence on me for years to come. They supersede school days, friendships, going away to camp and college, being in love and my first car. They helped erase the bitterness of having an alcoholic father, and the despair of my parents' divorce.

My stroke of luck in landing a job on the newspaper was the experience that put my life into focus and made me become an acceptable member of the human race. That little card that said, "Member of the Working Press," became my badge of integrity and prestige. It meant I had an obligation to represent the paper in the very best possible way on the Woman's Pages, which is where I started.

How I loved that pile of typing paper, those thick black pencils and that paste pot. They were my very own status symbols.

Getting a job on the evening newspaper was not exactly easy in war time. It was May of 1945. The men who had left their jobs to go to war would soon be coming back. It had been a make-shift, "make-do" era, where the skeleton staff, including the copy boy, went wherever they were needed to fill in the gaps and get that paper out. It looked like this was about to ease up.

It was clear I *needed* a job. I had first gone to the employment office at Eli Lilly and Co.; my mother had urged me to try to get on there because Mr. Lilly himself set the tone for fine morale and personal benefits for the employees. I could have normally qualified as a French interpreter, but due to the war, not many people were going to, or coming from, France, so there was no job for me at Lilly's.

There *was* a job at *The News*, however. It was only temporary of course, because of vacation times thinning the staff. I had a friend who was Fashion Editor, and over lunch she clued me in on the facts, but warned me not to get excited. Two weeks, *if* at all, she said.

I decided to go for an interview, which she also pushed my way. My formal education was in no way connected to journalism, and I began thinking about that. My God, I was a French major. Served breakfast in bed in the French House, rose on a tray. I had a lot of nerve trying to get a job on a newspaper! I began to back off, lose nerve. Newspaper men were notorious characters. They came in all shapes and sizes and varieties (and always will)! This particular staff would probably not be highly motivated to make friends with a young lady brought up mostly in girls' schools. The only saving grace was that I had finished my last two years of college at Indiana University. But as for experience—a single creative writing course was as close as I had come to any formal training. Being on the staff of school papers didn't seem to impress anyone. But there is one thing about news writing. . . you have to like people, understand people, and have a feel for people and human nature. Well, I did love people. That was a good start.

There are a lot more things you have to know about newspaper work. I didn't know any of them. Carl Sandburg was an old veteran newspaper writer from Chicago. He had gone on to other kinds of writing, but he always said newspaper writers didn't make much money. And he knew it was hard work and no lunch! He didn't go around telling others that writing was wonderful; instead, he had called me aside in that kitchen to tell me that writing was a rotten idea.

But I guess I wasn't listening. I was on my own now, and with trepidation I passed through the doors on the old Washington Street plant of *The News* that first day and smelled the odd smell of newsprint and ink that was to be such a part of my life for the next few years.

The interview went well. The editor who interviewed me, Herbert Hill, had a brother in Union City, and he and I found a common ground. The words and ideas flowed nicely. He seemed to think it would be an addition to the staff to have a recent graduate with my background, incongruous as it was. But of course he knew about Sandburg's visit to his home town, and he was most interested in my friendship with the poet.

I was hired, and it changed my life and style as a person and a writer. As I read over rough drafts of anything I write, I realize that still today, after forty-some years, I correct and revise the same way I did for the copy desk. Being society editor did not give me a license to misspell or make typographical errors. Nor could we make mistakes with facts. We researched, checked and double checked on times, dates, correct spelling of names and so on. It was a taskmaster job with headaches and heartaches, but you learned about yourself and life through it.

Those years, because they made me absorb the meaning of professionalism and because they taught me about human nature, have become dear, touchstone years for me. I started out the right way, as a novice, inexperienced, scared, just a green girl graduate—writing copy for the Society Department, cowering before the "pros," the real writers, the daily column boys and the editors. Still, something in me kept reaching. I threw my heart over the jump and hung in there, praying that the words "temporary, vacation help, assistant to" would give way to "permanent." I felt like a little seedling trying to root in the rich, warm corner of the editorial floor. Along the way I was lucky enough to make a few mistakes and one that was really serious, and heard the ominous words, "One more mistake and you are out of here!" (That was a big one!) Cut back all the way to the ground is not a bad way for seedlings to grow fast.

I was aware right away that I was working for one of the greatest afternoon dailies in the country, and that only added to my awe. I'd like to stop and take a look at *The News*, a really influential Indianapolis institution since the time of the Civil War, and maybe that will help you see why I felt so honored to be there right out of college.

The Indianapolis Sentinel was the newspaper of the 1860s and '70s; its building stood on the Circle. A new paper, *The Evening News* began operating out of *The Sentinel* office on a sort of subcontracting arrangement. Its first issue came out December 7, 1869—Mr. John H. Holliday, a Civil War soldier, wanted to print President Grant's address to Congress. According to Hilton U. Brown, long-time Editor and Vice-President of *The News* in his wonderful *A Book of Memories*, the paper changed its name in 1876 and continued to grow in popularity and eminence in the newspaper world ever since that time.

"The paper was never colorless," Mr. Brown said. "It battled for what it believed in." Hilton U. Brown came to work for Holliday in 1881 and succeeded to City Editor, Managing Editor, General Manager and member of the board, Secretary-Treasurer and Vice President. This remarkable man, whom I knew as an old-timer, visiting the city room most days in his nineties, had a career which spanned almost the entire history of *The News* from Holliday to Pulliam.

Mr. Brown mentions that early on he went to New York with Delavan Smith, where he met the editors or owners of many of the top papers in the country around the turn of the century. *The News* was involved with Associated Press and Newspaper Publishers' Association matters, and, as one of the top papers in the Midwest, joined other great dailies such as *The Los Angeles Times, The Boston Globe, The Kansas City Star, The New York Times, The Chicago News, The Philadelphia Bulletin, The Washington Star, The Atlanta Constitution, The Cleveland Plain Dealer, The Chicago Tribune* and *The New York World*. Interestingly, when I worked at *The News*, each day most of these very papers were brought in and placed on a table for all of us to scrutinize as "the ten top papers in the country." *The News* from earliest days set its standards of quality and knew its competitors.

Former editors of the paper say today that it was the human element that made *The News* different from *The Indianapolis Star*, its long-time rival and, eventually, sister paper. It was *The News* that had the flavor, humor, and immediate coverage of what people cared about in Indianapolis. *The News* really was Indiana personified, with all its small-town personal flavor, strong political cast, and feisty spirit. It was proud of being Hoosier and went out of its way to preserve the zesty originality of small-town Indiana.

Early on, the local literary "characters" found their way onto *The News*. Tom Hendricks, a leading citizen of the city, describes the way *The News* was in the twenties, when he served a stint on the paper.

> *In 1916 I was thrown directly out of college into the Idle Ward of the* Indianapolis News. *The Idle Ward was the comfortable area set aside for such great personages as Kin Hubbard, the creator of Abe Martin, Gaar Williams, the cartoonist who later went to the* Chicago Tribune *where his "Wot a Life" drawings became famous, and Bill Herschel who inherited Jim Riley's mantle as the Hoosier poet.*
>
> *The Idle Ward was the focal point for all the greats and near greats who came to Indiana. It was located on the eighth floor of the* Indianapolis News *and was the center of most of Indiana's literary activity after the turn of the century. It was there that O.O. McIntyre and Will Roger Montgomery and Stone Darling the cartoonist would come to pay their respects when visiting Indiana. A motto drawn by one of these famous visiting cartoonists hung over the Idle Ward. It said, "As work is such a good thing, let's leave some of it for tomorrow."*
>
> *To have graduated from any college was bad enough for them, but to have graduated from an eastern university put a fellow beyond any hope; so these three Hoosier musketeers gave me the works from the start. After an unusually thorough going over about the third day I was there, Kin Hubbard, who for a humorist could be as cutting and sarcastic an old sour puss as I have ever known, particularly after a hard night before, turned on me and said, "I understand you went to college."*
>
> *I admitted I had. "What college did you go to?"*
>
> *"Princeton," I answered.*
>
> *At that Bill Herschel, a 225-pounder rose from his desk, came over to me and held out his hand and said, "Put 'er there, pal. I'm a Princeton man, too. Princeton, Indiana."*

Hilton U. Brown describes Bill Herschel, who was an institution in himself at *The News* in this way:

> *Life has not been the same since Bill Herschel left us in 1939.*

> But The News *had him some thirty-seven years, and that made him unforgettable. Some men are so affectionately regarded that the world treats them as intimates and calls them by their nicknames, "Jim" Riley, "Tom" Taggart, "Kin" Hubbard, Bill Herschel . . . the public knew him as "Bill" . . . he had a laugh that preceded him wherever he appeared. For years Bill Herschel's laughter roared through all departments of* The News. *Neither his person nor his laughter could be restrained. He would go a-visiting to share a thought with a brother editor or friend in the printshop. . . . There was no dullness where he was and there were no deadlines in what he wrote.*

Bill Herschel had come from Princeton and found his way to Evansville, Terre Haute and finally to Indianapolis. John Holliday had seen in him a fine writing talent and brought Bill Herschel to *The News*. One of his first jobs there was the police run, where he brought a sense of humor to a dreary job.

He became a star journalist and during World War I wrote poems that so charmed Indiana readers, as well as men in the trenches, that he began to be in demand as a speaker. He wrote books and stories and poems, among them "Long Boy" and "The Kid has Gone to the Colors," and everything he produced was enlivened by his native good humor and wit. His most famous poem "Ain't God Good to Indiana" was recited by schoolchildren for an entire generation and hung, framed, on many a polite parlor of the twenties and thirties. His

> *Good-by, Ma! Good-by, Pa*
> *Good-by mule, with yer old hee-haw!*
> *I may not know what the war's about*
> *But you bet, by gosh, I'll soon find out!*

was typically Herschel, and exactly in the tradition of "down home," Hoosier dialect wit that marked *The News*, and lots of other things in Indiana, in the early part of the century. A lot of his work could be set to country music, I bet.

When I was at *The News*, his widow Josephine often dropped in to chat and wander among the various editors' desks. Since she never hesitated to come when people were working, and since she visited often, editors would sigh with relief as she went down the elevator. Then, in unison, they would say, "Ain't God Good to Indiana!" It was only later it dawned on me

AIN'T GOD GOOD TO INDIANA?
By William Herschell
(1873-1939)

Ain't God good to Indiana?
    Folks, a feller never knows
Just how close he is to Eden
    Till, sometime, he ups an' goes
Seekin' fairer, greener pastures
    Than he has right here at home,
Where there's sunshine in th' clover
    An' there's honey in th' comb;
Where th' ripples on th' river
    Kind o' chuckles as they flow—
Ain't God good to Indiana?
    Ain't He, fellers? Ain't He, though?

Ain't God good to Indiana?
    Seems to me He has a way
Gittin' me all out o' humor
    Just to see how long I'll stay
When I git th' gypsy feelin'
    That I'd like to find a spot
Where th' clouds ain't quite so restless,
    Or th' sun don't shine so hot.
But, I don't git far, I'll tell you,
    Till I'm whisp'rin' soft an' low:
Ain't God good to Indiana?
    Ain't He, fellers? Ain't He, though?

Ain't God good to Indiana?
    Other spots may look as fair,
But they lack th' soothin' somethin'
    In th' Hoosier sky and air.
They don't have that snug-up feelin'
    Like a mother gives a child;
They don't soothe you, soul an' body,
    With their breezes soft an' mild.
They don't know the joys of Heaven
    Have their birthplace here below;
Ain't God good to Indiana?
    Ain't He, fellers? Ain't He, though?

that she hung around because she missed him so. She was lonely and it was at *The News*, his beloved workplace, that she could feel his spirit and keep in touch.

    Kin Hubbard, one of America's all-time great humorists, was both of *The News*, and on *The News*. He has been dead for years, but a funny looking little guy named Abe Martin has been found ever after in *The News* sharing his homespun philosophy, as fresh and interesting as the day Kin Hubbard created him. This little guy looks a little like Sad Sack in appearance. But he is, truly, his own person; he has a thin frame and is lanky and lazy and wears ragged old clothes and a beat-up top hat smashed on his head. He usually philosophizes while leaning against a lamp post or an old barn or a tree stump—anything run down. He says something really meaty about human nature and its frailties. Hubbard had his tongue in his cheek most of the time, for this little Brown County humorist was always poking fun at someone or something. The piece below is not a cartoon, though; it's an essay:

> When Miss Tawney Apple returned from testifyin' before th' grand jury th' other day, she remarked, "it wuz simply wonderful." Th' way th' word "wonderful" is bein' abused and debased these days calls fer a stingin' rebuke. Ever' buddy's takin' advantage of it. Even ole Jake Bentley that lives almost three miles off th' road has caught on. We asked him how his wife's liver wuz actin' this summer an' he said, "Well sir, it's jest wonderful." Th' expression, "Fine an' dandy" had a long run, an' is still encountered now an' then in' sparsely settled river counties. An' strange as it may seem, th' expression finds its greatest popularity 'mongst those who look jest th' reverse o' fine an' dandy. People that speak of a 20-cent dinner, or a dandruff cure, as bein' simply wonderful are usually folks that have never been beyond ther own township. Still we wuz talkin' t' a women th' other day that had been around th' world an' she referred t' a new egg lifter she'd bought as th' "most wonderful thing she ever seen." But ever' buddy's overworkin' "wonderful." Th' film wuz wonderful, th' hash is wonderful, th' trip to Kokomo wuz wonderful, th' new baby is wonderful, th' rain, an' even the soup wuz wonderful. These things might be good, or nice, or tolerable, or out o' the usual or even extraordinary, but they all come many leagues from even approachin' th' wonderful. Think of a full grown, beautiful, well educated an' refined young miss sayin', "Th' bologna was perfectly wonderful," upon her return from a picnic. Think o' classin' bologna right along with th' Temple of Artemis at Epheses, or th' seven Sutherland sisters. Our real wonders are very few, not more'n seven, includin' th' Collosus at Rhodes, th' hangin' gardens o' Babylon an' maybe th' new fillin' station at Bloom Center. We have many things borderin' on th' wonderful,

but ther's nothin' t' eat among 'em. We have some exceptional paw paws, very toothsome ice cream, an' hot dogs, but ther not wonderful by a long shot. Loopin' th' loop on a bicycle, an' how some people git by, comes dangerously near bein' wonderful, but ther's nobuddy makin' wonderful speeches, writin' wonderful books, or servin' wonderful food, an' there hain't nothin' wonderful in th' whole United States but th' Grand Canyon. Niagary Falls can't help itself.

But this is the age of extravagances, not alone in spendin' money, but in forms of expression as well.

Kin Hubbard was from a newspapering family from Ohio, and was early known for talent in both writing and charcoal drawing. Kin, whose real name was Frank McKinney Hubbard, created his cartoon character in 1906, put him in Brown County and pretended he was a hick with homespun wisdom and satirical humor. He came to work at *The News* in 1916.

Make no mistake, Kin Hubbard was anything but a hick. However, he wrote, "a hick town is one with a speed trap, a yeller brick gym, and a Carnegie Library, an' no sidewalks." He was Will Rogers-like in philosophy, but much more productive.

He also said, "Come to think of it, human nature is here to stay." He lived in Irvington where many of *The News'* editorial staff lived, and then moved on to build a fine new house on Meridian Street, and was entertained by the "social set," who loved to hear him throw one-liners at his wife, a fine wit herself.

He said good things about women too, things that I wished I could use on the society page to illustrate a few women who had timeless and ageless characteristics. But "We'll say this fer women—they don't chew t'backer."

Marriage note: "Mr. and Mrs. Art Small's daughter wuz married today, an' in talkin' to a press reporter they said, 'We hain't got no definate plans as yit, but you'll be perfectly safe in sayin' that we're goin' t' take a good, long rest.'"

And for fashion: "Th' only decently dressed women we have left are Eskimos."

Bashful before audiences, he let Abe Martin do the talking in "chalk talks." He was considered a genius by many who knew him, but unusual for a genius, he worked with amazing capacity at a day's work, including in it not only prodigious amounts of written and art work, but also gardening and home improvement at the family home.

He and his cartoons remained as popular as the headlines on the front page until his death in 1938. A good collection of first editions of Kin Hubbard's Abe Martin books is very dear indeed. Edward R. Murrow sometimes ended his broadcasts with an Abe Martin quote. That made me like E.R. Murrow even more.

Most of all he was unique—the voice of the post Civil War Midwest— as well as the voice of the thoroughly Hoosier *Indianapolis News*. Mr. Brown has said it so well in saying that Kin Hubbard was a "philosopher, cartoonist and humorist in combination . . . [putting out] daily comment on current affairs, a book a year for a quarter of a century, besides a weekly feature. . . . he was himself, a timeless humorist, ever fresh, young and convincing."

As I said, it would have given me a great deal of pleasure if I could have written the wedding account of just one couple in the dialect of Abe Martin and told the things that no one wants known in the style of that beloved bedraggled character. Just once if I could have written, "POP'LAR COUPLE WEDS" in upper case, big print, top of the page.

The time when "Hoosier Greats" like Hubbard and Meredith Nicholson (to be discussed later) and Herschel sat in its editorial rooms were the "glory days" for *The Indianapolis News*. Its editorial excellence was easy to explain; the business side of the paper was a little more complicated, with ownership changing from time to time. One version of that story is given by Richard Fairbanks, whose grandfather was directly involved for years in *The News*.

> *My grandfather died in 1918, and I have been told it came as a great surprise to the city when it was disclosed at that time that he was the majority owner of the paper.*
>
> *According to what I have heard some time around the turn of the century he put up the money for his cousin, Delavan Smith, to take over the paper. When he died, Delavan Smith was still the publisher, but owned only a minority interest . . .*
>
> *In any event not long after his death his children bought out the Smith interest and his eldest son Warren C. Fairbanks became the publisher. He died in 1938 and therefore he ran the paper for some eighteen years, what you might call its glory years.*
>
> *During his tenure the paper won a couple of Pulitzer prizes; it had the largest circulation of any paper in the state and in fact*

was considered one of the top afternoon papers in the country, and it was dominant in Indianapolis and Indiana.

Those were the glory years for afternoon papers generally. This was before television. It was a time when men hurried off to work in the morning and returned home in the evening to read their newspaper from cover to cover.

But because his paper was so dominant, Warren Fairbanks became more and more reactionary. He refused to consider radio, which he despised. I am not in a position to comment on what other opportunities he missed, but there probably were several. I do know that he could have bought the Miami Herald when it was in dire straits after the Florida boom went bust.

When he died, he was succeeded by his next brother Fred. He was a charming man, but so far as I know had never worked in his life and knew absolutely nothing about newspapers or running any business. But very shortly after taking over, he was stricken with cancer and died a couple of years later.

My father was third in line and he became publisher in late 1940 or early 1941. At one time when he was young, he had an interest in the Anderson paper, but in all the years I knew him he had not worked. His tenure did not last long either. He was stricken with cancer in 1943 and died in 1944.

Therefore, after the death of Warren in 1938 the paper was pretty much left adrift. Mickey McCarty had been managing editor and became the de facto publisher during Fred's, and then my father's illness. When my father died, Mickey became president of Indianapolis News Publishing Company and publisher of the paper.

I went to The News in 1934 after I got out of college. Because I was the only Fairbanks of my generation who had an interest in the paper, Warren and Fred looked on me kindly. I do remember working pretty hard, six and even seven days a week . . .

But then the war came along, and I was gone right after Pearl Harbor. Then the paper was left to Mickey and Joe Breeze, who had been an advertising salesman in Warren's day but who had advanced to advertising director. Mickey was a charming man and a wonderful politician, but not a good businessman. Neither was Joe.

After the war I moved to Miami Beach and went to work for The Miami Daily News. But by 1947 it was evident that The

News *was doing poorly. I had urged my father to buy* The Indianapolis Star *when it was for sale before the war. But he refused, and Gene Pulliam got it instead. Now, with strong leadership, it was moving in on* The News. *I decided I had better return to Indianapolis to see what I could do.*

I did, and was as popular as a bastard at the family reunion. I asked for a hand in running the paper and instead was shunted off to WIBC which had been bought during the war and was losing money. I still kept poking my nose into the paper and concluded that something would have to be done.

The obvious answer would be to sell. But for many reasons I didn't want to do that. I discussed the situation with the husband of one of my cousins and told him of my plan. It seemed to me that we could do best by talking to Gene Pulliam with a view toward effecting a merger. He and I agreed and after a family meeting we broached the subject to Gene, who was more than receptive.

To make a long story a little shorter, our group and Gene's met in Chicago and after a week of negotiations we hammered out the merger which exists to this day, whereby we received debentures which provided for the old ladies who had been living off The News *and took a minority position in the new company, Indianapolis Newspapers.*

Despite the fact that most people believe The News *was sold and refer to the sale of the paper, there never was a sale, and we still have a substantial position in the newspaper publishing in Indianapolis. I was a director of INI for several years, along with Gene and Nina Pulliam. The merger took place in 1948, but three or four years later we were still contending for a TV station in Indianapolis, and I thought it best to distance myself from the papers.*

It was during this last period spoken of by Dick Fairbanks that I joined the staff as a lowly society reporter. I was aware of two of the things he mentioned—the fact that the staff was just recovering from the losses of men who went to the war, and the feeling of greatness as a paper that went back to before the turn of the century.

Besides Mr. Brown, I could be impressed by the editor Mickey McCarty. C. Walter McCarty (Mr. Mickey) was a lovable man, an affable reporter and Executive Editor of *The News*. I saw immediately that there wasn't a person on the entire editorial staff that didn't love the genial, dedicated Irishman.

Mickey McCarty's story had two chapters, always intermingled. They were journalism and Indiana University, and to both he gave generously of his time, his energy, and his affection.

I wrote the following for my friend Mickey when he died in 1965.

There is a new bright star in the heavens. The smile, the warmth and sweetness of Mickey McCarty is shining down on the people he has left behind. The head of The News *family has left the staff. Many have written simply or eloquently about Mickey and what he meant to many people. As a former staffer of postwar days, I remember how it was with Mickey as boss. It was like this. It was great fun to work near him. The society desk was outside his office. Everyone from the copy boy to the governor had to pass our desk to get to his office. It was hard to concentrate! He was the greatest example of firmness and fairness in his work. Once he brought me some copy to write: the celebration 50th wedding anniversary of a prominent couple. The news story was to serve as an invitation also; it was to be a black tie affair. It was important. These were Mickey's personal friends, and in his typical fashion, he told them he would see to the story himself. He gave me the copy, and I wrote the story. The story appeared in the early edition with just one mistake. I had written the wrong date. Some people appeared at the party on the wrong night. I was informed by Mickey fairly and firmly this could only happen once. And in the years that followed, as I cringed at the thought of this mistake, Mickey had long since forgiven and forgotten. After this I was vindicated by another story. William F. Fox Jr., the sports editor, sent me to cover the fights. I had never seen a fight, so I wrote a Dumb Dora type coverage that turned out pretty funny. I suppose that was why Fox had assigned me. Mickey called me into his office to tell me that it was clever and that he got a kick out of it. I knew why he did this: encouragement was his forte. In the face of a difficult task, he gave me a pat on the arm and said, "You can do it, honey." Time had changed my role but not his. You could count on his being the same, always. I saw him in the grocery, at the drugstore, at a party or at* The News *office. I'll miss seeing him in all of these places. But most of all I'll miss just* bumping into my old boss here and there and hearing, "How are you doing, honey?"

Things his colleagues said about him:

> The report of the death of C. Walter (Mickey) McCarty comes as a shock to his countless friends. He was truly a leader in his chosen profession. His influence has been a potent factor in establishing a high standard of fair, honest, and accurate reporting of the news of Indiana.
> Mickey McCarty has been a symbol of the best in Indiana journalism. A first-rate reporter and writer, he added to his luster being city editor, managing editor, president, general manager, and executive editor.

My obit for Mickey had begun this way:

> "Thirty." That is the way the printers express it. Thirty is a wonderful word which means "the mighty press is shut down—edition over" to newspeople.
> Thirty for Mickey, and a loss to journalism in general.

The biggest compliment I received at *The News* was when I was asked to take over a column called "Atop The Town" at the retirement of a pro of long standing. Columnist Filomena Gould was my mentor when I started on the Society Desk. She was also my friend, and she was a trouper if ever there was one. It was Fil who took over any task left vacant by any staff member in the armed forces. It was Fil who sat at the Copy Desk . . the News Desk . . . or the City Desk. And it was Fil who stayed later than the rest so the young with family could go home.

Her column was well enough read so that the stories usually came to her. The rich and the poor knew her. The butcher at the city market was her pal. A call from Fil would soothe troubled waters. Filomena was a writer with feeling, but she was also a friend. She proposed me for the Indianapolis Woman's Club, which is where I gave my very first paper on Carl Sandburg. And she had a sense of humor that was both sophisticated and Hoosier through and through. It was she who quoted Abe Martin with fluency, "The best way to stop dandruff is with a blue serge suit." She was a pro in the highest sense of the word.

Back in the First World War, when Fil was a girl and engaged to Jack Gould, he came back from the war feeling that she was his exclusive property. His first view of her upon his arrival home was from a parade downtown where the town was honoring the returnees. There she was smiling and laughing as she threw rose petals at the soldiers. Jack took one look at the scene and huffed, "Well, I'm not going to marry some goddamned exhibitionist." Which, of course, he did. Lucky for him!

Filomena Manley Gould was a lady. What this lady did for the newspaper that employed her, though, was keep it printed during the war when the boys were gone.

Fil was the *crème de la crème* and then some. She was beautiful, she had brains and unplumbed depths of talents. She was a Society Dame and wife who went professional. Today, this is the tone of our times; then, however, Fil was unusual, a forerunner of the "two income family" wife when options for women working were taboo.

Her accomplishments are legion. She was a founding member of the Junior League and a member of every important club in town, and she was a real community worker! She had purpose and drive and nerve. Having attended both public and private schools, she later went to Ogontz School in Pennsylvania where Amelia Earhart was her classmate and good friend. Later when Amelia was teaching at Purdue University, she spent weekends here with the Goulds.

Fil finished her schooling at Sophie Newcomb College in New Orleans, where she was an Art School student. All of the talents she'd cultivated up to that time put her in a good position to weather the Big Crash of 1929. Being a contemporary of my parents, she belonged to that fated crowd of young marrieds that "just had a wonderful time" doing the Charleston and partying and drinking and living it up, happily enjoying the bounties of life. And like the Titanic they were all about to sink. When the Goulds awakened to the fact that they too were left penniless and jobless, Mr. Gould suffered untold agony. He moaned, "We have been wiped out. Why, all we have left in the world is that old Cord car and Filomena's squirrel coat." Oh, woe was they. Some of that age group swam while others sank. Fil swam and she held up more than one fallen sparrow.

The Crash caused a universal suffering, with some suffering more than others, of course. A lot of tucks were taken, and life styles were changed overnight even for the "well off." Fil had a cook whom she depended on for everything at home. There was only one way to keep Agnes the cook. Go to work herself!

For generations, the best place in town to buy books was Stewart's Book Shop. Filomena, after the crash, took her many talents and ensconced herself in an indispensable corner of Stewart's—the party counter. There she dreamed up favors for special parties and events and place cards for the same. She blew out eggs and made tree ornaments at Easter and she made party-giving a big success. She was clever with words. She named the Junior League Magazine, *Pen and Inklings*, and then became its editor.

Fil was on top of things! Working Stewart's book department, she read the new books and proceeded to write reviews. Every newspaper has a book review section and this, I guess, is how Filomena got tangled up in newsprint.

Anyway, believe me when I say Filomena Gould was a trouper with class and ability. Fil joined the editorial staff in the late thirties before the men left the paper to serve in Germany or the Pacific for the war years. Is it any wonder that Filomena Gould took over, literally, during the war years? She wrote editorials, she filled in at the City Desk, she helped put out the Fashion Page and at the same time worked at the Copy Desk. She worked the Society Desk, covered interviews for various lectures and style shows and interviewed celebrities. She watched Helen Hayes jay-walk across the street below *The News* office and not get arrested. And that was news! So went her column! She could cover the City Desk, State Desk, chat in the press room and at the same time hold forth in the publisher's office on his turf with great ease. Fil by virtue of friendships and reputation often got "first breaks" in her column.

Her July, 1945 column was the harbinger of peace after a terrible war and a forecast of a new writer who would be our children's hero—for she wrote about Kurt Vonnegut's release from prison camp.

Filomena would be in her nineties now, and though she would no longer be writing her column, (or would she?) she would be right up there in the top ten for ability, history, memories, grand dame manner, good looks, style, nerve and verve. She would still be "Atop the Town."

The Indianapolis Sentinel Building stood on the circle. Out of *The Sentinel* grew the *Evening News* and then came *The Indianapolis News.*

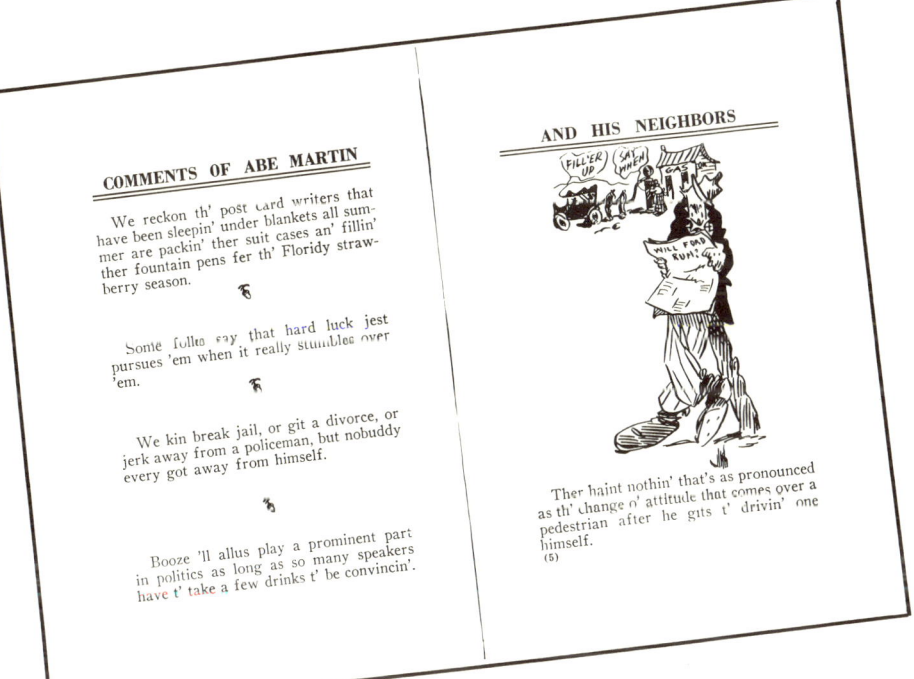

COMMENTS OF ABE MARTIN

We reckon th' post card writers that have been sleepin' under blankets all summer are packin' ther suit cases an' fillin' ther fountain pens fer th' Floridy strawberry season.

Some folks say that hard luck jest pursues 'em when it really stumbles over 'em.

We kin break jail, or git a divorce, or jerk away from a policeman, but nobuddy ever got away from himself.

Booze 'll allus play a prominent part in politics as long as so many speakers have t' take a few drinks t' be convincin'.

AND HIS NEIGHBORS

Ther haint nothin' that's as pronounced as th' change o' attitude that comes over a pedestrian after he gits t' drivin' one himself.
(5)

Abe Martin's grass-roots philosophy of man captured human nature as it is.

The "Perennial Four" of turn-of-the-century Indiana society—(clockwise) James Whitcomb Riley, Meredith Nicholson, Booth Tarkington and George Ade.

ATOP THE TOWN

The spirit and strength of America's young men, leavened by an incredible sense of humor in the face of the worst torment and hardship, is seen in the attitude of certain of our boys who survive, by the skin of their teeth, long, harrowing imprisonment as prisoners of war in Germany. To cite an example, take the case of about done from starvation, just getting to and from was no mean assignment.

For a time he had the dubious distinction of being his group's leader, thanks to having studied a bit of German while waiting around England and being able to make himself vaguely understood. His pre-eminence was short-lived, however. Came a day when he said too much in German in hotly protesting the way his crowd was treated. Calling upon the Geneva agreement, he made it clear what he thought of the pig of a guard, was clouted on the head for it

The first word about Kurt Vonnegut after his release as a prisoner-of-war was in Fil Gould's column.

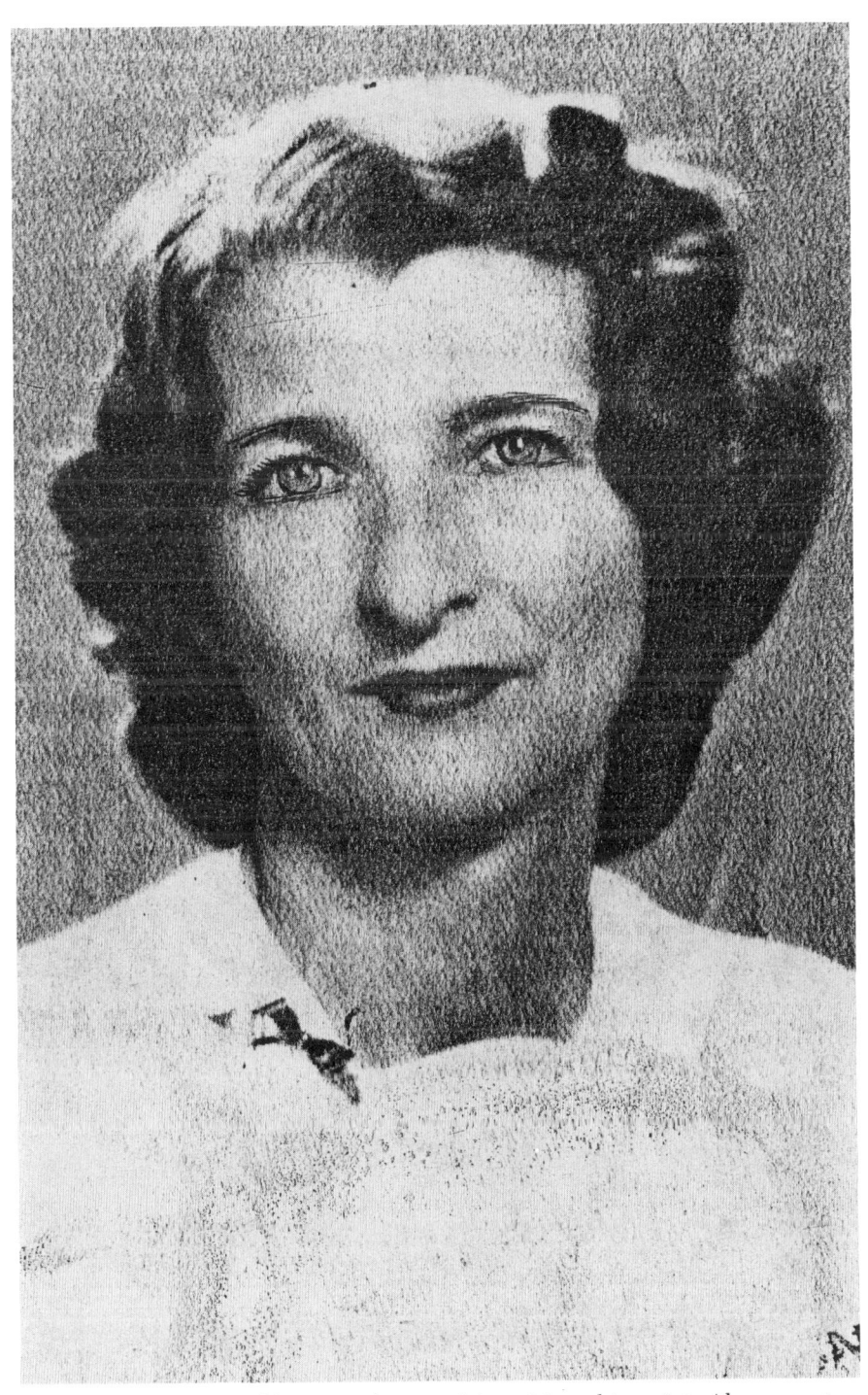

Filomena Manley Gould, "Atop the town" in spirit and in print. Always on top in the eyes of *The News* staff.

C. Walter McCarty, the genial host and toastmaster who was Editor and Publisher of *The News*. My boss.

3

OTHER GREATS ON THE NEWS

Paul Shideler was the dean of photography in Indianapolis in the late forties and fifties. Shideler's principal requirement for a photo was *action*. Never take a picture of someone standing or sitting, doing nothing. Action tells everything.

Bob Lavelle was Paul Schideler's disciple. Lavelle, by nature, had a feel for action in pictures.

Once Bob was sent to the airport to pick up Victor Borge, who came for a concert. Martha McHatton's (Ziegner later) job was to interview Borge for her story as "Drama and All Things Theatrical" editor, and Bob's job was to get a good shot of him. She rode along with Bob, and tells the following story.

Victor Borge had put four bags down on the curb for the doorman to pick up. Lavelle said, "Mr. Borge, would you mind picking up a couple of your bags so it will look like you are carrying them yourself?"

Borge said to Lavelle, "I can do better than that, I can pick up all four bags." His photo made the Blue Streak Edition (late edition) showing what a good guy was our guest Victor Borge, who was not above carrying his bags as he arrived at his hotel. Good action. Good press. Gets attention!

Bob Lavelle was also famous for action shots during the war. He served in the European theater, and while he was there, an outhouse caught fire. While it was burning to the ground, Bob saw an action photo in the making. He set his camera up, put on the timer, dropped his pants and made a beeline for the outhouse. As the camera clicked, he was caught coming from the burning edifice with his pants down. Just what Paul Shideler was talking about. Don't just stand there, *do something!*

(Would somebody please do something about pictures today in any form of publication where there are from two people to six, standing and grinning at each other with drinks in their hands and doing absolutely nothing? It shows a lack of imagination, energy, originality and intelligence on the part of the photographer and the editor. What kind of cutlines do you write for a picture that shows no substance at all?)

Ed Ziegner was one of the most knowlegeable writers *The News* ever had. He had newspapers in his blood; his father and brother had both worked for *The News*. Eddie came to *The News* when Wendell Phillippi was drafted, working on the copy desk for a mere $22.50 a week. Then Eddie had to leave his job to go to war, serving as a captain in the anti-aircraft division in Italy. While he was in Italy, Mickey McCarty wrote him a letter asking him to come back to the paper when he was discharged. The day after Christmas, 1945, Ed Ziegner came back to *The News* as a reporter. Forty years later he retired as Chief Political Editor. Except, of course, he really didn't. You never really do. You can't wash out all the ink, the heartbeats and the memories. Eddie belonged, and still belongs to politics in Indiana, as every governor from Shricker to Bayh could have told you.

Eddie's political preference was not necessary to define or explain; he was fair and unbiased in his coverage of facts and did not feel the need to insert his own opinion.

Eddie traveled the state with VIP's by train, by plane and by car, attending functions of import whether he liked it or not because he had a column to write. He was big on the readership scale. And controversial too.

He had a favorite politician—lovable, laughable Senator Homer Capehart. Capehart had a string of real accomplishments both in the business world and in public life. He had organized and run a radio company and then went on to Washington, where he was known and respected. He was also a master of malapropisms and mispronunciation. But that made him all the more colorful. He went to a flood area that had been devastated by high water and reported back that the "rooble" (rubble) and the "chauss" (chaos) were just terrible.

A beloved Indiana Senator, Capehart was revered by those in all walks of life until he was washed out of politics in the first modern PR campaign in Indiana history—that of Birch Bayh. Ed Ziegner relished every event of the senator's career that he covered.

Martha McHatton was Drama Editor Walter Whitworth's assistant, and as his health failed, she took over more and more of his work. An absolute whiz kid, she raced from one part of town to another in her job. She seemed particularly speedy in light of the fact that she did not own a car. During the war years a lot of celebrities came to this city as a part of tours. Martha had to hop a ride with the photographer and often go to Stout Field, a military air field, to meet planes, wait while the photographer did his work, then ride back to the hotel or wherever she was going to interview the person.

One of her "pick ups" was Bob Hope. She still describes him in detail as a "doll." Always a showman and always "on stage," Hope was so disciplined that he could fall asleep at the drop of a hat for a refreshing and needed cat nap. And he was a sport.

Martha took him to the Indiana State Fair, where they went directly to the hog barn. Martha, low key, sweet and unassuming, simply asked Bob Hope to pose with the pigs, which he graciously did—in profile. She also was assigned to interview Orson Welles, which terrified her because of his reported temper tantrums off stage. And of course, he was sweet and cooperative. This tells you something about Martha too; never did I see her raise her voice or show any sort of rage, although in the newspaper business there is often provocation for such behavior. Martha was just one of those gems. She still is.

It was not easy covering opera and the Indianapolis Symphony, seeing the movies as they came out, meeting the celebrities and interviewing or reviewing them all for her column. One day she went to five movies and wrote a review of every one of them. She also wrote a radio column and later added TV.

Martha loved Filomena Gould as much as I did. Fil helped Martha whenever she needed it. Time and newsprint were at such a premium during the war days that good scouts were angels on horseback.

Martha continued her work at *The News* until 1951, when she settled down into housekeeping and child rearing. Her press pass was kept polished because she had married Ed Ziegner. In June, 1990, they celebrated their fortieth anniversary, an affair thronged by members of the fourth estate along with many other well wishers from city officials to governors, past and present. They were real pros who worked like dogs, and were an essential part of the spirit of *The News* when I worked there.

The man I related to most at first at *The News* was Cornell (Duke) Acheson. He joined the staff with more odds against him than I! He was trying to become a newspaper reporter without knowing the ropes. Happily preppy in dress and attitude, he seemed to be too blue-blooded to be readily accepted as one of the guys. He did finally achieve that station. Short, wearing thick glasses, he brought a little touch of *Esquire* to the usually shabby newsroom with his gray flannels, tweed vest and jaunty bow tie. His cultivated voice, slightly eastern accent and gentlemanly manners caused him no end of ridicule, rejection and anguish!

When I was still a novice trying to prove myself, Duke was given a desk next to Chris Albion, assistant city editor. Chris was a good hardworking "pro" who commuted daily from Shelbyville by bus. Duke lived in one of our suburbs and drove his sports car downtown. Duke drove Chris to drink. He didn't mean to; he didn't do it on purpose.

Whenever the phone rang on the desk, Duke would answer it promptly and say, "Mr. Albion, sir. Telephone, sir." He might do this twenty times a day.

It wasn't too long before Chris had had enough of Duke's "to the manor born" manners. One day Chris turned to Duke and said, "For Christ's sake, Acheson, will you please stop calling me sir?!"

Duke replied, "Yes, Mr. Albion, sir. Sorry, sir."

Well, you can't make a sow's ear out of a silk purse overnight. In time Duke did himself proud. His dear friend, Eddie Ziegner wrote about it.

Former News Staffer Got Wish, Saw World
by Edward Ziegner

Cornell "Duke" Acheson came to work at The News *in the spring of 1946, and my first memory of him is that he either didn't know how to type, or maybe he could type, but, at first, at a glacial pace.*

It was nothing to be ashamed of. Most of the staff of that day, new to the paper or having worked there briefly before World War II, used the hunt and peck system, never having darkened the door of a typing class in high school days.

Duke Acheson had a science degree in foreign service from Georgetown University, and, as he says, had been "lightly seasoned in journalism as editor of a college paper." These were somewhat unusual credentials for a starting reporter of those days.

He also came from Philadelphia's Main Line, a rare source of newspapermen.

But The News *of 1946 was a good place to learn, even if Wayne Guthrie, then city editor, stood beside your typewriter as you wrote, and cracked his knuckles and urged you to greater speed.*

Acheson spent two years at The News, *doing the itty bitty stuff with which you start, and gradually evolved into a very good reporter.*

In the spring of 1948, he became a foreign correspondent for The News, *with the paper paying him a salary. But Acheson, "temporarily in funds," paid most of his own expenses.*

It was the beginning of a career as a foreign correspondent which was to last some thirty years, and take him over a great part of the world.

He went into Palestine, now Israel, then the scene of the first Arab-Israeli war, and covered that conflict. Acheson came back to The News, *but longed to get overseas again. He soon did, as a correspondent for several newspapers and magazines. His work found him in London, Algeria, Cyprus, Rhodes, Greece, Italy, and Africa, where he lived in Rhodesia for a long time, becoming a farmer-rancher (he once was chased out of his melon patch by a cobra).*

He edited a local paper and took part in civic affairs, but Rhodesia was falling into civil war and terrorism, and he left with his family.

He was never a "name correspondent" in the tradition of the ones from The New York Times *or* The Washington Post, *but he was a very good one.*

Some of the best people weren't blue bloods. Far from it. Freda Ash was from Loogootee.

Pronouncing odd Hoosier towns in funny ways was a standing joke on *The News*. Russiaville was "Roooshaville"; Loogootee (which was supposed to be pronounced Low-Goatey) was "Looogooooteey." The town itself was no joke, although it was pretty far out in the boondocks of Martin County. Once when Robert Kennedy was stumping in Indiana with his press corps, they stopped there. One of his staff wandered off and couldn't be found. When they did find him he was writing a post card which said, "Can you imagine getting stranded in Loogootee?!"

Well, Freda didn't get stranded there long. She came to the city and went to work on *The News* switchboard. That's where you get to know everything that is going on and everybody who is doing it. And there she was well trained for her next job as unofficial receptionist for Editor Mickey McCarty (Alice Cole was his secretary). When Wendell Willkie (the 1942 Hoosier presidential candidate from Rushville) came to see Mickey, he was so rumpled and wrinkled she led him right into the office so no one would see him looking like he had slept in his suit. She was the single most important person on the whole editorial floor, sitting behind a counter which was directly in front of the society desk. As one stepped off the elevator, he or she came face to face with Freda, separated only by the long counter that was interrupted by a small swinging gate, a little protective but not obstructive. There was a good feeling of openness on the whole floor in those days. When anyone had a visitor, Freda called the staff member up front where he or she could either proceed or lead the guest right back to the elevator. It was a minimum of fuss for a maximum of prevention.

The governor often stepped up to Freda's desk. Celebrities all stopped at Freda's desk, and just plain "nuts" stopped at Freda's desk. These were the days before security guards kept everyone off the news floor, and all the staffers had at least one try at walking through a crisis with a disturbed person and helping the person into the elevator with a big "Whew," as the door closed. It was good to know that Freda was watchfully backing you up.

Freda was also a pro. A short little lady with a very round face and rosy cheeks, not quite five feet tall, she wore stilt shoes and walked accordingly. She was straight-up-and-down, but showed off exceedingly good-looking legs. Her hair was mouse brown and stringy, dragging on her shoulders. Good grooming was not one of the requirements for working at *The News*, anyway.

But Freda was tough as she was funny, and she was a devout Catholic to the bone. Actually, she talked tough, but she was God-fearing and good hearted and her whole life was wrapped up in *The Indianapolis News* from nine to five. She learned tact by practising it every day with about one hundred irascible, over-pressured human beings. She was especially practiced at keeping very important people occupied until executive editor Mickey McCarty could come out to greet them.

During the Indianapolis 500, the office buzzed with famous people popping in and out. There was an excitement during this event that was missing the rest of the year, and Freda steered the big and little wigs around the office without a stir.

And there were the hawkers and con men and salesmen—you name 'em, Freda got 'em and took care of 'em in short order. If some reporter had something unexpected come up or got sick or had a tragedy, there was Freda right up front to know, sympathize and to help. And Freda got the word around fast so everybody pitched in. Freda was Miss Know. I can't tell you what Freda didn't know about *The News*—it probably wasn't important anyway.

Freda may not have had much education, but she was street-smart and people-smart and had a native sense of intelligence that got her off the switchboard and into the job as the executive editor's receptionist, the most important station on the editorial floor. But not before I begged her to teach me how to run the switchboard. She did that and I loused up more calls and long distance messages than any other stand-in operator, including Martha McHatton, who also thought everyone should know how to work a switchboard. It was so much fun to pull those plugs and wear those earphones—and to pass the buck to Indiana Bell if I made a mistake.

And funny? Was Freda ever funny—and profane! She was so much to all of us and so strong that it would never occur to any of us that Freda would get sick. She did. She died of cancer, breaking our hearts.

I don't recall if Bess Watson wrote Freda's obituary. She probably did, since she wrote most of the obits in town. If Bess Watson didn't write your obit, you didn't die right. She gave death class and she gave it space. Every bereaved person felt the genuine sympathy of Bessie, and the departed was given that due dignity that passing deserves. When Bessie hung up the phone or shook hands in person with the bearer of the statistics, he or she always left with a good warm feeling of having dealt with a newsperson who cared and was really sorry. "Eastside Man Cared About Dogs," the headline would say, and someone would read it in Irvington and weep with gratitude to *The News*.

Bessie herself was really corny, a big woman with a heart of gold and a frustrated performer. At *News* picnics Bessie had a whole repertoire of barnyard imitations. The renditions were tolerated only because she was such a good scout. But Bessie could pound out a good obit!

And there was Louise Lee, the Church Editor. She had a little more to work with than Bess. Louise was perfect for dealing with the clergy and the church groups and activities. A cheerful, pretty, middle-aged, rotund woman who wore silk dresses, Louise always looked like she was on her way to a church social. She was well-bred and savvy about most everything and everybody and wrote the Church Section of the paper with the same feeling that the Woman's Page Editor or Fashion Editor gave hers.

Frank Salzarulo was Farm Editor. The Agricultural Desk was one of the busiest and most demanding, and I learned, long before my own son became a farmer, that farming is fraught with problems. After I left, Frank took on the additional assignments of Auto Editor and labor reporter. He retired in 1985, four years before his death.

Albert was just Albert, although his real name was Albert Woodruff. He was the copy "boy," a misnomer in his case. His age was unknown, but he was certainly not a boy. Albert took life at *The News* very seriously and was very efficient and loyal and hard working. He passed out the first editions with dispatch to the whole staff. This was important, because we had very little time to catch any errors in time for the street editions. The black pencil went to work and then Albert would take the corrected copy back to the copy desk where it was sent in haste to the press room. Albert was good. And after the papers were back, he had a sweet way of bringing coffee to anyone who wanted it.

Actually, Albert was the one who did everything no one else would do. He lived with his mother, who took care of him. We never knew what his physical problem was exactly, but he had a slight speech impediment and seemed a little limited, though not limited in willingness, cheerfulness and desire to please. Albert did please, and the whole staff was fond of him, and what's more, needed him.

One gentleman who was as colorful as the American flag was Sports Editor William Fox. An impeccably dressed, white-haired man who was very dignified at all times, he was not what you would expect of a sportswriter. He looked more like a nobleman you would see at the Ascot Races, sitting in the royal box. He had a stable of sports writers that was hard to beat, and he ran his department with charm and grace.

He was beyond my reach as far as I was concerned. I stayed away from this gentleman who looked more like Douglas Fairbanks, Jr., or Cary Grant than a sports editor, lived in the *haute* neighborhood, drove the latest Cadillac and had his clothes tailored in New York. He had a beautiful wife and a beautiful life, and I was pretty far away from his milieu.

Now about the story of the fights. I knew nothing about the fights. Nothing. Not where they were held, or who fought whom, or where these fighters came from. But there was one redeeming fact. I wasn't going alone. This was a gimmick. Something to relieve the sameness and boredom of the same old thing. It was probably February!

The good news was that I was to be accompanied by a real pro sports writer. This was the Greek god of the whole newspaper editorial staff, Angie Angelopolous. A word of introduction about Angie. When he came home from the Navy, Angie bee-lined it down to *The News* in his Navy Whites, wearing his beautiful white smile and tanned skin and went right up to the staff floor.

Freda took one look at him and said, "Oh God, here comes the ugly Greek, Angie, back from the war." Followed by a shriek and a long hug. He was beautiful in every way. And I got assigned to go with Angie to cover the fights. *Hot Dog!*

What I knew didn't matter. This was to be the Society Editor's coverage of the sport of boxing. Still, I wasn't too much of a powder puff. Neither hitting nor the sight of blood did a thing for me; I certainly didn't feel like fainting. The only thing you could say was the sparring was dull. Finally I would have welcomed a good hook to the left or right or middle. The nearest thing to excitement was when the fight was over. The lady behind us stood up to put on her coat and her husband tried to help her by holding her coat for her. Her arm missed the sleeve and she socked her husband right in the jaw. Bill Fox thought that was great. I thought it was an evening wasted.

Angelo was a gifted sports writer. I joined the collection of girls who were in love with Angie. Every time he passed my desk I had palpitations. He was more than handsome, however; there was compassion and humor and modesty mixed with his ability as a good writer. *Sports Illustrated* recognized this as did other magazines.

And then Fate did a terrible thing. Angie got leukemia, and in the early 1960s, he died. There wasn't a room big enough to hold all of the people who loved Angie and wanted to come to his funeral. Sadly, Angelo had survived the war as a Navy Air Corps lieutenant, but in one sense the war did actually account for his death. Members of his family said that after Hiroshima the Navy asked for volunteers to fly over the city to ascertain the damage from the atomic bomb. Twelve pilots volunteered, and Angie was one of them. All took off from the carrier *Hancock* and flew their mission into the depths of the horrible radiation. There was damage all right, but it appears to have been to him and the rest of the pilots. All twelve of those pilots eventually got leukemia and died.

And It Had to Rain

Mary Jane Covers Her First Fights Amid Some Difficulty

By MARY JANE ALFORD

Well, I covered my first boxing match Thursday night—in the pouring rain. It seemed pretty silly to even think of fighting then, but the others didn't seem to mind. I took along my knitting in case there was any blood, so I wouldn't have to look. But the rain shrunk the yarn.

Crowds always fascinate me, and I like to look around and see if there is any one I know. I was just saying hello to an old neighbor when Mr. Ashley was knocked out by Mr. Peak. I think it is perfectly horrible for people to yell and scream when some one gets hurt. They were all saying "Atta boy, good work," and things like that and the referee was shaking his fists at the poor unconscious man and mumbling to him. I just didn't look.

The drizzle seemed pretty determined so they had the best fight next. That was with that cute blond curly-haired Denson and a man named Brown from somewhere or other. I was very excited when they came out looking very mean with their black satin shorts on. I was getting on to the game now.

Friendship Flickers

They smiled at each other and I thought it was nice that they were friends, but then the man by the ring rang the bell and they seemed to hate each other. They snarled and snorted and spit and slapped each other in the face, and then they would put their arms around each other and the man in the middle would yell, "Now break it up."

Once in a while they would smile at each other when the bell rang. I smiled, too. How can people concentrate when the crowd is yelling, "Hit him in the kidney" or "Counter him" (whatever that means!). I tried to quiet the people near me by saying "Shhsh," but I gave that up.

And, incidentally, my ribs should be black and blue, because some man next to me kept poking me with his elbow and screaming, "C'mon baby, kill 'em," and what not. I was very annoyed. I got tired then and looked around the crowd for relief. There were some very attractive women there all wearing pretty raincoats and colored scarfs to keep their hair from coming down in the rain.

Once Brown hit Denson right above the eye, and a steady stream of blood poured down his face. This made me dislike Brown intensely because I could see Johnny was getting tired and his eye hurt. I think the whole thing is absurd. When the fight was almost over Denson was knocked between the ropes and he headed right straight for my lap.

That's when I moved back a row. Finally the referee held up ten fingers and I was so glad because I thought those poor boys could use a ten-minute intermission. But I found out he meant tenth round. By this time the rain was serious and people were leaving in bunches. I was soaked and the ink on my notes ran together so now I have no idea what I was going to tell you.

The fighters were so wet their mitts just slid off each other and was I glad! Some people behind me had the nerve to complain about that! Johnny's poor eye kept bleeding and he could hardly see. Then at last the bell rang and some man yelled, "It's a draw." I guess that meant the fight was over. Both the boys smiled when it was over so I guess they weren't mad any more.

The best part of the fights was when the woman in front of us stood up to put on her coat, missed the sleeve and socked her husband right in the eye.

The News honored its own with an obituary editorial, which included these tributes:

> Not only was Angelo a great writer, with a warm human insight that few experience, but he was one of the kindest men we ever knew. He could always find time to search out the good and write about it . . .
>
> His warm style of writing was admired throughout the country. He was at his best when a few years ago he visited his father's birthplace in Greece.
>
> Of his arrival there, he wrote, "I swung off the horse, 14 hours after we'd left Athens and stepped down into a pitiful little hut. Aunts and cousins I had never seen before and could hardly see now in the faint light of a coal oil lamp embraced me. Here is where Pop was born.". . .
>
> We have lost not only one of this newspaper's greatest writers ever, but we have lost a dear friend.

And I say *The News* and the sports community lost one of the most beloved men ever to grace the editorial playing field.

Angelo was only one of the "boys" from the armed forces who came back to *The News* to return to their old jobs. It was a colorful parade of intriguing personalities, most of whom returned in their uniforms. Sometimes they came into work with the uniforms on, for a day or a week or more until they got "civvies." And Oh, Glory, they had to pass the society desk where they were in full view and could be overheard as they told their tales.

Herb Kenney appeared in a Navy uniform to take up his job as Amusements Editor and charm us all with his kindness, decency and phenomenal use of the English language. He was ever alert for the pun, the malapropism, the upside-down use of a word by a young and inexperienced writer, but he corrected you with such good humor that you felt blessed, not insulted.

Herb knew the arts, but he also knew the Navy, tournament bridge and finance. What he did not know was how to wear tastefully chosen neckties. When Herb died in the eighties, he had been with *The News* for almost fifty years. He was remembered by everybody who knew him as a friend as well as an editor.

The day I opened the paper to find that Filomena Gould, in her "Atop The Town" column writing in particular about another of these returning heros, Kurt Vonnegut of Indianapolis, I realized that many of the exuberant boys of my high school friends group from Shortridge had been swallowed up into another dimension for the years of their youth. Though they returned, they were forever changed.

Fil said this:

> The spirit and strength of America's young men, leavened by an incredible sense of humor in the face of the worst torment and hardship, is seen in the attitude of certain of our boys who survive, by the skin of their teeth, long, harrowing imprisonment as prisoners of war in Germany. To cite an example, take the case of Pfc. Kurt Vonnegut, Jr., who is home now, the better for the sight of Indiana and for the regaining of forty-odd pounds, thanks to Army care following his liberation.
>
> Kurt's experiences make the wildest adventure thriller pallid reading in comparison. But what gets us is that he has the gift for describing appalling situations with liveliness and humor. One finds oneself laughing with him over the most grueling episodes merely because he relates them with fresh and cogent humor. Afterward, one digests his comments and wonders how crumbs of comedy could be wrung from them. He has jotted down a log of his adventures which in my opinion surpasses any firsthand account of an American soldier's existence in enemy hands. Kurt enlisted in the Army from Cornell where he was studying biochemistry as well as taking an active part in university publications. After a varied pattern of military training in this country, he went over with the ill-fated 106th.
>
> Here is his letter:

Dear Folks,

> I'm told that you were probably never informed that I was anything other than "missing in action." Chances are that you also failed to receive any of the letters I wrote from Germany. That leaves me a lot of explaining to do—in precis:
>
> I've been a prisoner of war since December 19, 1944, when our division was cut to ribbons by Hitler's last desperate thrust through Luxembourg and Belgium. Seven Fanatical Panzer Divisions hit us and cut us off from the rest of Hodges' First Army. The other American divisions on our flanks managed to pull out.

We were obliged to stay and fight. Bayonets aren't much good against tanks: Our ammunition, food and medical supplies gave out and our casualites out-numbered those who could still fight—so we gave up. The 106th got a Presidential Citation and some British Decoration from Montgomery for it, I'm told, but I'll be damned if it was worth it. I was one of the few who weren't wounded. For that much thank God.

Well, the supermen marched us, without food, water or sleep to Limberg, a distance of about sixty miles, I think—where we were loaded and locked up, sixty men to each small, unventilated, unheated box car. There were no sanitary accommodations—the floors were covered with fresh cow dung. There wasn't room for all of us to lie down. Half slept while the other half stood. We spent several days, including Christmas on that Limberg siding. On Christmas Eve the Royal Air Force bombed and strafed our unmarked train. They killed about one-hundred-and-fifty of us. We got a little water Christmas Day and moved slowly across Germany to a large POW Camp in Muhlburg, south of Berlin. We were released from the box cars on New Year's Day. The Germans herded us through scalding delousing showers. Many men died from shock in the showers after ten days of starvation, thirst and exposure. But I didn't.

Under the Geneva Convention, officers and non-commissioned officers are not obliged to work when taken prisoner. I am, as you know, a Private. One-hundred-and-fifty such minor beings were shipped to a Dresden work camp on January 10th. I was their leader by virtue of the little German I spoke. It was our misfortune to have sadistic and fanatical guards. We were refused medical attention and clothing: We were given long hours at extremely hard labor. Our food ration was two-hundred-and-fifty grams of black bread and one pint of unseasoned potato soup each day. After desperately trying to improve our situation for two months and having been met with bland smiles, I told the guards just what I was going to do when the Russians came. They beat me up a little. I was fired as group leader. Beatings were very small time: one boy starved to death and the SS shot two for stealing food.

On about February 14th the Americans came over, followed by the RAF. Their combined labors killed 250,000 people in *twenty-four hours and destroyed all of Dresden—possibly the world's most beautiful city. But not me.*

After that we were put to work carrying corpses from Air Raid shelters; women, children, old men; dead from concussion, fire, or suffocation. Civilians cursed us and threw rocks as we carried bodies to huge funeral pyres in the city.

When General Patton took Leipzig we were evacuated on foot to Hellensdorf on the Saxony-Czechoslovakian border. There we remained until the war ended. Our guards deserted us. On that happy day the Russians were intent on mopping up isolated outlaw resistance in our section. Their planes (P-39's) strafed and bombed us, killing fourteen, but not me.

Eight of us stole a team and wagon. We traveled and looted our way through Sudentenland and Saxony for eight days, living like kings. The Russians were crazy about Americans. The Russians picked us up in Dresden. We rode from there to the American lines at Halle in Lend-Lease Ford trucks. We've since been flown to Le Havre.

I'm writing from a Red Cross Club in the Le Havre Repatriation Camp. I'm being wonderfully fed and entertained. The state-bound ships are jammed, naturally, so I'll have to be patient. I hope to be home in a month. Once home, I'll be given twenty-one days recuperation at Atterbury, about $600 back pay and get this—sixty (60) days furlough.

I've too damned much to say, the rest will have to wait. I can't receive mail here so don't write.

Love
Kurt, Jr.

And thus were the seeds sown, and the scars laid, for Slaughterhouse Five.

The editorial staff of a newspaper is a family, and like any family, there are all kinds of people filling it out. There are the loveable, the hateful, the talented, the dedicated, the impossible, the irascible, responsible and irresponsible. The smokers and the non-smokers, the drinkers and the non-drinkers, the hard workers and the enjoyers . . . and on into infinity. Some news writers are there for a living and some for the sheer enjoyment of using their talents. But all are there working, feeding hungrily on newspaper life. This is, of course, why they stay.

Bill Wildhack probably embodied in himself most of the contradictions I've just listed. He was the author of "Don't Quote Me," one of the best-written, most well read pieces of writing in the paper each night. It was a tongue-in-cheek and tears-in-eyes column. Bill, a naughty boy himself from one of Indianapolis' leading families, brought out the naughtiness in people. He knew everybody well, from the cop on the beat to the son of the publisher. He called me "kid," and after my days at *The News* were actively over, he got quite a bit of material from me. This was later, of course, after I'd left, but I'll tell the story here anyway.

As a young mother, I was always in the middle of a happening, like getting the mumps when I was about ten days from having my third baby. Someone who is as short as I am has to work very hard to keep from looking like a barrel, and I had put on weight. A full-blown case of the mumps had me so sick I couldn't even drink water, which made me look like the Goodyear blimp with two balloons on the top of it. Bill stopped by the house, saw me at the window, doubled up, and I was soon in the "Names in the News" column. When my baby girl was delivered—beautifully healthy, thank God,—my clothes hung on me, and I called Bill and told him so.

Another day I was in our dining room using the phone that was right beside our big dining room window. I gasped and stopped talking. It couldn't be! A dog was driving a car across the street up our front bank across our lawn and heading straight for the dining room. I was frozen; luckily, the car with its dog chauffeur stopped just short of the dining room, coming to rest in the cedar hedge. Bill put that in, too, and lots of people didn't believe it really happened and called him up. How did the dog drive? He knew the answer. Our neighbors across the street had parked their car, leaving it open and their small dog had jumped in and knocked the car out of gear. The excited dog got behind the wheel and stayed there. The story appeared nationally in the syndicated "Freak Accidents of 1958."

Bill loved a good story and casual dress in the newsroom. His usual outfit was khaki trousers, white or blue frayed oxford cloth shirt and dirty tennis sneakers. One day he came back from lunch with a beautiful periwinkle-blue cashmere sports coat.

"Wow," said the whole editorial floor. "Where did you get that?"

"My grandmother took me to lunch and thought I looked shabby, so she bought the sports coat for me." In unison we looked at his feet. No, she did not buy him new shoes.

Bill befriended me immediately, in and out of the office, taking me to places I shudder to think about now. One was the Fox Burlesque theatre, where his favorite stripper, Rose La Rose "took it off." She needed no press agent in our city; she had Bill Wildhack!

After I was gone, Bill suffered from various illnesses and lay off for a while, having a good part of his stomach taken out, with a lot of trauma. Bill came back to writing, and it was at that time that he initiated the very popular "Don't Quote Me" column at Gene Pulliam's request. Some of the time, though, he seemed to be without his usual buoyancy and bounce. We all lost a good friend and Indianapolis lost a fine journalist when this man, who looked like a combination of Jack Nicholson and Jack Benny and warmed everyone's heart, went . . . forever.

When Griff Niblack died in 1992, he had been on the staff of *The News* for over fifty years. That was a lot of beat-covering, re-write work, editorial writing and hometown nostalgia. Clay Trusty, the wry and competent city editor of *The News* in the fifties, said about Griff, "He was the only re-write man I ever saw who could come at you with a story backwards. He could do the last columns and then bring in the fast-breaking lead right before deadline." When Griff graduated to the editorial page, he continued another of those purely Hoosier special touches *The News* specialized in: the Ebben Stebbin character, who told wry truths about Southern Indiana and human nature in general and helped us recall with pride and appreciation the simple and decent qualities of our roots. Griff particularly loved animals, and the way he wrote about his dog Henry in his column "Hoosier Homespun" made Henry seem wise indeed.

One of my favorite of Griff's columns was on squirrels. Here it is, another sample of the kind of excellent writing we can all learn from:

> *The gang of squirrels in University Park continues to get free board and room, following a tradition established by the late Frank Fitzel. And judging from their sleek plumpness, they are doing rather well.*
>
> *There are believed to be five in the group, which is the same number that Fitzel used to feed. The feeding is now done by a kind caretaker of the little downtown oasis. He buys peanuts for them which they accept with alacrity and quickly scurry up the nearest tree.*
>
> *Fitzel, who lived in the nearby Essex Hotel, used to coddle the squirrels with handfuls of expensive nuts from City Market, but they seemed just as grateful for peanuts.*
>
> *It seems strange that wild animals live in the heart of a large city, but it seems to be a mutually enjoyable situation with squirrels getting fed and humans having fun watching them.*

> *There were three baby squirrels some weeks ago. The caretaker reports that somebody killed them. Obviously there are some humans who haven't advanced much beyond the wild beast themselves.*

That was Griff.

When I began this book I wrote to my old friend Fremont Power asking for his "take" on the newspaper business during those early days as compared to the trade today. His reply follows.

Dear Majie:

> *As for the old days versus the new days, I suppose that it is expected of old gaffers that they say the old days were much, much better. I don't know. Good writing is good writing, whether new or old, and we had some of both then, as we do now. There is no doubt that the newspaper is better designed now—but then I don't think design ever saved a paper. Example:* The NY Times. *It's looked the same since I can remember and I don't think anybody buys it because of makeup, which is very pedestrian, except for some of the Sunday sections. You must remember I've been gone from the wax works for more than eight years now and so I know scarcely anyone who works there now. But from what I hear, it seems to me we had more fun then than the present staff has.*
>
> *White wine as the drink of choice had not yet appeared in our time and it seems to me now we operated with a bit more élan and abandon.*
>
> *Who has a sportswriter now who goes to a Big Ten game and then wires the paper to "use AP" as he is much too soused to file a story? That would be Chris Hankemier, whose name I'm sure I'm not spelling write. (yes write).*
>
> *Who else had a sports editor (W.F. Fox, Jr.) who wrote poetry in his column? And some of it wasn't too bad.*
>
> *Do you remember Guthrie's system by which we rewrote every single snippet of an item? And* The Star *apparently did the same thing, after which we might rewrite it again, until one time both papers had carried the same item for three days running until some perceptive operator cut it off.*
>
> *And do you remember the days before Christmas when the day's festivities would begin when Mickey McCarty came out and set a fresh fifth on the copy desk?*

It was not considered bad personnel policy then to have fun with your colleagues. Of course, it's a wonder we didn't all get killed going home, but then none of us did.

This is not to say all our enjoyment was alcoholic. It's just that we seemed to live without so damned much obsession with the future.

In many ways, I think the investigative reporting now is much superior to our own, particularly when I consider that Guthrie might explain he was killing a story because it was "controversial." Damn, that used to gall me then—and it still does.

[Guthrie was Wayne Guthrie, City Editor, a stickler for rules who paced and cracked his knuckles, as has been reported. He was a nerve-wracking boss who drove us all crazy, and I also remember him as having a brilliant intellect and being a "dear little man."]

We operated in a time when if you called somebody up and said, "This is The News," the party knew who he was talking to. Before I hung it up, it used to scorch me no end when the party called would respond, "News what?"

"News newspaper, dammit, in business since 1869. No we're not on a channel. We print stuff to read."

Well, as you can see, there is a bit of bitterness under all this someplace, so I think I better wrap it up for now before this typing gets any lousier, as you put it in your letter. Very refreshing hearing from you, Majie.

All my best,
Fremont

Back in the seventies, Kurt Vonnegut wrote "Fremont Power is something of a novelty. A man who can write!" He was a novelty anyway in word and deed. A champion of the underdog? Not exactly. More of a champion of causes and conditions. He would bore into unfair practices like a dentist looking for a cavity. He would find it, dig into it, and try to fix it by letting it out in the column. Fremont was a newspaper WRITER—the kind of a writer I would like all newspapers to have.

Martha Ziegner, Eddie Ziegner, Wendell Phillippi and I were going to meet Fremont at Shapiro's Delicatessen one day and sit around the table with our corned beef on rye and talk about how newspaper reporting had deteriorated, and dream up ideas to clean it up. "Free" was not feeling well. The word was that he had lung cancer. I was crushed to hear of his illness, but grateful that at least I had his letter about our old staff days. He didn't show at Shapiro's.

The presses of Fremont Power's good mind shut down in '91. I had an out-of-town engagement and could not go to his funeral or calling. But on my way to the airport I stopped for a minute at the mortuary. No one was there, so I walked up to his open casket where he was reclining big as life to say a quick goodbye and to thank him for being what a good newspaper man is supposed to be, and more, for always being supportive and a friend to me and for caring about people in our town who didn't have a good shake. So Fremont, here's to you. The flowers I would have sent you are herewith sprinkled around your own words. The following are two articles published in *The News* on September 20, 1991.

Fremont A. Power
When Jack Averitt, former Statehouse correspondent for The News, *was a cub reporter, he was struggling with the wording on a rather routine police-beat story.*

Fremont Power, who was then on the rewrite desk, asked if he could lend a hand.

"Fremont just changed a thing here or there," Averitt later recalled, "but by the time he had finished, that story was completely different. It just sparkled. He was just incredible that way with words and the language."

Power, a reporter, columnist and executive editor of The News, *was indeed one of the best to ever practice the craft of newspaper writing. He was also a marvelous person.*

Born in 1915 in Home Place, a Hamilton County farm community, Power managed to attend Indiana University despite the Depression. In 1938 he gravitated into journalism, going to work for the Indianapolis Times. *His career was interrupted by the war. After the war, in 1946, Power was hired by* The News, *initially to put out a Saturday Magazine. Although the magazine never got off the ground, he was kept on as a feature writer and rewrite man. In 1965 he was given a daily column and named executive editor.*

During his career, Power interviewed virtually anyone from Mae West to Maurice Chevalier. He traveled from Dallas, Texas, while covering the assassination of President John Kennedy to

Bimini in search of Adam Clayton Powell. He won numerous awards for his work.

Power was also an accomplished medical/science writer. In 1958, former Purdue University President Fredrick L. Hovde cited Power as the only newspaper reporter in the state who met the qualifications for acceptance into the National Association of Science Writers.

But, what Power is best remembered for is his writing about the dispossessed of society—the homeless, those in institutions, the activist, the eccentric, the artist. He gave voice to the voiceless.

And, around here, he is remembered for the generous help he gave to legions of young reporters.

Volumes could be written about Fremont Power. But nothing speaks better for him than his own words. We commend your attention elsewhere on this page to a reprint of one of his columns.

*The Legion is Minus One
by Fremont Power
(reprinted from 9/16/68 The Indianapolis News)*

They were part of the street scene, these two women, and what they had was each other. If nothing else.

And it never appeared there was much else; the old papers they carried about and whatever else they might find in the trash baskets they searched. That was about all.

They lived on the vague fringes of society. And they were forever on the move, walking, walking, walking, as if there might be danger in stopping. Perhaps then the "regular" world would close in on them and somebody, in great officious kindness, would decide that something should be done for them. And that might involve separation, a danger to be avoided.

They were members of the Indianapolis Legion of the Damned, a rather noble legion when you come to think of it. They don't live in society, really, nor in society's big brick institutions for the damned, and yet they survive. Or at least they do until the heat or the cold or pneumonia or some disaster takes them from a world in which they never seem to belong.

There are several members of the downtown legion: The bearded old man in the aviator's cap who occasionally startles unwary passers-by with his irascible outbursts . . . the thin, unwashed one who, standing out on the sidewalk, is forever rocking back and forth on his feet . . . the bird-like woman, always heavily clothed and carrying something wrapped in linen—her precious silverware, it is said.

Mostly they go alone, these supreme individualists, but the two women were invariably together. In fact, togetherness seemed to be their bulwark and refuge.

In some circles they were known as "George's girls," after a social worker who used to see them occasionally. Once about 10 years ago, when times were particularly hard for them, arrangements were make to send them to the Julietta home, where they made a reasonable adjustment.

But then, it is said, a man "took a shine" to the younger, taller of the two, the one with the long, tattered fur coat, and so they left and went back on the streets.

Occasionally, they were able to earn a bit with telephone soliciting. Mostly, it appeared, they were on the verge of destitution.

But it was not always so. Both had been to college. The shorter, heavier one, who sometimes wore two or three men's jackets under a mackinaw, was once a legal secretary. She also wrote poetry and was the author of three books of verse.

But there was a quirk of personality—a failure to relate satisfactorily to other persons, that impelled them out of the ordinary channels of society.

And there also seemed to be something of a social protest in their way of life. Once it was suggested to the older, shorter one that she try to return to secretarial work.

"I've given up that part of my life," she protested. "We're together."

But no more. The older one was stricken last month and taken to General Hospital. She died at 61. Official cause of death: heat stroke.

There was a proper funeral and a proper burial. Remaining now are those books of poetry—and the younger woman, 41, crushed and alone.

So alone she will have to try to go into the society where most people live.

The legion is minus one, maybe two.

That superb piece of writing, typical of *The News* at its best, is a fitting close to this chapter.

Dapper Bill Fox, *News* Sports Editor, surrounded by allstar staffers (L to R) Angie Angelopolous, sports writer, Fremont Power, feature writer, and Wayne Fuson, sports.

The good-natured, fun-loving, helpful, mischievous newsman—columnist Bill Wildhack. He's covering his favorite event, the Indianapolis 500 Mile Race.

A rare combination: Virginia Nicholson Fairbanks, granddaughter of author Meredith Nicholson and Richard H. Fairbanks, grandson of Vice-President Charles Warren Fairbanks, whose family owned *The Indianapolis News*.

Wendell C. Phillippi, handsome officer of the Indiana National Guard, and, in 1952 its youngest brigadier general. Wendell was Managing Editor of *The News*.

Ed Ziegner, a newspaperman's newswriter, with his phone in its typical position.

Angie Angelopolous, one of the rarest and most beloved writers of an era. Sportswriting was his field, compassion was his seal.

The intelligence and productive capacities of Martha McHatton are enhanced by a bright smile.

4

SOCIETY EDITOR

So, I eventually found myself with that odd and sometimes maligned title on any newspaper—that of Society Editor.

The News had the Woman's Pages—made up of stories about fashion and child-rearing and recipes and food analysis. But the most popular part of the Woman's Pages was the Society Page, or pages. I had trained myself to think that a paper would be delivered by a paper boy in the late afternoon and that the lady of the house would run to get it before her husband got home. She would turn right to the Society Page, my page, and what I had put out on that page made up everything a woman needs to know about the social side of life! Where and when the "meetings" and "important functions" were, who was who, and what people were getting married. Those three things made up the society pages. What else is there? Anyway, it was enough for most everybody who was female. Even men were not immune to it.

Every wedding on any particular day is going to be the most important day in somebody's life, for sure. But the Society Page was also the place to find out what went on at the parties you were invited to and the place to spill coffee on the parties you weren't invited to.

The Society Page was for information and reporting events that were considered *Social Events*. It was my job to get the first break on anything big that was going to happen or just did! We read the rival papers and compared our stories. I would hope to have something more or something new on "my page." Sometimes we could bargain a little. "If I can have the scoop on this, you can get first break on that." This sort of negotiation depended upon the importance to that particular paper of a particular event.

Society editors attended very special events, some by invitation only, and then duly reported them. The Managing Editor sent the society department to cover charity and public events like horse shows, home tours, Junior League projects, garden clubs, auxiliary groups, art museums, other museums, the symphony, new groups, alumnae groups, *women's* groups in general, clubs in general, groups in general, *and* the biggest annual event of the year in the city of Indianapolis, the 500 Mile Race.

Every society news item was printed on the page in a spot that was commensurate with its importance to the community . . . sometimes to the paper itself. Weddings were given space by that same yardstick.

How did "Society" operate, while "Cityside" was busy doing its own thing on the other side of the newspaper office?

Here is how it went, at least for me.

You walk in the door, and before you put your purse down the phone rings.

It's a woman with a notice to put into Tuesday's paper. Not Monday and not Wednesday, be sure to get that straight. Put down the phone, say hello to Herb Kenney, who is out at his desk in the editorial department editing something for the early edition. Say a mannerly and sweet good morning to Louise Lee, the lovely Church Editor. Look around to take the greeting of Freda Ash—"How the hell are you?" Now you can start the day. If you cleaned up your desk the day before, you take out your folder and start going through your notes and written copy marked, "For Saturday," or whatever the future day is. You go to the wedding file and this is when you reach for the aspirin bottle—these details have to be here *now*. Flowers, colors, where, when—why aren't they all here?

Now it's time for the phone to really get ringing off the hook. You can't hide—they know you are there by this time. And it could be something important. If it is, you sit down, concentrate, and try to ask the right questions, which you can do by rote from the many times you have taken these calls.

By now, 9:30 a.m. anything that has to go to the copy desk this morning had better be corrected, edited and ready to go, because it is getting on towards 10 a.m. deadline.

Albert comes in, bless him. "You want a cup of coffee?"

"Damn right. Oh, and Albert, would you bring me some fresh pencils? Atta boy!"

Phone again, rinnnging—never ends. You make calls, check wedding and club meeting details, when you can get into the lines. "Hello, yes, no, okay. We'll do the best we can. Who? Oh yes, love to, how nice. Oh, we'll use all of it. How do you spell that middle name?"

And now, a face at the door—"Please sit down, I'll be right with you."

And finally, it's noon. There are some of the guys standing by the elevator. You look up, wistfully.

"Hey, you want to come to lunch?"

"Be right there! Hold that elevator."

Our break of the day. We walk to Fox's Deli for a heavenly baked ham sandwich on fat egg bun. Delicious. Then we talk about what happened in our departments in the morning, then walk back to the west Washington Street offices of the paper, to Sports, to City Desk, to State Desk, to Copy Desk and to my Society Desk.

And then we all start on tomorrow's paper.

This is on an average day. A few times during the year were definitely not average times—Christmas with its plethora of parties, the Dramatic Club Cotillion, and of course, the super extravaganza for the society pages, the most exciting time of the entire year and demanding the most of us in the women's office—The 500 Mile Race.

The month of May is known in Indianapolis as the month of "The Greatest Spectacle in Racing," now referred to as the Indy 500. I belong to the ancient group—old school—that recoils at the word "Indy." Please, for us, Indianapolis?

Almost as if it were Christmas, there is an undefinable something in the air . . . a smell, a spirit, that is in the city at race time. It has festooned itself in a setting of black and white checkered *everything*. From flags to tuxedo jackets, eyes cross with black and white checkers. There is some relief from checkers with the myriad of red geraniums planted everywhere. A big party is in the air during the entire month of May. You can't describe it, you can't eat it and you can't fax it. But it's there and it is enhanced by the freshly mowed lawns, the tulips and peonies and iris blooming and the downtown becoming alive with pansies planted in boxes and with the pride of its citizens.

The Race belongs to all mankind from Maine to Hawaii and the rest of the world. Racing fans live for this, whether they're sleeping on blankets in the infield, waiting for days for the race to begin, or relaxing in grandeur in the suites with closed circuit TV, open bar and luncheon á la gourmet.

This event draws people from all over the world and every walk of life. There is nothing else like it in this country.

In addition to being one of my biggest jobs of the year, it was also very big for the staff of photographers, and an awesome job for the sportswriters. It was, of course, an even bigger job for the radio announcers, and bigger still for the TV cameramen. There is no way to describe the "hype" for the camera men and radio reporters during the month of May at the Indianapolis Motor Speedway. The Sports Page reporters and writers were swamped.

And I discovered that the responsibility of reporting for society is not limited to the subject of women.

It was my job to put on my press pass and go with our best photographer to interview the spectators in the boxes. First, there was the research job: where would all the important people be sitting? I found that out and put family and corporate names beside notes which said "north turn," or "straightaway stretch." We went out at six in the morning in a caravan of cabs, and by ll a.m. at the start of the race I had all the material and was done. Since my press pass took me anywhere, except the pits and pagoda area, I could be wherever I pleased when the "Star Spangled Banner" was sung and millions of bright balloons climbed skyward. That spectacle was soon followed by Speedway President Wilbur Shaw's instructions, which always sent chills up my spine, "Gentlemen, start your engines!"

Then I craned my neck to see the pace car lead a team of thirty-three drivers around the pace lap, with excitement mounting as speed increased. The pace car pulled off the track and the race was on, with the loudest accompaniment of screaming, clapping and va-rooming you can imagine.

With that very emotional high over, I would return to the quiet office, my ears still ringing with the roar of the engines, to write my copy and cut lines for the photos we would spread across a full page of the race from "socs" point of view. In those days the race was a sporting event and a tremendous social happening, as well as an opportunity to test all kinds of automotive improvements in a town where the automobile always was, and still is, important.

As a woman covering the event, I was once asked to leave the pagoda area because women were not allowed beyond the tall fence that surrounded those places. I thought that was a silly rule, and I ignored it. I was, after all, with other reporters from *The News*. I was noticed, and word was sent down. "No women allowed. Please don't make it embarrassing for Mr. Shaw." I would have to vacate the area immediately. Stupid rule—I again ignored it.

Another message! Mr. Shaw himself was coming down from the top of the pagoda (an old, tired, frame dump that impressed nobody). Ha! I thought, with irony, that will be a good way to meet the exclusive Wilbur Shaw. Of course he didn't have to come down and oust me, because I had to go and work on my page assignment.

You will have to make a "pit stop" here as we are talking about the subject of the 500 mile Speedway Race. I have to tell you here about Filomena Gould's son, and my friend, J.D. Gould. Fil's son was a contemporary of mine. J.D. and his wife, Sally, have been two of the most talented and wonderful people it has been my pleasure to know.

J.D. Gould was a man for all seasons. His best season of all was the month of May. J.D. was a businessman, (manufactured valves), a musician (guitar, banjo, country music) and orator, and like many other friends of ours, he was a race fan. His family and many of their friends were a part of that "auto-mania" I spoke about that happens in May when the racing world descends on our city. A lot of people were race car owners, and there was a fever among those people that only the first day of June would break.

For three generations our friends the Goulds had had a spot on the old popular North Turn at the track, and that was where the "500" North Turn T & T Society held its meetings. It's where people could go and watch and picnic and mill around and "dress casual" and get sunburned and exchange stories and culminate the whole month of the trials and qualifications in one glorious day of noise and fumes. There was nothing peaceful about any of it, but it was tradition. No one ever told me what T & T meant. I figured it was none of my business.

J.D. got the black flag on his own race track in 1991 and so he won't be watching from his favorite spot any more. But he lives on in verse about the Speedway.

John D. Gould, Jr.
Chief Observer, Retired
"500" North Turn T&T Society

Hardly a fan is still alive
Who remembers the Race of Thirty five,
Or braved cold May in the Old North Turn
To hear the Novi and Ralph Hepburn
Or observed the Balloon hook the Ladies' commode
This is enough of this terrible Ode.

Henry Wordsworth Gouldfellow   1923-1991

The 500 Mile Race and glamorous weddings and big affairs were not the only things we covered, of course. But our job was to see that important people doing important things got in the paper. Every club had a publicity chairman. Today it's the public relations person. And if you have any idea how many organizations there are in a city and how many auxiliaries and all the other organizations and institutions I mentioned a few pages ago, you too would begin to wonder where the newsprint is coming from—that is, the paper the news is printed on.

And all those people who hold the publicity chairman's jobs for that year are supposed to take the Society Editor out to lunch at least once. That act is to give a feeling of identity with the person and, hopefully, to get good space. If possible, I avoided these luncheons, preferring to grab a quick bite at the local nip and sip with the boys, or once in a while to have a Hotel Lincoln special sandwich, which was sliced turkey, tomato, bacon and blue cheese covered with thousand island dressing—on toast. You have to relax sometime during the day even if it was in an orgy of eating.

Our greatest attention, of course, went to weddings, and they had their own unique kind of PR person. In those days of Society Page editing, a wedding was decribed in great detail. We needed full descriptions of gowns and bridesmaids' dresses. Those usually came from the bridal bureaus of the department stores or specialty shops. The details used were proportionate to the prominence of the family of the bride (or the aggressiveness of the bridal department). Then came the next biggest headache, the florist. There were probably more harsh words between the Copy Desk and the Society Desk and the typesetters over descriptions of bouquets and "arrangements at the club" for the reception than any other matter. One florist in particular *never* got the copy to us in time and *never* answered our calls pleading for details.

Customarily, this information was sent in to the paper on little forms in plenty of time and any details could be confirmed by phone. Reader interest dictated what was used on sentimental occasions. Colors, flowers, schools, parents, grandparents, ancestors, satin, silk, tulle, arm bouquets, nosegays . . . and on and on. But never, in those days, did the Society Desk tack on the occupations of the bridal couple, unless it was of national importance. It would have been considered in very poor taste.

If there was a problem with the florist, it was routine to call and say, "Madame, if you cannot get your copy to us by our deadline, then perhaps you will understand if we omit all descriptions of bouquets and floral arrangements." This was like being stung by a hornet, which they deserved on occasion. Florists often assumed a style and then a reputation and then a feeling of importance second only to the mother of the bride!

Wedding portraiture by Noble Bretzman was *de rigeur*. Bretzman, from one of the old families himself, officiated from a studio on North Meridian Street, where young women whose profiles were illumined with the softest of lights gazed off in a sort of romantic reverie into the unfathomable future. He charged by the square inch, but it was worth it. Nobody touched his work for engagement or wedding photos.

What an ego trip the whole wedding write-up could be. And a giant pain in the neck! But the worst pains were the parents of the bride. It was indeed the prerogative of the bride's mother (or the father's secretary) to send in all the details of the wedding and the wedding party. It was her obligation to have names of the bridesmaids and groomsmen correctly spelled, but it was our obligation to check on these. It was fine to include the schools attended, the colleges and universities, additional degrees etc. Some of the information was more than needed and often more than wanted. The key to a family's real makeup was often revealed in the way the information was presented to the Society Editor. Some people are pushy. Others have a very false sense of importance. There are also total fakes who make things up. Some put on airs. Some think the word "society" is the key to the kingdom—social climbers. We learned to spot the species! The authentically important people, of course, are often more modest, the least assuming and the most cooperative. These are the ones who know where they are coming from and are the understanding ones.

Only one wedding write-up made me angry enough to throw my paste pot across the room. Unfortunately, it was a family who was considered high society. There was some difficulty getting the details together and the same prima donna florist was not getting her information in to us.

It must be known that some folks were adamant about being in either the morning or the evening paper, depending on the time of a wedding. This is understandable, because in those early days, an early writeup would tell secrets about the bridesmaids' dresses, bouquets, etc. and totally ruin the whole production, which could be akin to a grand pageant in the gardens of Versailles, of course. I must say I do miss some of the theatrics involved in weddings.

But in this case, I was getting nowhere. At the close of the day I still had too many missing facts. Evening paper, they had insisted. Socially prominent, of course. No one could reach the family. Finally in desperation, I called the boss. "All you can do is call them first thing in the morning, if they want the wedding in tomorrow's *News*."

First thing the next morning, around 8:30, I called. The bride's mother answered the phone. I explained our dilemma. She would have to give me the necessaries over the phone in order to get in the evening paper, which I represented.

"Well, of all the inconsiderate, stupid, insipid people I have ever encountered, you are the most. How *dare* you call me at this hour of the morning, the day of our wedding. I was sound asleep!" It was hard to keep from screaming at that point. What she got from me was a fantasy banana cream pie in the face and complete disinterest in her wedding.

We had a wonderful staff and there was a good spirit of caring and camaraderie between Cityside, with all its variety of characters, and Society. And the Copy Desk had great sympathy for the Society Desk. We always tried to help each other.

Look in any newspaper today and you will notice that weddings are no longer "written up," they are reported. There are rarely full length or three quarter length or half length pictures of brides. Instead, one sees postage-stamp-size snapshots or informal photographs of the happy couple.

Now all the information needed for a wedding story is: name, parents' names, time, date, church, maid or matron of honor, and best man. Schools attended and present jobs of both parties are often described and that includes produce manager at the A & P. That may be very democratic, but in my opinion not of real "social note."

Nowadays, if there is a wedding involving very important people or other readable interests, it will come from the wire services or appear in a column. Local columnists often miss some of the most newsworthy items because their access comes from what they know about or hear about or is mailed or called in to them. The *crème de la crème* are often silent and private. Some of the most wanted are often not reported at all. Then an editor gets hot because his paper didn't get the real news.

In all fairness, lack of space or lack of newsprint is the reason for much mediocre reporting today. Also, many of the so-called old families have been replaced by the new rich or the "new element" and nobody but the older folks know who the hell anybody is or even was anymore. This tends to eliminate real old-fashioned society as we old society editors knew it and wrote it.

Why did a newspaper writer put up with all of this clap-trap? Imagine being a department head on the editorial staff and making $47.50 per week! Imagine the same kind of condition at Christmas. The women were given a pair of hose and a box of candy. What the men got I never knew. I hope it was an extra pay check because most of them had families and low pay.

Perhaps it was love of the "game" that kept us at it. Newspapering bites you and is like an incurable virus. All the rest of a newsman's days he will smell a story in a situation that goes over the layman's head. Part of it was the pride of the byline. To see your first byline on a story is a great thrill. To cover a story that merits a byline is the ultimate. The real coup is to write a column and have that name under the heading.

There is a cast of characters in every newspaper situation. And real life is even more colorful than TV or the movies, especially when it comes to the press. One professional bonus was the fact that we all helped each other. We often ran into stories that were not pertinent to our own department and we always passed it along to the right reporters.

The handling of all the complicated aspects above in society-page writing implied a very important knowledge, or should I say pseudo-knowledge. That was the knowledge of "who's who" in Indianapolis, and to some extent, Indiana.

I had had some knowledge of which families in the Hoosier capital were considered prominent from my childhood and youth and schooling, but there was a lot to learn about the unofficial bluebook. When I said pseudo-knowledge I meant what I said. God or the governor of Indiana didn't decide who was a "member of an important family" in Indianapolis, who was old money, who was new rich, and whose engagement we should put in with a big Bretzman photo and whose a tiny two-line announcement. We just sort of intuitied who the socially prominent were supposed to be, a knowledge which seemed to ooze out of the pores of downtown buildings like the Athletic Club or the Propylaeum, or maybe it was the houses on Meridian and Washington Boulevard.

Let's be hard-nosed about this. The bottom line was that names make news, names sell newspapers. We were given to understand from the first day that in the society pages we cover people who are considered important in important ways, people who aren't known get short shrift. Ladies want to read about social doings, and they want to read most about people they've heard of and consider social doers. So there was a certain stratification and snobbishness about all this.

Consider the way we covered church circles. If the church circle contained Lillys, we gave it probably the biggest play of all. Eli Lilly and Company had been the most important business in our community ever since the turn of the century, and I knew first hand who the Lillys were. The most magnificent coming-out Indiana had ever seen was the debutante party of Evie Lilly at the Lilly house overlooking White River on Sunset Lane.

The year was 1938, and Eli and Ruth Lilly and Eli's headstrong young daughter Evie greeted guests in an elegant garden setting. Women in white chiffon evening dresses, men in summer formal wear sat at tables around a dance floor where a big band played. Benny Goodman had come from New York, with Lionel Hampton, and Indianapolis society was agog. Gorgeous food, and a perfect summer night added to the magic. Evie Lilly danced so much during the evening that her dress was tattered by dawn, when the party broke up.

Eli and Ruth Lilly, his second wife, were not usually extravagant entertainers. They were unassuming, gracious people with a fine sense of artistic beauty and commitment to community service. They were usually only extravagant with their bull terriers, whom they were known to indulge with scraps from the table. At both their places was a little gold pick and the table bits were quietly delivered to the little canine mouths with gold service!

Eli's brother Josiah K. was the other "First Name" to watch in Indianapolis society. From his memorably planned and beautiful estate across from Woodstock, on White River, he set the style for quietly gracious Indianapolis living. Oldfields had extensive gardens, quaint bridges, and miles of walks. Josiah Lilly's estate was left eventually to the Indianapolis Museum of Art, which has created on its grounds one of the most beautiful art museum sites in the country. But that, of course, was later.

Tarkington. Another famous name in town. All loyal Hoosiers had read Booth Tarkington's *Penrod, Seventeen,* and *Magnificent Ambersons,* and many of us had heard the interesting stories which came to light during the Centennial celebration of the Dramatic Club. Booth Tarkington had helped organize the club. He also wrote and acted in some of its early productions. Haute Tarkington Jameson, his sister, was a founder of the club and often on stage. They were, of course, involved in many civic and social projects. Booth Tarkington was still around when I was Society Editor, and his family set social standards from their house on Meridian Street and their summer home in Kennebunkport, Maine.

We gave those names big play whatever was happening, and went on down a secondary list that was always understood and never talked about much. That didn't mean we didn't cover other church circles or club meetings; it was a matter of prominence of display. If the garden club had women who were members of the prestigious country or service clubs, it got a bigger article for its flower show than the newly formed, unknown-person garden club.

We did try for balance. We covered Jewish women's affairs very carefully if the women were "socially prominent"—those who were culturally and economically important, with names like Efroymson, Goodman, Block, Bloch—to name a few. We mentioned Broadmoor Country Club almost as often as Highland or Woodstock.

Black women's society doings weren't covered to any great extent in those days. A women from the black community came in each week with information on social happenings, which we ran in a column on Saturday, but we did not feature events at other times. That was the way things were in those earlier days, and nobody seemed to question it much. Madame Walker or Robert Brokenburr's families were covered on Cityside, too. Madame Walker was a household name, very powerful in the city. Years after her death her importance, her business acumen and her success are beacons for many who are proud of her accomplishments.

Now, this raises an intriguing question: how did society editors on *The News* and *The Star* decide who these socially prominent people were beyond the two or three main families whose social authority was unquestioned? What groups were considered important clubs in Indianapolis? Exactly what was that indescribable institution we all covered known as "society" in the Hoosier capital?

To answer that will take us back a while, all the way to Victorian Indianapolis, where society was really formed in this city. Remember that then, as now, society was all a perception. Social importance didn't really have anything to do with what kind of people they were deep down, what their private integrity was, or what sorts of decent families they had.

Society is a funny word. Webster defines it as "that part of the community which marks itself apart, as a leisured class with much time given to formal social affairs, fashionable sports etc. As in a busy week for society." Looked at that way, "society" has to do with surface perceptions. Some of what is implied in the word, some of what society pages cover is meaningful; some isn't. Let's go on to see what that means.

The Board of Directors of the Dramatic Club

requests the pleasure of your company

at

100th Anniversary Dinner Dance

and Annual Meeting

on

The crème of Indianapolis society, the Dramatic Club, initiated the annual Debutante Cotillion in the early 1950s. Mrs. Conrad Ruckelshaus was first chairman. (Backrow l. to r.) Moxley, Nicholson, Ruckelshaus, Schullenberger, Taggart, Zaring (Front row) Alig, Failey, Hanley, McFall.

The Founders

Miss Melle Colgan   Miss May Shipp   Miss Nancy Baker
(Mrs. Evans Woollen)

More of the Founders

Miss Emma Ayres
(Mrs. William B. Wheelock)

Miss Jane Graydon

Miss Mary Allen
(Mrs. William Mode Taylor)

Miss Alberta Johnson
(Mrs. Joseph K. Sharpe, Jr.)

Miss Florence Malott
(Mrs. Woodbury Treat Morris)

The founders, a group of ladies of social note, played all the parts in early Dramatic Club plays—women and men. Early on they decided "it's no fun without men." Thus the membership expanded!

Ivy covered the early University Club of Indianapolis.

Indianapolis' Propylaeum served many purposes in its early days.

University Club of Indianapolis

Dinner for William M. Rockwood on his seventieth birthday, March 14, 1944, at the Clubhouse, 970 North Delaware Street.

5

VICTORIAN

Of the truly meaningful stories that society pages have always covered, weddings are the most pleasant. Marriages, after all, are very important.

Wedding fashions do change through the ages, just as other fashions change. I have a picture of a late Victorian wedding. The bride is posed on a typical Victorian chaise upholstered in green satin damask. Her gown is awash in seed pearls embroidered in a sort of arbor and floral combination. She looks wistfully out of the window she is posed against. She is swathed in tulle, and her right fist is clenched in a white knuckle situation. What could she be thinking? She could be wanting to jump, she could be wishing this was another day, she could be sad that she is leaving her girlhood and popularity behind.

Or she could be a typical Victorian bride-to-be and not really thinking very much about anything in particular. Just the fluff and the myriad of wedding gifts, the floral designs that transform the home into a wedding scene, the bringing of the outdoor garden into the November afternoon—all that flurry could make a bride look apprehensive.

Victorian, as a lifestyle and way of thinking, began in Indiana before the Civil War and spilled over into the early 1900s, and wedding fashions followed. The Victorian weddings, when compared to weddings of the thirties and forties seem outlandish. However, and whenever, though, the wedding of the year was the wedding that was happening in the home of the bride.

Between 1890 and 1910 the first true society sections of newspapers began appearing. Although there had been women's magazines such as *Godey's Ladies Book* before the Civil War, newspapers didn't begin to really notice women's affairs until after the turn of the century, and then not in any regular way.

Early society articles were not usually arranged on separate pages which appeared in regular places daily. Mostly the items consisted of small-town snippets about goings and comings placed at random: "Miss Caroline Warner is visiting friends in Columbus, Ind. for a few days." "Mrs. Samuel Pierson has issued invitations for a military euchre tomorrow afternoon." (Whatever that was.) Occasionally there were small advice pieces. "If you add salt to whitewash, it will stick better."

Little by little the irregular society articles showed themselves as popular, and by about 1900 editors began to run double page spreads, with pictures of particularly fashionable people doing fashionable things and regular society news. In 1908 *The Indianapolis Star* was carrying information about teas, "In the Theatres," garden parties, sorority affairs and special events. The formula had finally evolved that became the stock-in-trade of every later society writer: clubs, weddings and important people. At that time, though, pictures were a rarity.

The main interest then in Indianapolis' Victorian heyday was the society wedding, of course. Newspapers began to send reporters to homes and, as the century evolved a little, churches. The society editors of the times attended nuptials looking important, wearing proper things like white gloves and hats with little veils. Personal comments and editorializing were the order of the day. They described the wedding as "one of import" or the families as "socially prominent" without a shade of a blush. Or, if they didn't attend, they made it up.

Below I have two descriptions of the same wedding taken from two different papers about that time. You can tell which one was attended by the staff writer and which just came from a second hand report or someone's imagination.

> *An exquisite floral setting for a wedding at home was arranged for one of the autumn brides not long ago. The rooms were emptied of furniture, pictures and rugs. The walls and ceilings were hung with Southern Smilax. A frieze of smilax was festooned with rose buds and from the stairway to the bow window, where the bridal party stood, there were ropes of tulle fastened with choux of tulle. About every three feet was a rosette of*

> tulle in which was thrust a pink rose. The stairway itself was almost hidden in the smilax. In the ceremony room were bay trees adorned with pink roses that made them look like large rose bushes in full bloom, and when the ushers, who brought in the tulle ropes, reached the altar space, they fastened the ropes to the rose trees. Tall candles were so placed as to give the effects of Cathedral lights. Into this room the bridal party entered to the soft music of stringed instruments. After the wedding and the feast following, the bridal pair were ready to leave on their trip. Instead of the limousine ordered there was, at the door, an electric motor car with a note.

The car was the mother's wedding gift and in it the bride and bridegroom rode to the station. Hearts and flowers and an endless supply of newsprint. Here is another paper's description of the same event. (Don't believe everything you read.)

> The floral setting was of Grecian garlands of laurel and yellow roses and the bridal party stood in the bow window, which was filled with maidenhair ferns studded with yellow roses. The bride wore a beautiful gown and veil and carried a bouquet of white roses and lilies of the valley.

Somebody clearly didn't do her homework. Take your pick, pink roses or yellow; tulle or maidenhair ferns. I'll take the pink because from the text, I think that was correct. It was my mother-in-law's wedding. The second writer took a long shot and missed. The year was 1913. The wedding was in the old-fashioned setting of the home in deference to the death of the father of the bride a year earlier. The bride's mother remained in mourning the rest of her life, as some bereaved women did in those days, following Queen Victoria's mourning tribute to Prince Albert.

Times may change, newsprint may get scarce, papers may have their own formats, weddings take place in a tree house or a balloon or on the ski slopes or a gondola on the canal . . . but a wedding is the occasion of the beginning of a marriage, and a marriage should be properly recorded. And as I have said, what I think of the way the Society or Woman's Page handles the printed account of a wedding today wouldn't take much newsprint space! Tiny pictures, routine descriptions of place and attendants—like a job resume, short-change one of the greatest events in a young couple's lives. It saddens me that the newspapers can't find a happy medium for reporting weddings.

And so, it pleased me to find a clipping from a Greenwich, Connecticut, wedding announcement recently. It was a happy mixture of facts (though all details and the things that women like to read about were deleted) and a traditional, old fashioned gracious engagement announcement. This paper, in one of the most exclusive and traditional towns in the East, seemed to have retained some of the mannered sense of what is proper.

It includes a two-by-three-inch formal photo.

>Mr. and Mrs. Philip M. Drake of Greenwich and Marion, Mass., have announced the engagement of their daughter, Susan Holly Drake, to Todd Michael Sylvestri, son of Mr. and Mrs. Rocco J. Sylvestri of Greenwich and Palm Beach, Fla.
>
>A June wedding is planned.
>
>Miss Drake, a graduate of Greenwich Academy and Lake Forest College, is a Montessori teacher at the Montessori Discovery School in Norwich. She is the granddaughter of Mrs. Joseph W. Drake of Rye, N.Y., and the late Mr. Drake, and the late Mr. and Mrs. Lew Wallace. She is a descendant of Gov. Lew Wallace, the author of Ben Hur, Governor of the territory of New Mexico and Minister to Turkey. Her father is a senior partner in the law firm of Cummings and Lockwood.
>
>Mr. Sylvestri, a graduate of Brunswick School, holds a Bachelor of Science degree in Civil Engineering from Purdue University. He is a principal of Sylvestri Contracting Corp. His father is an industrial real estate developer.

I like the history involved in reporting ancestors. That makes the reader relate in some way, either by memory or reading or actual association. In this case, for instance, almost anyone would be interested in the fact that the ancestor wrote the famous *Ben Hur*.

Even though much of the reading and viewing public associate Charlton Heston with *Ben Hur*, it has been produced many times, and is a version of one of the most popular books in American literary history. The author was from Indiana and was pure Hoosier Victorian. The time was the Gilded Age—1870-1900.

Is it possible that some people (other than myself) who read of ancestors in wedding write-ups even go to a research source as I did in this case? If anyone did not know about Holly Drake's great, great grandfather, General Lew Wallace, he or she could spend days learning. I wonder, for instance, how much the bride even knew.

This engagement notice, connected to Indiana and Lew Wallace, takes me into my next subject in this look at "Victorian society," which is— "Important People" in Indianapolis at the turn of the century. It's interesting to note, and perhaps not well known by everybody today, that Indianapolis society near the turn of the century was dominated not by industrialists and the extremely wealthy, but by the Hoosier State's artists and writers. Literary lights were all the mode, and of these the brightest by far was the author of *Ben Hur*.

Governor David Wallace, governor of the state of Indiana from 1837-1840 had a son Lew who became a symbol of worldliness and success in the Indiana of the Gilded Age. Lew Wallace finished *Ben Hur*, his greatest novel, between going west in a buckboard wagon to the New Mexico Territory and returning east on the Santa Fe Railroad train. While out west, he got mixed up with the *real* wild west and the Lincoln County War and killings of Billy the Kid. Some museum somewhere has these letters; copies were furnished me by various Wallace family members.

It's an odd irony that this Hoosier wrote the story of the life of Christ while he was out chasing outlaws and trying to protect his wife, Susan, from not only dust and critters of the desert, but from being murdered by honest-to-God gun-toting outlaws and fugitives. Lew Wallace always liked important political appointments, but when this one came, as a result of his Civil War career, it took the Wallaces to the wild west. Lew Wallace was appointed Governor of New Mexico Territory, and Mrs. Wallace's staid Victorian furniture was a real anachronism in this unpredictable territory . . . not yet a state!

I located the material given below in a biographical sketch, *"Lew Wallace: Father of Ben Hur,"* prepared by Bridgie Hackstaff, and written in the small town of Crawfordsville, Indiana.

After 1878, when Wallace received that political appointment as Governor of New Mexico Territory, his interests were divided. He was kept busy maintaining order with the Indians, managing the state legislature, looking into gold mining, capturing real outlaws, and writing the last three chapters of his book. He pardoned Billy the Kid once and later signed his death warrant. (Later Billy was "allowed" to escape.)

Looking further, I found more on the ancestors of the Greenwich bride-to-be. In a letter from the Governor's Executive Office, Santa Fe, New Mexico, dated July 29, 1880, addressed to his wife, "Dear Sue," we learn that the train has started working again "both East and South." And he goes on to say,

> The engineer who laid out the track of the A.T. and S.F. has by this time found out that the novelties of New Mexico are not limited to the climate, the air and the vegetation; even the common soil is full of them; and that very particularly, it won't do to think it don't ever rain. A well of water went roaring down the Rio Sapello, another down the Galistio, and when passed, there was nothing of the railroad but a beggarly account of smashed ties and iron, the latter intertwisted and bent like tangled telegraph wire.

Another letter from the General to Sue, dated September 6, 1880. In part . . .

> The railroad is once more repaired and giving us regular mails and trains . . . . The daily newspaper here is the merest nothing, a feather afloat in the Newspaper world and a provocation and a blister . . . .
> Last week—Thursday I think, I read and returned to New York the last pages of Ben Hur. When I came to the words The End they looked beautiful. What a long job that has been! How many hours and days it has consumed! And, When the book will be issued from the press, I am not yet informed.

November 12, 1880. *Ben Hur, A Tale of The Christ* was published by Harper and Brothers in New York. In general, sales were slow for the first two years, then the book caught on and its popularity became epidemic, making it one of the best selling novels of all time.

And so, after gift copies were sent to several important men of the time, including President Rutherford B. Hayes and president-elect James A. Garfield, the following letters were sent from the Executive Mansion. This one, sent to Mrs. Wallace on January 9, 1881, from President Hayes, indicates he had read certain parts of the book and looked forward to having time to read it all.

My Dear Mrs. Wallace:

We are greatly obliged by your kindness. With too little time for reading to finish the book now it has given us great satisfaction to read the parts you indicate. After we come home we hope to have time to indulge our fondness for good books, and will reckon among the pleasures in store for us the work which you have sent.

With best wishes,
Sincerely,
R.B. Hayes

From the Presidential Mansion, dated April 19, 1881, is a letter from J.A. Garfield.

Dear General,
I have this morning finished reading Ben-Hur *and I must thank you for the pleasure it has given me. The theme was difficult but you have handled it with great delicacy and power.*
Several of the scenes such as the wise men in the desert—the sea fight—the chariot race—will, I am sure, take a permanent and high place in literature.
With this beautiful and reverent book you have lightened the burden of my daily life—and renewed our acquaintance which began at Shiloh.

Very Truly yours,
J.A. Garfield

After reading Ben Hur, James Garfield apparently was influenced to appoint General Lew Wallace the Minister to Turkey . . . and so came the *Prince of India*, published in 1893.

After Lew Wallace received the advance for his novel *The Fair God*, he came to Indianapolis from Crawfordsville and built a residential hotel, the Blacherne, which became the toney place to live just before the turn of the century. Like some of the other literary lights in the Hoosier state, Wallace was a shrewd and sensible business man.

There is a story that David Laurance Chambers, the president of the Bobbs Merrill Publishing Company, was walking with an author downtown in Indianapolis. The man complained that he wished he could have an advance on his book so he could make an investment like Lew Wallace had.

"Well, you didn't write *Ben Hur*," Chambers announced to him.

Lew Wallace was Victorian through and through. He had been a general in the Civil War and then became a novelist in an age where novelists were idolized. This was especially true in the Gilded Age, which turned its literary men into social lions. They became the "big names" at dinner parties if they could be induced to attend. If they dropped by the Indianapolis Public Library or attended a meeting, the newspapers covered them. Their wives were fussed over and described in the society stories of their day. Real writers! (Sigh.)

Nathaniel Owings, the architect, wrote of the intellectuals of the era gathering to talk in the balcony of W.K. Stewart Bookstore. Book-buyers or celebrity gazers could see George Ade, Meredith Nicholson and Booth Tarkington.

Meredith Nicholson had not been to college, though he later got an honorary degree. He came by his sensitive and lively literary ability naturally. His mother was an intelligent woman who was widely acquainted with literature. Nicholson first wrote poetry, then went to the *Indianapolis News*. His books, *The Hoosiers* and *The House of A Thousand Candles*, became standard classics beyond the Hoosier state. (Odd how paths cross in Indianapolis. His granddaughter Virginia Nicholson Claypool Fairbanks and I seemed to be always in the same place—we were together first at the Church of the Advent on Meridian, then went to Tudor Hall and on to Dana Hall and finally to Indiana University together.)

George Ade had written plays and novels which created memorable humorous characters like "Artie" and "Doc Horn." He had a bit of a national reputation, which fed the desire on the part of people in Indiana in the Gay Nineties to get away from the reputation the state had for being a backwards, hick place.

Booth Tarkington was the perennial gentleman from Indiana. He wrote *Penrod*, a charming and funny narrative consisting of episodes rather than a chronological plot. Penrod is a boy about to have his twelfth birthday, and the book details his life with his dog, his friends, and his childhood enemies. Tarkington drew from his own Hoosier world and his own three nephews' antics to give us the story.

Tarkington liked to sign his name in autograph books by caricaturing himself along with the signature—a custom that Kurt Vonnegut sometimes does today. Everyone called Tarkington "Tark," and enjoyed his genuinely friendly and witty presence at the University Club, the Dramatic Club and

First Edition inscribed for Louise Nicifora

Booth Tarkington
Indianapolis, May 3.33

other groups and gatherings. But he particularly seemed to like going to Stewart's to be accessible to his public and join the other lights of the book world.

When James Whitcomb Riley came by Stewart's, his arrival caused a hubbub. As Owings says, "Not so routinely, there was an exciting invasion through the back shipping entrance by James Whitcomb Riley in his cups, declaiming at the top of his lungs one of his lesser known odes such as 'The Outhouse Built for Two.'"

Riley's picture was often taken with Tarkington and the others in the days after the turn of the century; newspaper readers heaped praise unceasing on the Hoosier poet whose writings made him one of the most read poets in America—and even internationally—in his time. Any club worth its salt expected to have a Riley program; women's groups and school classrooms honored his birthday.

All of us in Indianapolis grew up knowing that James Whitcomb Riley was the poet of childhood and visualized him looking fondly through funny pince-nez glasses at kids clustered all around his knees. His home was venerated even at the time he was living in it on Lockerbie Street. Lockerbie Stret was a fashionable gaslight neighborhood on the edge of downtown Indianapolis, platted by James Lockerbie, a Scotch emigre. Because of its easy access to downtown it was soon built up, and many of the original families lived there until after World War I.

Among my mother-in-law's effects I found a small brown journal, in which she had written an article called, "In the interest of truth." She was a cousin to the John Nickum family with whom Riley lived, and was aware of the circumstances of his boarding with the Nickums. (The house is now the Riley House in the Lockerbie Historic District.)

The story blasts the picture of the "dear children's poet" into bits. And even though a realistic picture of Riley is now accepted by some in the Hoosier state, others may not know it, so I'll tell it as it was told in the diary.

> *The "Riley house" on Lockerbie Street wasn't really Riley's, of course. Riley came home from a weekend at French Lick with the Nickum family who owned the house. "The wagon carrying Mr. Riley's valise was relieved of his luggage by mistake of the dray men. Therefore, it being late and not for any other reason Mr. Riley was urged to 'come on in and stay the night.' The dray men would pick up his luggage on Monday and return both to the hotel*

where they resided and belonged. Twenty-four years later he still was living in the house as a boarder."

The little brown book also firmly states that Riley didn't always care much for children.

James Whitcomb Riley, tragically, was an alcoholic in an age where alcoholism was not regarded as a disease and so he went on embarrassing himself with drinking he couldn't control, though he tried. Once, so the story told at the Greenfield Riley House goes, he let his friends lock him in a hotel room for a few straight days to see if he could "break the habit." But, tormented, he called for the bellboy and had him furnish whiskey through a straw under the door.

This has nothing to do with the fine imagination and enjoyment of "Little Orphant Annie's come to our house to stay," and "The Raggedy Man." But it does have to do with how the Victorians created their own myths and then laughed at those myths behind their backs.

Some of the credit for the literary boom in Indianapolis at the turn of the century has to go to the Bobbs Merrill Publishing Company. Samuel Merrill had one of Indianapolis' earliest businesses, and his bookstore grew until it became a printing company which specialized in regional books of good quality. Riley's books were put out beginning in the 1880s by the predecessor of Bobbs Merrill, Bowen Merrill, and the later company continued to issue new books until the time of Riley's death in 1916.

Bobbs Merrill also issued the books of Johnny Gruelle, the son of one of Indiana's premier artists of the day, Richard Gruelle. The younger Gruelle's literary career had begun in an interesting way. Gruelle lived near Riley in the Lockerbie neighborhood, and worked as a cartoonist for *The Indianapolis Star*. His daughter Marcella ran into her father's room with something she had found in the attic—a faceless, worn rag doll.

Gruelle thought he remembered it as an old rag doll of his mother's, and since Marcella was disappointed because the doll had no face, he fixed it with a red-ink, one lined smile. Gruelle also painted a heart on the dolly's chest, and, as they looked at a book of favorite poems by neighbor James Whitcomb Riley, decided on the name Raggedy Ann (from "The Raggedy Man" and "Little Orphant Annie"). Marcella clutched the doll to her and loved her the rest of her short life—which, sadly, lasted only two more years.

John Gruelle wrote of the doll's doings and invented a boy companion, Andy, and the books which followed their adventures became all-time best sellers for Bobbs Merrill.

Society in the Victorian age in Indiana wasn't just elaborate weddings or prominent literary characters. It was clubs, and clubs are another positive part of what made up the term we know as "society."

Women's clubs had become important in almost every town in Indiana after the Civil War. They had grown out of the sewing bees and church socials of earlier times; now that women were being educated in academies they formed groups with names like the "Shakespeare Coterie," "Forensic Forum" and "Philosophical and Spiritual Inquiry Club."

Indianapolis' club structure as we know it now, though, was generally set up between 1880 and 1920. In one way you can say that the "first families" set up the city's social structure, because somebody had to be the founders—of such things as the theatre, the opera, the arts support organizations, and the churches. In the Victorian Age it was an article of faith that if you got from the community, you gave back. The club founders did that—they gave intellectually, socially, culturally and economically. That has been a cornerstone, an absolute foundation of Indianapolis society—that those who had should give, and it still is today. Noblesse oblige!

The 1942 yearbook of the Society of Indiana Pioneers, quoting William Wesley Woollen, spoke of early Hoosier town builders as men who "plant civilization in the wilderness, who organize backwoodsmen into communities and who throw around them the protection of the law." The Society of Pioneers told us not to forget these societal organizers. "They render mankind a priceless service, and those who come after them and enjoy the fruits of their labor and their sacrifices should never tire of honoring their memory."

Founders and leaders of the Society of Indiana Pioneers themselves fit the description of being community leaders. Early presidents of the group were John H. Holliday, 1916-1921; Mr. Amos W. Butler, 1922-1924 and Charles N. Thompson, 1925-1929. Life members in the Society of Indiana Pioneers in 1941 were Elizabeth Brady Ball, Arthur Voorhees Brown, Katharine Malott Brown, Byron K. Elliott, Eli Lilly, Josiah K. Lilly, Norman A. Perry, Charles J. Lynn and Charles N. Thompson.

Most of the earliest clubs were for men only, but, interestingly enough, one of the first and greatest of clubs in Indianapolis was the Indianapolis Woman's Club. According to its history, the club's founding was a dignified sign that Indianapolis women were not to be denied identity. "Born in an academic neighborhood, cradled in the intellectual yearnings of its twelve founders, the Indianapolis Woman's Club first raised its collective head on a cold February afternoon in 1875."

Mrs. Thomas Hendricks, the First Lady of the state, was elected president, but she never appeared again, probably because the group had some suffragette connections, and that was not a good political association for such a high-ranking wife.

Founders of the Woman's Club were Eliza T. Clarke, Katharine L. Dorsey, Laura Giddings Julian, Belle Thorpe Manlove, H. Kate Martin, Martha N. McKay, Henrietta Athon Morrison, Elizabeth Nicholson, Jane F. Nicholson, Sarah R. Perrine, Nancy G. Roberts and May Wright Sewall.

The original membership was drawn from the College Corner area clustered around Northwestern Christian University (later Butler,) north of Thirteenth Street and east of College Avenue. The founding women wore cloaks and gloves and bonnets. The gloves and bonnets, according to proper etiquette, were not removed for the entire length of the meeting, so the applause must have sounded rather thumpy when papers were read.

After the reading of those papers, the women in their floor-length bombazine skirts, and hats laden with velvet flowers, drank oolong or Darjeeling tea amidst the horsehair, rich brocade, and rosewood parlor furniture of the first families of Indianapolis.

Many of the husbands belonged to the Gentlemen's Literary Club. This witty and impressive assemblage included the leading citizens of its day—governors, senators, judges, artists, "names" like Riley, Benjamin Harrison and Charles Evans, Head Librarian of the Indianapolis Public Library. Maybe they stood about smoking Cuban cigars and expressing bewilderment about what "the women were coming to" as the wives over at the Woman's Club discussed such topics as "Housekeeping—should it take up all our time?" Soon there were other literary clubs—The Fortnightly Literary Club and Over the Teacups were two.

May Wright Sewall, a gracious and intelligent woman in "society" in her day as well as an active member of the suffrage movement, devised a delicious comeback to the Gay Nineties all-male mindset I just mentioned, the idea that women should stay with their knitting and men should stay with their cigars.

Her brainchild was born on September 25, 1890, and her explanation of it was this:

> In the spring of 1889 at the personal invitation of my husband and myself, a small company of men and women who, among our friends, seemed best to unite intellectual order and clubbable personality, convened at our home to consider they knew

not what, for the object of the gathering had not been thus far indicated.

What she was forming was a club in which men and women would hold equal positions, listen to the same programs and function in complementary ways as equals. "I had not ventured to let anyone but my husband know that a new club had been born in my brain," she went on.

"Already clubs were so numerous in Indianapolis and of such variety that a proposition to limit would have seemed more reasonable than once to increase this form of mental cooperation. In the constitution was something not provided by other existing clubs—'Its membership shall be open to men and women on equal terms.'"

In her new club, men and women would associate equally and there would be no excluded subjects, no forbidden ground. And thus was Indianapolis' Contemporary Club born.

Charter members included Reverend and Mrs. John Baltzly (but they were listed separately; Mrs. Sewall took great care that each person should have his own line.) Mr. and Mrs. Frank H. Blackledge; Mr & Mrs. Noble C. Butler; Prof. & Mrs. Scot Butler; Mr. & Mrs. William P. Fishback; Mr. & Mrs. William Dudley Foulke; Mr.& Mrs. John L. Griffiths; Dr. & Mrs. Edward F. Hodges; Dr.& Mrs. John N. Hurty; President (of Indiana University) & Mrs. David S. Jordan; Mr & Mrs. Harry J. Miligan; President (of Purdue University) & Mrs. James H. Smart; Mr. & Mrs. Alexander P. Spruance and assorted single people. There was intellectual prestige here; both university presidents were represented as well as the Butler family and Miss Nebraska Cropsey, the first Elementary School Supervisor of the Indianapolis School System.

George Ade, Booth Tarkington, James Whitcomb Riley and Meredith Nicholson—the perennial four—could be seen gracing the meetings.

The meetings were held in the drawing room of the Sewell's house until the Propylaeum had finished building its imposing meeting center—a spacious, three-story structure where many clubs met and where people of some means could eventually rent rooms and have meals. The Contemporary Club was the first tenant of the new building. Dr. David Swing was first guest speaker and the likes of Cornelia Otis Skinner, Dr. Karl Menninger, H.V. Kaltenborn, Gertrude Stein and Carl Sandburg eventually spoke there.

Here, later, Mrs. Byron Gates would train generations of children manners and ballroom dancing—or try to, whenever she could drag the boys in from the fire escape long enough to waltz across the entire third floor with her or dance the conga to spirited piano playing.

Two political figures were very important to the social scene in the Hoosier capital in the period just before the turn of the Century. Benjamin Harrison was President of the United States, 1888-1892. Charles Warren Fairbanks was Vice President, 1905-1909. The Harrison home on Delaware, and the Fairbanks home on Meridian Street at 30th were pointed out to gawking visitors being driven in carriages to tour the sights.

In the Gay Nineties, University Park was the political, and sometimes social center of the downtown area, with bunting everywhere, speeches the occasions for lots of people to gather, and great torchlight parades the order of the day. To further the candidacy of Harrison, a marching club had been formed in 1888. The entire club went to the nominating convention to march and cheer and soon became an honor guard for visiting dignitaries who might wish to see the President in Residence in his home town. When he didn't get elected in 1892, the marching club went permanent anyway, and continued as the Columbia Club in headquarters on the northeast quadrant of the Cirle.

Some members believed the political air, or Republican cigar smoke, were a little too thick and established a social and intellectual organization known as the University Club.

In February, 1898, the newly incorporated club held its first meeting and elected former President Benjamin Harrison, just returned home from Washington, as first president. His portrait, by another member, T.C. Steele, hangs in the living room in the modern-day University Club.

Many Steeles were acquired by the club, supposedly because every ten months or so Steele would present another painting to the club in lieu of dues. The newel post at the foot of the staircase had a removable top. Underneath were tokens; if a member didn't have money for the streetcar he could borrow a token from the pot, but the rule was, it had to be replaced the next day!

The University Club became a center for entertainment and social gathering, and the city's Victorian leaders met to eat chicken à la king after attending the English Theatre or to hear Booth Tarkington recount scores of stories. Ladies were thrilled to receive invitations to go in their own special side entrance to attend parties with prominent people.

A roster of names listed in the 1898 Greater Indianapolis BlueBook lists names in the University Club which have been active in Indianapolis society ever since: Atkins, Ayres, Bobbs, Coffin, Dean, Fairbanks, Fortune, Frenzel, Hanna, Hollett, Holliday, Jameson, Landers, McKee,

Mothershead, Nicholson, Pantzer, Ruddell, Sweeney, Vonnegut and Williams, for instance.

Some of those were "old names," from the earliest days of Indianapolis—one of the early Bobbses, a doctor, had performed the first gall bladder surgery in America in Indianapolis. The first Clemens Vonnegut had come when Indianapolis had dirt streets, married a waitress and produced five civic leaders for the Gay Nineties generation who became a part of the "north of Washington Street Germans." McKee was related by marriage to the former President of the United States.

The Dramatic Club, which has been mentioned before, was founded in 1889. Several well educated young women, among them Haute Tarkington Jameson, Miss Nancy Baker, Miss Melle Colgan, Miss May Shipp and Miss Emma Ayres formed a group for the purpose of acting theatrical productions. Men were soon added because "things are not much fun without men anyway." The club's first stage was constructed of boxes, and the actors had to watch their steps as they came on stage. Booth Tarkington, who had already founded the Princeton Triangle Club, wrote and acted for the club and was elected President in 1894. The Dramatic Club was a bastion for old families. They passed their memberships on as legacies which were treasured more than stock certificates.

By 1895 some of the new money and social power, however, was passing to a generation of manufacturers who had put up buildings in the new manufacturing district south of Washington. The most important of these was the family of Eli Lilly. Colonel Eli had been a dashing and respected officer in the Civil War. Before the war he had been a chemist, and he returned to Indianapolis after the conflict to open a pharmaceutical firm. This firm rapidly expanded until it occupied a square block on McCarty Street by the 1890s. Josiah K. Lilly, the founder's son, lived in the fashionable section north of Washington—on Tennessee Street, which today is known as Capitol Avenue.

The Old Northside, between Washington and Sixteenth Street from Capitol to College, was a gay, friendly place in the days when Indianapolis was feeling the first bloom of industrial success. It was a neighborly area where children chased dogs and rolled hoops and rode bicycles, and in the winter sleighs dashed down the streets. Little Eli Lilly, grandson of the founder, was sent to the fashionable Farquhar's Kindergarten, and his family attended Christ Church, the lovely gray stone church on the Circle, where he sang in the choir.

He, and many other Indianapolis children who were from first families, had their elementary school experience at School #2. By the turn of the century in School #2 and others like it, new educational theories which let children play and experiment were mixing with character-building academics, including Bible study and poetry and strong grounding in the "Three R's."

Robert B. Failey was one of the children in Eli Lilly's class at both the Farquhar's Kindergarten and School #2. These two men stayed close friends all through their lifetimes, and valued the early friendships above all others. Their relationship was typical of Indianapolis "small town" flavor in those early days.

Social and intellectual life continued to intermix. Carnegie branch libraries opened and were sure to thrive, parties were thrown for men going off to the Spanish-American War, and the first automobiles were being assembled, and even driven in Indiana. The Gay Nineties was in full swing.

What goes around comes around as the saying goes. Here we are, well into the 1990s and it looks like a century later we have come full circle. Only today gay means "homosexuals," not "a happy time."

It was certainly a slower-paced age. Newspapers of the last decade of the last century reflected a time for gracious conversation and consideration. Life and the national vision in Indiana were focused on pleasant times and happy homes and comfortable living and women being placed on pedestals. The kitchen was a warm, inviting haven where the most delectable dishes were invented and consumed. And because this era preceded central heating, it was often the warmest place in the house. It was a time when manners and courtesy were rigid requirements. A time when emotions were kept hidden and when tears were not allowed. It was a beautiful time of unreality, and the older population, rooted in those days, have a very hard time understanding the 1990s. It has taken us a hundred years to realize there were some problems with the idyllic Victorian Age.

A hundred years ago we were barely getting started as a country—we were still young. But were we proud! American families took part in a sense of national pride and patriotism that was very intense. They read at least two newspapers a day in Indianapolis, every article. Some newspaper headlines from 1890 explain our place in history at the time Benjamin Harrison was president of the United States.

Four states were admitted to the Union: North and South Dakota, Montana and Washington. And in South Dakota there was an Indian outbreak by the Sioux and the Cheyenne. On the international front, Africa was being carved up by the European nations. Across the nation women began to ride bicycles and pneumatic safety tires on safety bikes started a craze. Can you imagine being a bicycler back then! Cardinal John Henry Newman died that year, as well as Sir Richard Burton and John Ericson. Being obit editor would have been a fascinating job back then, too. Bessie Watson would have had a field day for sure!

Somewhere in Woodruff Place or Irvington or on Meridian Street, someone attending a fine dinner party with a seven course meal could have raised sherry in Venetian glass to offer these light-headed and light-hearted toasts:

>*Here's to love on every breast!*
>*Liberty in every heart!*
>*Learning in every American head!*
>   and
>*May three great generals be forever in power:*
>*General Peace, General Plenty and General Satisfaction.*
>   (Try that in 1992!)

>*May the tree of liberty bloom around the grove,*
>*and every human being enjoy its fruit.* (Don't we wish?)

Food has always been a perennial interest in everybody's home, but in Indiana groaning tables were a specialty left over from hungry frontier times. Here's a piece of advice from an 1890 newspaper, from a time when hostesses were trying to forget the frontier cooking habits of their parents and dine in a cosmopolitan way.

> *Embarrassing to many hostesses who have not had the benefit of finishing school, is the use of French terms. Therefore it is recommended that these be memorized.* (And remember the word for recipe was then "receipt.")

A few of the "Frenchies" are herewith sprinkled from the sugar and spice shaker. Darling.

> *A la fourchette—with the fork . . . meaning a substantial luncheon, usually not seated formally.* (We can do that!)
> *Coquille-shell—real or a shell of pastry.* (Not coquette)
> *Entrée—an introductory course; usually the light course preceding the roasts. Term is often misapplied to the main course.* (You could have fooled me!)

Glacé—frozen or glazed.
Panade—bread helper, a soup whose basis is toasted bread.

This can give you a terrible inferiority complex if you were born on the wrong side of the tracks or were a "woman of questionable character" before you married well!

And we now understand that women's lib is in terrible conflict with the Victorian concept of gentlemen. Among other things, if you were served fruit at the table you never bit into it. You pared it with a fruit knife, but usually the gentleman next to you peeled it for you, because that is just one of the things that gentlemen did in those days. (Not after smoking that cigar! Please!)

And while we are at the table, here is the 1890 cookbook recipe, "receipt," for Delicious Potato Salad:

> *Boil and peel potatoes; let them get perfectly cold, and cut in dice shape. Seven large potatoes, one goblet of rich cream, one half teacup of vinegar, one teaspoon of black pepper, one teaspoon olive oil (more if you like), three onions sliced thin; salt, and pepper to taste, and garnish dish with radishes and lettuce leaves.*

How about "medium potatoes?" Or how about small potatoes!

And there was etiquette, an important topic in those Gay Nineties "women's interest" articles. Proper manners were very important to both sexes.

> *Be on time.* (Important in any era)
>
> *It is vulgar to smack your lips or suck your teeth.* (Oh spare me!)
>
> *Never make disparaging remarks about the food, or state to your neighbor that you do not like a certain dish. Disturb the food with your fork and refrain from eating it.*
>
> *Bread should be broken with the hands, not cut with a knife and it should be buttered as eaten in small pieces. Never lay it on the cloth to butter it, and never bite into a slice or a roll. Break off a piece.*
>
> *Never put elbows on the table or play with the cutlery, tracing designs on the cloth. When not eating, the hands should lay quietly in the lap. Never tilt a soup plate when finished . . .* etc.

And on and on. Now I'm getting a complex.

We could edit and update some fine points of manners and courtesy and eating habits from the Victorian days. To me the time was idealistic and moralistic and intelligent. Also amusing, dreary, unattractive, overstuffed and overdone. But never uninteresting.

Here is a taste of some of the "women's interest" fare we spoke of from that era. The following excerpt was taken from the *London Saturday Review* and was published in 1884. It tells a lot about the values of the Victorian Days. It also tells us that human beings change with the times and yet human nature remains the same. This is good 'Victorian' at its best.

> *Pumpkins are among the most imposing of all groundling growths. They have fine showy flowers, handsome leaves, roving stems, and they bear solid looking fruit of a goodly size and gorgeous color. To see them spreading over their domain with such rapid luxuriance, one would imagine them among the best things growing; but a critical examination proves their flesh to be about three parts water, while as for their stalks, they are of so pithless a nature they can only creep along the earth, unable to stand upright without support; which tells something against the pumpkin's claim for extra consideration. Still, their showy largeness attracts the eye, and not a few of us believe in pumpkins, and admire both their mode of growth and the fruit resulting. In like manner the human pumpkins—those beings of imposing presence and loud self-assertion—get themselves believed in by the simple; and, as occasions by which their watery fibreless nature is revealed do not arise every day, they are for the most part accepted for the substantialities they assume to be, and the world is deceived by appearances as it ever has been.*
>
> *These human pumpkins abound everywhere, in all states, and in both sexes. We find them flourishing magnificently upon the face of the earth, taking the lead in their society, and setting themselves out as the finest fellows to be found in their respective gardens.*

Look out for pumpkins! These flourishing, crawling, pithless plants are also alive and growing in the 1990s in every state and country and have established a root system of scams and fakeries in every garden of endeavor!

Consider the S and L scandal, the Wall Street scams, the bad checks written by the very men who run our government. There is plenty of "water, fiberless nature" around.

I think Eli Lilly would have forsaken riches and almost anything he had before he would have taken himself, or anyone else down through the pumpkin patch of dishonesty.

There was plenty to live down about the Victorian Age, but also plenty to appreciate. Sometimes I wish for the security of it all. Corny as the Victorians were they were sort of—predictable.

Ah, give us, oh, give us those nineties again, when "women" were ladies and "guys" were gentlemen. Their dwellings in beautiful Irvington, or around Thirteenth and College and between Capitol and Illinois near the downtown, were castles with turret and gable. Though bathrooms were lacking in homes of the able (except for Eli Lilly's) the kitchen was warm and the place for a dip, and to keep from a cold, everyone took a nip. Though it be ever so humble each house would be cheery with gray, horse-hair sofas as rest for the weary. People saw beauty in abundant decoration; they "gilded the lily" as well as the nation. Flowers and bowknots and birds in profusion, and art nouveau objects to give the illusion of grandeur for barons and "kings," self-created, who fiddle-dee-deed while the unemployed waited and some people felt snubbed.

Snubbed. The history of the Indianapolis Woman's Club stopped the chronicling of those prestigious and privileged intellectual ladies to ponder:

> *One wonders about the outsiders looking in. Did they resent or envy the intellectual snobbish? The apparent nepotism? There must have been women who felt equally qualified and longed to be among their peers or those who looked with haughty dismay at this censure of progress.*

There were recessions in the seventies, eighties and nineties. Privation was brief, though, for there was always the Klondike for gold, and the Indian lands offered wealth to the bold. Or, you could open up a gee-gaw store or cafeteria along Washington Street in Indianapolis or in the many outlying neighborhoods, like Spades Park or Fountain Square, as well as the various bustling suburbs. A "prince of a fellow" sans brains, might progress; and his wife, sans ancestors, be "queen" or princess, decked in empresses' jewels as signs of success. Even in Indianapolis.

Victorian. I see little gold cherubs peeking behind banks of maidenhair ferns and garlands of green wrapped around marble columns and spun sugar cakes dancing around tables. The Victorian age strikes me as being gooey and sweet. The nineties we are dwelling in now seem to be anything but sweet.

That Victorian Age was so full of false values and so full of complex contradictions that after all the fun and ridicule are over, we can see that there were great hurts and much pain that spiraled through the branches of those family trees; there was so much restraint that it encumbered even the furnishings and colors, with everything seeming to be dark and heavy.

As for malfunctions of the human psyche caused by the "ignore it and it will go away" mentality of the time, we may be in for a few more decades of change before that mind set fades away. That is, "Let's pretend it didn't happen" or, "Keep a happy face" and, "If it hurts, say it doesn't." It is much like the dentist who was doing a root canal on a patient and said, "I can't find the root of your tooth. I know it's there but it is so covered with calcium I'll never find it." In the most rigid Victorian mores, emotions and the ability to express real feelings are so calcified you can't find them.

And . . . "Come to think of it, human nature is here to stay."

Kurt Vonnegut speaks of his mother, financially devoid of all old luxuries—yet still feeling it mandatory to get out her best china and polish the tarnished silver, and put on a "good show" for company. Many families of the "Old South" may have lost their money—but never their inbred sense of gracious living. I speak of the upper class. But all classes suffered varying degrees of repression of true feelings. That was the Victorian Age in essence.

Is it any wonder that a revolution of expression and searching would follow in the next century? Maybe the rest of the 1990s will bring . . . something else.

I would love to have been "Society Editor For a Day" back in the Victorian era, to have attended the wedding I described, with the green dress and the ferns. But after writing a few of these descriptions I would have wanted a drink of vinegar.

I hate "fluff." I like femininity but not wrapped in a vast armload of tulle. All of that sweetness and light was covering something else on the inside.

When Indianapolis people wanted to "escape" from their already escapist Victorian lives, they headed for "the lake." In the Gay Nineties, and after the turn of the century, this could mean perhaps the Chatauqua in New York, or Harbor Springs or Burt or Higgins Lakes in Michigan. There, in the country where Ernest Hemingway loved to hunt and fish, a Hoosier contingent spent warm evenings stirring cool drinks and took long walks up Indian trails lined with hemlock and pine. It took a while to get to Paradise. When the family of Berkley Duck went to Harbor Springs, the old Model T had to have over thirty tire changes on the bumpy, rutted road, and trains changed many times before reaching the spot. Mr. Duck deposited his family in June, then rode home on the train to work his 9-4 job at the Spann Company downtown, taking only a couple of weeks off in the summer to go back up to where the cool breezes blew.

The Michigan cottages passed on, like the people, into the twenties, with a second generation of children coming to spend the summers. Other Indianapolis families came to visit or rent, and stayed to swell the "Hoosier" settlement. Mrs. Susan Comingore Parrott, widow of a downtown baking magnate of the Gay Nineties era, came to visit and stayed. When her husband Burton Parrott died, he left money which she invested in a cottage. Here is the way her own daughter, Mary Parrott Failey, the same mother-in-law who was married in 1913, told the story in her own journal:

> In 1923 we rented Mr. and Mrs. George Hume's cottage at Burt Lake. Billie Failey was four months old. Mrs. Gladding had just finished her stunning cottage on Glen Drive. She invited us over for lunch, and Sylvester Johnston said, "Mrs. Parrott, you'd better buy that point out there. If you don't, [somebody else] will" . . . Bill and Bob walked over and came back saying that there was one high dune that could be called a hill. The price was a dollar a foot for 1700 lakeside feet. The land had been plotted into a subdivision, "Harbor Point Park." This was the start!
>
> While the purchase was being completed, we went to Prouts' Neck, Maine for the summer with cottage ideas and Maine antique shops, Mama did some superb shopping. She sent Mr. Herbert Foltz the architect down to Ashville, North Carolina to see a cottage in Albemarle Park which she wanted to copy. Mrs. Wallace and Jody had rented it while Lew was in France, and Lew III was born there . . . Mr. Foltz, with photographs of "Crow's Nest" (as it was called) drew plans. In the late winter of 1925 Mama and Mr. Foltz came by train to Harbor Springs, decided on the exact site and let the contract . . . In June we came up to stay at the Dunewood, to wait until the cottage was finished. We waited all summer . . . The end of September the furniture arrived from Indianapolis. Mama had thought

> *everything out so well that they placed the furniture easily. Ayres had made the curtains . . .*
>
> *Mama had loved the fuschia plants the village florists raised with such success, so decided to "do" fuschia coloring and have lots of potted fuschias around . . . We had the local mill make the turn-top table, a copy of an old one the Charlie Bracketts had. We struggled with the local painter who said, "There ain't no such color, ladies," but we mixed it and we love it . . . the cottage is a memorial to the imagination and sense of beauty of my mother.*

If it is possible to feel an affinity for someone you never met, then I know Susan Comingore Parrott very well. I know how she felt about children's picnics on the beach and tanbark trails from everywhere leading to the magic of the woods and a rippling brook, and getting to know the chipmunks and great horned owls on a first-name basis.

If it started as a barren sand dune, it soon became a thick wooded haven for all who visited it. Sandland! Kay Vonnegut (Kurt) is one of those many kids who posed for a dune picture with as many of the place's cairn terriers as he had lap for. His manners outshone "certain" other kids' manners that I know about! He was imported from Indianapolis along with other playmates for the young ones at Sandland. He and Skip were pals at Orchard school in Indianapolis and elsewhere even before they were together at Shortridge.

Other northern Michigan enclaves of Indianapolis folks were at Petoskey and Leland, where associations were formed. Country and golf clubs were built and long, sunlit sailboat races occupied the summer afternoons.

Often, however, in Indiana "the lake" meant the two prestigious but not particularly large bodies of water in the state, Lake Wawasee and Lake Maxinkuckee. In his book *Early Wawasee Days*, Eli Lily has written of Wawasee as a refuge, a special spot to retire from the cares of the business world, to sail and swim and be informal. He tells of a long childhood trip to Wawasee in 1895, in which days before the departure from Indianapolis, trunks would be readied for the huge, one-hundred mile trip.

> *Each day, there were two local trains to the Lake, one leaving at about seven in the morning. After an interminable wait at Milford Junction and a transfer to the B&O, the exhausted passengers would arrive at their destination about two in the afternoon . . . Day coaches were far from being as comfortable as*

those of today. Stiff, double, red plush seats whose backs were capable of being turned over enabled a family or a group of genial friends to ride facing one another if they boarded the train early enough . . . At each of the twenty stations, the conductor would call out its name in each coach, and groups of passengers, carrying babies, handbags, bandboxes and bird cages, would file from the cars . . . There being no dining facilities on these trains, passengers had the choice of packing fried chicken, jelly sandwiches, fruit "in season" and other picnic fare into the proverbial shoe box or dashing from the train at Anderson to snatch a sandwich or two from a small, stale-smelling restaurant next to the station . . . [Then finally] as the train slowed down, came the ecstatic thrill for the youngsters—every bit as good as Christmas morning—of catching from the car windows a blessed glimpse of the back of the cottage, across the cornfields, almost hidden in its grove of trees, with the glittering Lake beyond.

There was a certain robust, sports-centered, hearty good-times atmosphere at Wawasee, and there still is today.

Maxinkuckee was much the same, but with a gentile, relaxed feeling. You could see the same socially correct people there that you saw on north Central Avenue, except that you could look at ducks and sailboats while you talked to them.

Who in Indiana didn't sometime in their lives spend happy hours at Maxinkuckee or Wawasee? Lew Wallace is credited with writing his famous chariot race scene in Ben Hur near "Lake Max" at English Lake, and Booth Tarkington spent his honeymoon there. It is surmised that Cole Porter's sense of rhythm was developed by spending time, much time, on the sightseeing boat where the old upright piano and the noisy engine gave off a distinct beat, "The beat, beat, beat of the tom-tom," as he began "Begin the Beguine." It's logical! The Charles Coffins and the Walker Winslows and the Glossbrenners and the Hendricks were on the fashionable "East Shore." And the Vonneguts, en masse.

Here is what Kurt Vonnegut has written of "The Lake." He said:

If ever I were to write a novel or a play about Maxinkuckee it would be Chekhovian, since what I saw were the consequences of several siblings inheriting and trying to share a single beloved property and with their own children, once grown, moving to other parts of the world, never to return, and on and on . . . The closed loop of the lakeshore was certain to bring me home not only to my own family's unheated frame cottage on a bluff overlooking the lake but to four adjacent cottages teeming with close relatives. The heads of those neighboring households, my father's generation, had also spent their childhood summertimes at Lake Maxinkuckee, making them the almost immediate successors to the Potawatomi Indians . . . [Culver Military Academy] was at the head of the lake, and, after all, was the principal employer of the town, also called Culver. It was like a little West Point, and Annapolis combined, with a cavalry troop and a big fleet of sailboats and noisy parades and so on. They fired a cannon every night at sunset.

By the turn of the century, wealthy Indianapolis families were sending their boys to Culver to "receive a sense of discipline and learn good, sound American tradition." They also were picking up on the eastern preparatory schools I talked about earlier, and after that, Harvard and Williams and now even Vassar and Smith. "Going East" could be an important part of being correct; it also gave you a splendid education in the process. That does not mean Indiana University and DePauw and Wabash and Purdue didn't get their shares. It didn't matter where you went, just so you went "to a four-year college, certified," as my grandfather used to say.

You could get ready for these experiences by going to Orchard Country Day School, founded by some parents in 1922. And, if you were a boy, Park School provided local polishing. Its campus was located on Cold Spring Road. And we have spoken of Tudor Hall, earlier Miss Allen's School. There came to be something about those names. I have already said I didn't think the education in the private schools was any better than the education in the good public schools in Indianapolis.

The Twenties roared in and with them increased emphasis on society and its stratifications. A look at the 1925 Indianapolis Society Blue Book shows who was who, or at least who that book thought was who. The book issues a disclaimer against anyone who might think it was undemocratic to issue a book of "prominent residents arranged alphabetically and by streets."

We do not claim THE BLUE BOOK is either a City Directory or absolutely an Elite Directory; neither do we pretend to pass upon the social or financial standing of the parties whose names are contained therein. It is simply a compilation of the most prominent householders and residents published in the most convenient form for reference by our patrons.

... So there!

Reading the Blue Book roster one comes across not one but eight Vonneguts, M&M Alex, M&M Anton, Mrs. Bernard, Mrs. Clemens, M&M Franklin, M&M George, M&M Kurt, M&M Ralph C. In reading maiden names there is a whole segment of the early German families of prominence connected with the Vonneguts—people like the Schnulls and Liebers.

The Blue Book had everything. People were cross-referenced according to streets. Consult a few of the pages we have included from that Blue Book if you want to see who was included.

Clubs were also given for both male and female prominents. There were one-hundred-thirty-seven clubs important enough to be included in the Blue Book by the twenties; some of their names were the Aftermath, Catharine Merrill Club, four chapters of the DAR, including the General Arthur St. Clair Chapter, the Caroline Scott Harrison Chapter, the Cornelia C. Fairbanks Chapter and the Anthony Wayne Chapter, Irvington Fortnightly Club, Late Book Club, Matinee Musicale, Over-the-Teacups, Propylaeum, St. Mary of the Woods Club, Colonial Dames, University Club, Broadmoor Country Club, Indiana Association of Wabash Men, The Players, Indiana Historical Society, Indiana Wellesley Club, Hoosier Motor Club, Indiana Audubon Society, Yale Alumni, Harvard and Princeton Clubs, Exchange Club, Altrusa, Smith and Bryn Mawr College Clubs and the Rolling Ridge Polo Club.

Goodness gracious sakes alive!

The Indianapolis Athletic Club and the Columbia Club were in their glory in the Twenties. The Athletic Club, as a matter of fact, was founded in 1920 during a time of interest in sports. A Committee of Sixty helped the embryonic club get members. Harry C. Stutz, H.H. Barrere, Jr. Henry F. Campbell and Herbert L. Bass were instrumental in helping get the property at Meridian and St. Clair. Members of the site committee were Fred Hoke, T.A. Wynne, Eugene Darrach, Arthur Baxter and L.C. Huesmann.

The Athletic Club was unofficially Democrat, while the Columbia Club continued to be a Republican stronghold.

So—all of these intellectual clubs, church clubs, interest clubs, neighborhoods, ethnic groups, and institutions constituted, yes, SOCIETY.

But it was more than that. Society is described by Ring Lardner as "Upper Crust, Swells, Blue Bloods, *leading families.*" That's what the Blue Book of 1925 was talking about, even though they denied it, and that was what it was all about.

And that's what I had to learn when I came to be Society Editor at *The News* in 1946. It was twenty years after that Blue Book had been put out, but things hadn't changed much in Indianapolis. I liked the "who was who—names make news" part least of all the work—but there it was.

And so, sitting down at my desk, with paste pot staring me in the eyes, I faced the fact that I had to know who was *important*. I have mentioned a good many of the clubs, but what I had to know was which were *worth writing about.*

Well, first of all, from my growing up time, I knew that country clubs were important, and if they were doing something, we had to take note. The Country Club of Indianapolis was considered to be a great social club but a great distance from most of the Northsiders, since it was on the *far* west side, fifteen miles from the Circle. Woodstock was old money and old family. Its golf course fronted on the back yards of the lovely Golden Hill area. Meridian Hills was the newer, corporate club.

Highland was organized in 1903 with articles signed by William W. Carter, I.N. Cleaver, William Donaldson, Arthur F. Hall, James E. Kepperly, Edward L. Lennox, E.D. Moore, Samuel E. Rauh, William R. Root and H.F. Waterman. Eventually the Eastman estate deeded 144.56 acres of land, on which the Club's present golf course is located, to the group which was incorporating the club. Highland became known as the "golfingest" club about—mostly for doctors and dentists and—in the twenties and thirties—leading Catholic families.

Then there are the clubs I've already talked about as being prestigious in the past. At my Society Desk I caught on fast that they were still prestigious today. The Contemporary Club was continuing to maintain its leadership place, and along with the Progressive Club represented the intellectual as well as social aspects of society. The University Club, located by now on the near Northside was still the men's club: during the forties a small group was going to the club for lunch and then quietly dispersing to the upstairs where they played Sniff (the same domninoes game Booth Tarkington had played) all afternoon. The Vassar Club and Wellesley Club and other college groups functioned with varying degrees of involvement and dedication to alma mater.

I wished somebody had sent me to cover the Trader's Point Hunt Club affairs—the doings of the mink and manure set. The TPH was officially recognized as a member of the Master Foxhounds Association of America on September 14, 1934. It was founded by horse lovers and equestrians who loved the sport and wanted to initiate drag hunting with horses and eight fox hounds (coon hounds). It was not for social status that these people put down the scent of a fox with a live coon led by a chain. It was love of the sport!

Fox hunting as Trader's Point Hunt Club did it was a particularly colorful country sport with a lot of excitement and action and barking of dogs, as the riders galloped over the fields and took the jumps through the woods and over the countryside. A lot of them "came a cropper," which means, you guess it, landed on the ground sans horse. Organizers and first officers of the Board of Directors were Cornelius O. Alig, Russell Fortune, Sr.; Ralph Lockwood and Charles Mayer. Their first board consisted of Nate Davis, Kiefer Mayer, Thomas Ruckelshaus and Samuel B. Sutphin.

Early on this elite group had a "Croppers' Party," where only those who had "uh," fallen flat could attend. On Thanksgiving Day, 1936, the first Blessing of the Hunt was done. The Blessing of the Hunt is a French custom going back to the original use of stag hounds. On that Thanksgiving Day, the little Salem Methodist Church in Boone County farm land became the scene of a touching and humble tradition which included local farmers and guests, children and cousins as well as those who would actually ride to the hounds. They bowed their heads in prayer before the hunt began. Nice! From that day on the Traders' Point Hunt Club was lovingly referred to as the mink and manure set—at least by those of us who had to put pen to paper about the doings of all these people and clubs.

No doubt about it, as the phones rang and the notices came in, I realized there was a pecking order in all these organizations. For women it was definitely the Junior League, always at the top and always in the news. Most of the time it was for good reason; the members consisted of young women who had the time and the desire to give volunteer hours to better the community. During World War II the Junior League had given thousands of volunteer hours to the war effort.

Their big cause in the days I was on *The News* was the James Whitcomb Riley Hospital for Children. The Junior League worked long hours in the wards and gave knowledge and expertise to help build or buy whatever was needed, whether equipment or entire wings. Big money had to be involved, so there were the Junior League Follies, and the Junior League Balls and whatever and wherever, the Junior League was big time news in the society pages. They always had a Publicity Chairman and getting news for the league was easy. We needed them. They needed us.

The Children's Museum Guild was directly beneath the League in the P.O. (pecking order/prestige order). They had been organized in the thirties and were a working group supporting the Museum at Fourteenth and Delaware, with such people as Peg Hiser, Rosemary Sisson, Marge Rocap, Dorothy Gallahue, Jane Baxter, Lou Ramey and Margaret Clark providing energy and effort. There were many others; this was an age when women were at home, and volunteerism brought vital energy to society.

The Children's Museum under Grace Golden was developing into a first-class museum during the time I was on *The News*, giving promise of the world class institution it was to become. "In a troubled and oftentimes dishonest world, the museum extends a calm and soothing hand and shows us that our culture lives on," Mrs. Golden said.

Lots of the group I knew had been directly involved in helping build the Children's Museum, and I had heard of it all my life. Kurt Vonnegut's father had designed the seahorse pin, a button all children could wear if they brought their quarters to school to join. That pin is now a collector's item. Kurt's father, Kurt Vonnegut, Sr., was on the first Board of Directors. Nancy Kriplen, author of *Keep an Eye on That Mummy*, the history of the Children's Museum, states that Kurt Vonnegut, Sr., proved to be an indefatigable worker during his many years on the Museum board. When he died in 1956 he had given many years of service—since 1925—AND Sidney the Sea Horse.

Peg, Mrs. Walter, Hiser from the old growing-up neighborhood was one of the staunchest and most devoted workers on the Children's Museum Board, as were Ruth Lilly, Mary Stewart Carey, who was the first Board President and worked very hard to get the museum started, Christopher B. Coleman and Mrs. G. H. A. Clowes. Some board members had come onto the Children's Museum Board by serving in the Guild, which was a mainstay and fund-raising arm of the museum.

There were other auxiliary groups we had to be aware of. Among the important ones were St. Margaret's Guild for hospital work and The Children's Bureau.

Some of the clubs provided community service and were also strong on social life. Possibly the most elite of all social clubs in Indianapolis was still the Dramatic Club. Its members represented the "oldest" families and "most important" names in Indianapolis. It was never easy to get in and the best way to accomplish that was to "marry in." The Dramatic Club has been the most family oriented of all clubs. Generation after generation became members and took part in their plays. Just before Christmas, readers of the society pages rushed to pick up the paper and find out about the Dramatic Club Cotillion. Who were the debutantes? How did they all look? Who were their escorts, who had the prettiest dress, what were the bouquets? Pictures and stories for the Cotillion were organized in a great flurry of activity.

In spite of its constant social whirl, a significant focus in the Dramatic Club was always the stage performances. Famous and semi-famous "names" came and went. A little later, in the sixties, Mary Tone Atkins became one of the best known names in local dramatics. Franchot Tone was her uncle, and Mary actively represents the theatre in acting and directing in Indianapolis.

Garden clubs have been popular for years in Indianapolis; The Indianapolis Garden Club was considered to be the most elite in the late forties and fifties. An affiliate of the prestigious Garden Club of America, its gardening emphasis is demanding and serious. Garden Club meetings are gracious and entertaining. At age 102 today Mrs. Bowman Elder is still actively involved with her greenhouses and prize-winning orchids, as she was at the time I wrote society stories.

Being a society reporter mandated that all of this background and all of these clubs and organizations were as familiar as your middle name. The best way to learn all of this, of course, was to jump right in and start learning by writing. Names make news, the friendly editors told me, and important names make important news.

It was second nature daily to sort your mail and your notes into proper categories, and you had better know which notes went into what category. Names like Lilly, Ayres, Noyes, Fairbanks, Holliday, Ruckelshaus, Vonnegut, Madden, Efroymson, William H. Block, Goodman, Levy, all went to the top of a certain pile. Then there would be another pile for things probably due to get in if there was space, with secondary names. And so on down in little piles to things that weren't going to get in because there wouldn't be space in the newspaper for everything.

It did not take long to figure out that among names on the top piles family friends had married, and everyone was related to everyone else in this little old overgrown village of Indianapolis. As I have said, we tried to have some balance, Catholic and Protestant and Jewish.

And black clubs? The call for equal time and space because we try to be equal by law and our own consciences? As I have said, these things did not exist in the same sense in those days. Indianapolis blacks were a community growing in importance; pride in Crispus Attucks High School and other institutions had sparked awareness of Negro importance. Pretty new homes had been built in a neighborhood north of Fall Creek and west of Capitol Avenue, but it was not yet the day of integrated neighborhoods or integrated society page coverage. That was for a time to come.

By the way, in that mostly male newsroom, never did anyone do anything that I could at all interpret as "sexual harassment." If somebody thought my dress was sexy and said so, I took it as a compliment. Mostly they spoke to me as a human being and co-worker. That was all I wanted and that was all I got. I knew how to take care of myself, anyway. If anybody had said or done anything I didn't like, I would have let him know it.

Romance and marriage entered my life finally, and my career in active journalism had to mesh with learning to cook and keep house. When I left *The News* in 1948 it was with tears of sadness and regret. I loved the wonderful conglomerate of personalities and characters, each so different and each so important to the paper. I had been having a wonderful time and had been getting paid for it. Not much, but paid. I was programmed for the pace and the mind-set of newspapering, and I wondered how I would get along each day without this team around me. This was not going to be my cup of tea; I would be out of the mainstream. Was I cut out to be a wife? Housekeeping didn't thrill me at all. Cooking thrilled me less. But what about children? Now, that did thrill me. All children were important to me. To ensure myself a place in the archives, my departure from the staff was heralded by a full page story about children which I researched and wrote personally.

The Marion County Juvenile Center was a very poorly run and inadequate facility for delinquent children and chronic runaways. Its shortcomings needed to be aired, so I decided to expose them. And I felt the community should go to bat for these children. So many of them were cast in the wrong roles. Often the parents were, in fact, the ones who were delinquent. Aided and fortified by a social worker whom I knew well, I determined to write a productive and constructive feature page, pictures and all. There was a very good reason for my interest in misunderstood children. Today, the same page would be written on child abuse, and I was knowledgable enough about that! Not all abused kids came from the slums, though, or were illiterate; many children who suffered on the right side of the tracks were ignored and thus twice abused. This is still true. Finally, we realize abuse does not always mean physical abuse and have taken legal and practical steps to combat it.

My parting feature story hit its mark. In a fairly short time a new facility was built and a new program implemented by the Junior League which, as I have said, had a history of doing good things for the benefit of children. Though the project was also helped along by a very good Juvenile Court judge, the work was moved forward by the League until the County was able to carry it alone. It was a good feeling to know that maybe I had lit a match to the kindling.

And so it was goodbye to my fondest friends and my learning years as a member of the working press. That part of my life would always be with me. There would be stories and I would always seek to find them, feel them or smell them. And you could have *Society!* That had just been my transportation!

Soon afterwards I went to the West Coast as a tourist, and before I could say "Press Pass," I was back at it. I was still a representative, and I went into action immediately. Newspaper work had spoiled me and I wasn't quitting just yet. The first thing I did was call the MGM studios publicity department. I got to the right person who knew who I knew and we were in business. A visiting press member gets the VIP tour of the studio, one-on-one and rejoices in the fact that she isn't on a little tour trolley with the proletariat.

I picked a good day because we were privileged to see a scene on the set of "State of the Union" with Katherine Hepburn and Spencer Tracy. The piercing brown eyes of Frank Capra, one of the all-time great directors who recently died, were watching them closely. I stood by very quietly so as not to miss a word of that lilting Hepburn voice or the casual attitude of Spencer Tracy. Hepburn's navy and red costume was probably a Chanel, and I remember the pencil line skirt that had a cape tailored to hit her in the right place. She was smashing, and it was thrilling to be there. As we left the set and were walking toward the commissary, Spencer Tracy left and walked just ahead of us with his hands in his pockets, with his typical nonchalant and jaunty walk. He greeted many of those he passed on the street of the MGM lot with a simple "Hi-ya," or "How are ya?"

No one who isn't at least a certain age is ever going to know about those days when actors belonged to the studios and to their public. These were the good old days for sure. The word glamour was the key word. As we walked, June Allyson cruised by right beside us in a sea-green Cadillac convertible. I was so startled I forgot who the actress beside her was. The "family picture" of all the actors contracted by the studio was very impressive and read like a Who's Who in the movie industry. One famous face after another—elbows touching—family style.

Through the years quality stars have shone brightly and faded and gone. But the still sparkling one whom I admire greatly is Katherine Hepburn. I see her now and think of that set. She has that strong New

England strength and fiber and she's all quality. Gritty, gutsy, outspoken, a beacon of hope in the sea of immorality and decay that her industry has become—she's a fighting spirit, and I respect the eccentricities which are as delicious as her acting. Her book *Me* is her message of inspiration for those who can look a lot farther back than forward. Stay on and on, Kate!

These were the "upper crust, Swells, Blue Bloods and Leading Families" of the American screen, the real darlings of American "society." No, I couldn't leave newspapering behind, even in Hollywood.

I reflect and wonder if I would have been a better switchboard operator. But then I would have been replaced by a bunch of little wires and conductors and buttons.

No, what could have been better than getting a job that you just loved, with people whom you hated to say goodbye to in the evening, in a place that pulsated with excitement and happenings all day long? Well, I'll tell you the only thing that could have been better. Getting paid enough to live on!

A wistful bride contemplating a moment when Victorian mores and concepts were about to undergo a real change—on the eve of World War I. Mary Parrott becomes Mary Parrott Failey.

The Victorian Age, illustrated by the marriage license above and the Indianapolis Blue Book, provided drama, propriety, some superficial values and too much "sugar and spice and everything nice."

MRS. BURTON ELLSWORTH PARROTT

REQUESTS THE PLEASURE OF

Mr. Howard's

COMPANY AT THE MARRIAGE OF HER DAUGHTER

MARY REBECCA

TO

MR. ROBERT BURNETT FAILEY

ON SATURDAY, THE EIGHTH OF NOVEMBER

AT HALF AFTER FOUR O'CLOCK

AT TWO THOUSAND, NINE HUNDRED NORTH MERIDIAN STREET

INDIANAPOLIS, INDIANA

Tiffany and Co. provided much that was fine in Indiana Victorian preferences. Lamps, stained glass window pieces, elegant silverware—even the 1913 wedding invitation calling for a society editor's astute attention.

Two little tads taking orders from grownups at "Sandland" in Harbor Springs. Dune buddies Billy Failey and pal Kay Vonnegut in 1932.

```
              Boats

     The boats are sailing on
              the sea
     And the birds are flying
              with glee
     And the sea is roaring, Oh!
              so loud,
     If you could come with me.

                   Kay Vonnegut
                     Group II
```

1934 "Boats" was written by second grader Kurt Vonnegut at Orchard School.

Mrs. Farquhar's Kindergarten was the socially-in pre-school of the era just before and after the turn of the century. Eli Lilly is in second row, far left. *Courtesy of Lilly Archives*

Booth Tarkington always had poodles. "Where's Lulu?"—Lulu was Booth's sister-in-law, who resided with the Tarkingtons.

Relatives always say B.T. really wanted to be a cartoonist.

Kay V. was a poet and an artist from earliest days. Some relative had probably crossed on this German ship.

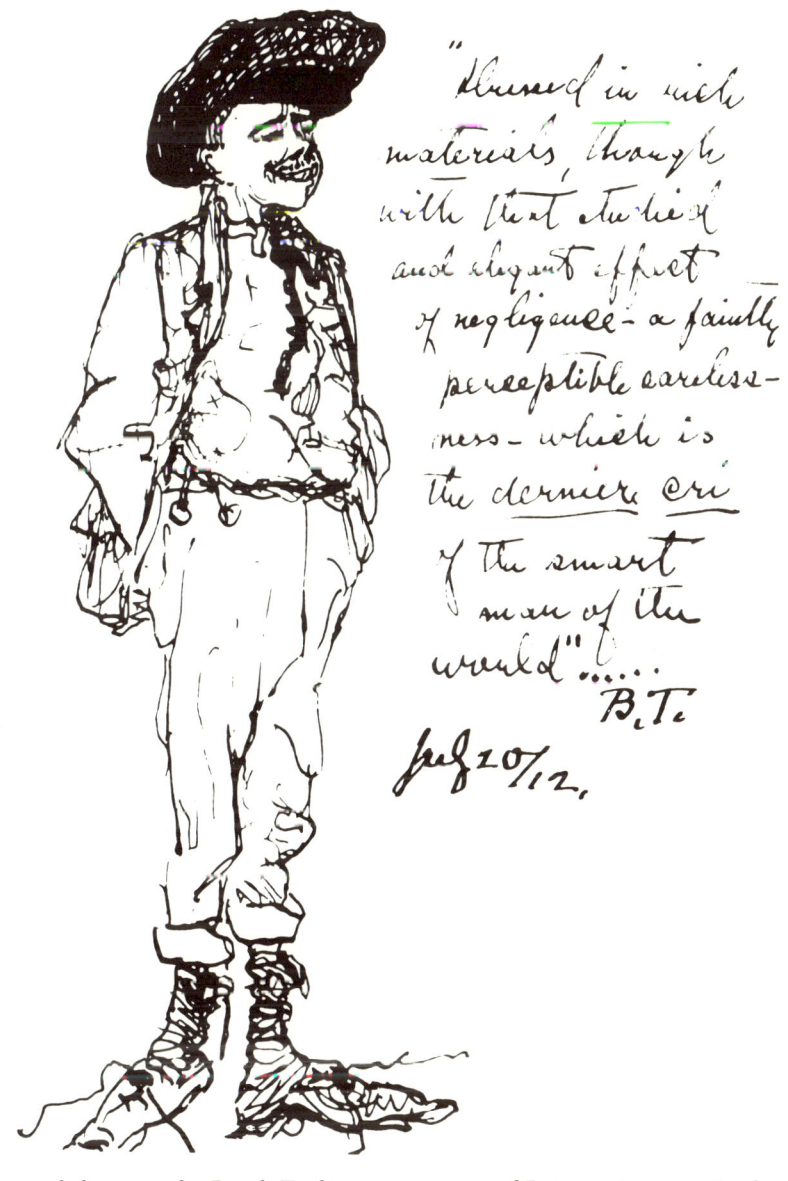

Original drawings by Booth Tarkington courtesy of Patricia Jameson Cochran

6

CARL SANDBURG

Recently while sorting through papers, I came on the following letter. I looked at it, realizing what a bridge it was in my experience from the time in my college years when I met the person who was to have the most influence in my life to the reawakening, the re-finding of that person years later. The letter had told me a wonderful woman was writing a book about one of America's greatest poets and authors—and she wanted to talk to me about Carl Sandburg.

Dear Mrs. Failey:

I am pleased to hear from Peter Sterling that you knew Carl Sandburg and that you might be willing to talk with me about your memories of him. Since 1980 I have been interviewing Sandburg's family, friends and associates, making tape recordings which are deposited in the Carl Sandburg Collection at the University of Illinois Library, Urbana, and in the Sandburg Archive at Connemara, his final home in Flat Rock, North Carolina and now a National Literary Park. In addition, I am writing the first comprehensive literary biography of Sandburg, and I find that shared memories animate my understanding of Sandburg in unique and invaluable ways.

I understand that you are away just now, but if you have time when you return, I would be happy to drive over for an interview. I will be away until August 17, and will telephone you upon my return, in the event that you are at home and that your schedule permits time for a Sandburg talk.

In the meantime, I enclose some material about various Sandburg projects. Sandburg said that Abraham Lincoln was such good company that he was sorry to finish writing about him! I feel the same way about Carl Sandburg and the wide fellowship of his friends and family. I look forward to meeting you and to sharing your perceptions of Sandburg.

All good wishes to you!

Cordially yours,
Penelope Niven McJunkin
1985.

The years rolled back for me when I received that letter, all of them filled with memories of my wonderful, far-off "uncle," my mentor, my friend.

It was 1956, early March *The News* was past history for me. And I was following Carl Sandburg's instructions. "Get married girl, and settle down with a man and have children." Ah, yes. I now had three of those, one quite new, almost a Christmas baby. Reading the morning paper and drinking my coffee, I read that Carl Sandburg was coming to speak at the Caleb Mills Hall of our Shortridge High School. He was being sponsored by the American University Women's Association, and I was a member of that group.

Wondering if I could even arrange to go hear him, I mused that maybe I could go backstage and say hello and maybe he would remember our meeting twelve years before in Union City, Indiana. But I knew not where he was or how to reach him before he came to our city.

I re-read the article, trying to find a place to reach him. Mr. Sandburg was at the University of Illinois and arrangements were being made to acquire the multitudinous volumes and writings of his personal library. He had moved from the cold, windy, Michigan Dunes and now lived somewhere in the foothills of the Blue Ridge Mountains—Flat Rock, North Carolina.

Well, being a university graduate, I thought it all out. At the University of Illinois there would have to be a union building; the same as Indiana University, I imagined. Why not write him there and hope those people would get the note to him? It must have been a bit more than a note. I was not only a busy little mother, I was a very absent-minded little mother. Do it and forget it! And so I wrote it, forgot all about it, and went on about the business of changing bedroom arrangements to accommodate the newest member of our family, and changing diapers, too.

It was time to put the baby in her own room now. Really, we needed a fourth bedroom. But the five and the seven-year-old could have the big master bedroom, the parents would take the small bedroom, and the baby, Gaye, would have the middle room for a crib and baby things. This home-management upheaval was going to have reverberations. Like the hurricane, a crisis was on its way!

Almost immediately I could see this was not going to be a good arrangement. The phone was in the big bedroom. Damn! That would wake up the two kids. Well, worry about that tomorrow because that would *have* to be changed somehow, or another room would have to be built! We were saying prayers, and tucking in, when the phone rang. I grabbed the phone, mouth open to say, "I'll call you back." A deep voice stopped me cold. "Mrs. Zaring? This is . . ."

"Yes?"

"This is Carl Sandburg." Speechless. Paralyzed. Terrified. That voice again after all those years. I do not know what my reply was. His was, "I liked your letter." He had analyzed it for me!

"Thank you." Quivering, "When are you coming? Where are you staying? How long will you be in Indianapolis? Can we get anything for you? Can we meet your train?" And finally, "Mr. Sandburg, I would love to have you stay here with us. But I have three children now and one is a three-month-old baby."

I was totally unprepared for a very long deliberate pause. "Well, we raised three children and we got along all right with that." After I gasped for more words, it was all arranged. He would love to stay at our house. *Three days* he would stay!

"Well!" I thought to myself, "Majie, girl, you've got yourself in one fine mess now. You've invited one of the all-time greats in literature to stay here and you don't even *know* him. No extra room, and the house is totally disorganized. You don't have a baby sitter. You are NUTS! And where are you going to get a guitar? He needs a guitar for his songs. It's part of the show. And what are you going to cook for his meals? And when are you going to have time to get things ready for him?"

"Oh shut up," I said to myself. "I'll manage."

I paused and wondered where to begin. I remembered my grandfather always saying, "Just be yourself." Boy, what a help that was!

I bought a nice leg of lamb and got our cleaning lady to get things in order while we went to the station to pick him up. She agreed to stay through dinner. I wondered if I would recognize him at the station and tried to recall what he looked like when I last saw him. I wondered if he would recognize me. Would he be hard to talk to? Will he think we're stupid? Oh dear God! Are there enough blankets on his bed? Are there clean towels in the bathroom?

I was having a sinking spell. I was terrified driving to the station. My husband was clutching a guitar . . . and wondering if it would be all right. We had two Lincoln volumes in the car to read at every stop light! Bone up on Lincoln in a hurry! Really stupid!

We parked the car in front of our old red brick Union Station, where half of our lives seemed to have been spent meeting trains and getting on and off them. We went to the stairs with the train number on it *and waited*, while person after person passed in front of us. No Sandburg. Finally, a man wearing a heavy coat with a shock of white hair under a big brimmed hat appeared. He wore a great, worn, loden green coat and carried an equally worn carpet bag. His face was ruddy and craggy and a little like an Indian's. He was about six feet tall, but he impressed me as being extremely tall . . . because he ought to have been. He thought tall. He wrote tall. He stood tall.

There he was. That was the man. Oh God, my knees were not strong. We were at the door. We stepped forward and I introduced myself and my husband. Easy. We took the bag and I looked up and asked, "Do you remember me?" He smiled and said, "No. But you are very kind to take me in."

"Oh boy," I thought. "Why did I cancel his hotel reservation? He would have been happier there." In reality, he would have been miserable there! We all got ourselves into the car, checked out the guitar, it would do fine, and from then on it was easy street. He would join our family, come what may. We had all afternoon to get acquainted, as I had had no time to tell anyone he was staying at our house.

The baby was there and the other two children would be coming home from school soon and we would be doing what we always do. When baby Gaye woke up, I would just have to deal with that, and he might have to help. Indeed, as it turned out, he helped beyond measure. (Thank you forever, dear Uncle Carl.)

Gaye wishes she could remember the time she spent in his lap giving him many happy moments as he sang about pink toes and gumdrop noses. Thank Heaven for little girls . . . tum de dum.

There began the most heart warming, leisurely, three-day visit one could ever imagine. One day just purred into the next, and I began to feel that maybe we should add on a few more days. In the late afternoon we were in our den and the children came home from school and kindergarten. Carl untied his shoes and began to relax. Oh, were his feet tired! He seemed too relieved to be able to unwind.

For some reason this bothered my five-year-old Cathy, and she kept tying his shoes back. When she did he would untie them again. Finally, after about five tries at this game, Cathy parked herself directly in front of him, hands on both hips and a mock frown said, "Mr. Sandbogue, can't you tie your own shoes *yet?*"

We whiled away the time, and as the day passed a whole story began to unfold. It was the story of his daughter, Helga, and her divorce. It made him very sad and he mentioned enough for me to pick up on how much it bothered him. What I didn't catch then was that two very stubborn people were involved here!

Later, I would find that Helga was a chip off the old block. Stubborn. And while the father was suffering the sadness of the situation, he was not "letting on" to the daughter. Nor was the daughter, Helga, going to share her pain with her father.

He was very nostalgic that first day and throughout the visit. It was a fine afternoon, and it felt as if we were old friends who hadn't seen each other for a long time—that he had so much to fill us in on. We went through his whole family history: back to the Swedish immigrants, back to Galesburg, Illinois, his birthplace, then on to Michigan, and finally to Connemara, his final home in North Carolina. He touched on everything except the present. The present would come later.

During his stay at our house he told us the following details of his life. His father had never had any desire to learn to read or write. That bothered the boy Carl and the man Carl. His mother at least had bought a set of encyclopedia. He had loved this fair-haired and hardworking woman. The family's religious preference was Swedish Lutheran. When we walked him by a German Lutheran church near us, he said the Sandburgs worshipped the "All Seeing God." He wanted to talk about his life, and although he was seventy-eight years old, the past still bothered him. I'm sure that there had been no burning desire for greater horizons on the part of his parents. But then hard-working people have little time for curiosity.

It was a big family. Carl slept and read in the garret. He did chores before school and after school. He delivered newspapers, and he learned about politics and business. He told us his secret ambition was to be a big league baseball player. He said as a child he did play baseball. He pointed to his foot and described how stepping on a broken piece of glass had ended in four stitches and ended his baseball dreams. He still grieved over the loss of two of his brothers who had died within minutes of each other of diphtheria. That is a very strong dose of sadness for one who missed the chums that should have been: a lesson that life deals cruel blows. Antibiotics had not been discovered, nor was the practice of medicine very sophisticated at this time. His grief gave way to a restless period of adolescence in which everything seemed to come to a dead end. He has written all of these things, over and over, but when they are forever in your heart and the pain is still there, you tend to repeat.

It was clear that he was carrying a sadness in his heart while he was at our home that somehow relaxed, releasing his innermost feelings. If he had wanted to, he could have stayed on and on, because we loved having him with us. He was very comfortable. We were very comfortable.

We moved into the living room where he sat near the piano and picked up the guitar, trying its strings. It was okay, compliments of our good friend Tom Riddick, who owned the Riddick Piano Company, on loan to the balladeer.

Sandburg said, "The guitar is a noble instrument. It takes someone who is devoted to it, like Segovia, to bring out its possibilities. If I'd gotten a prison sentence, I'd have probably become pretty good on the guitar."

So with seven-year-old Billy at his feet and five-year-old Cathy still regarding him with some reserve, and me holding the baby, he sang his myriad of songs with repeated requests for "Goober Peas." He also sang "Frankie and Johnny," and

> *Papa loved Mama*
> *Mama loved men*
> *Mama's in the graveyard*
> *Papa's in the pen.*

Cathy was somewhat confused about this man with the thick white hair and the deep voice, who had trouble with his shoe laces. She kept studying him. Finally, she pulled me into a corner and pulled my head ever so close to hers and whispered, "Mommy, is *he* God?"

I answered, "No sweetheart, he's not God. He's a poet."

We were having a wonderful time by now. Cathy was no longer afraid and Billy was practically standing on his shoes, mesmerized. The doorbell rang and I had to answer it. I put Caye in his lap, saying, "Mr. Sandburg, would you please hold the baby while I answer the door?" I had forgotten that this was dancing school day. A neighbor taught ballet, and parents who were friends often stopped by our house to kill the hour while their kids were in class. This one was a man. A big man. So big we called him Moose!

So Kenny Moeller walked into our sanctum and I introduced our guest. "Mr. Sandburg, this is Kenny Moeller. He was well-known in college as a football player. We call him Moose."

Kenny lost his cool. His little cigar stub fell out of his mouth and he was speechless. But in a few minutes it was he who was answering a zillion questions about football and college and the insurance business without even realizing they were talking about *him*. There was no mention of poetry or Pulitzer prizes or anything Lincolnian. Kenny never got over the fact that Sandburg was so easy to talk to, so genuinely interested in *him*. Or that Carl Sandburg was staying at our house and nobody knew it. Yet! When he left, Sandburg said, "Now, who would have thought that I would be lucky enough to meet a big-time football player from Indiana University?" This was a keystone to Carl Sandburg. Always the learner. Often the listener.

By this time it was six o'clock and getting to be dinner time. Tomorrow was a big day and some of it would be spent getting ready for his lecture and picking out his ballads and getting his political comments ready. He stayed in his room until noon. We were all relaxed and into the routine by now. He was comfortable. We were comfortable too and, so far, we had kept his visit quiet and the press and phone were not bothering us. Everything would change tomorrow. Baby fed and back in crib, children ready for bed, and we, tired but happy. We called it a day.

And indeed it was to be a great and happy three days in which we all grew very close and adopted each other forever. He enjoyed our family and children. They loved him, and he seemed to feel that he belonged there in the bosom of our household—chaos and all.

The next day, on the way to Caleb Mills Hall for his presentation-performance, we unexpectedly met a friend of ours coming up our walk with a gift. Our neighbor and dear newspaper friend Ed Ziegner approached us, carrying a bottle of Jack Daniels under one arm and one of Dewar's White Label under the other.

Ed and Martha had recently had a terrible furnace blowup which destroyed everything they had in their house. My husband, Bill Zaring, was their insurance agent and had done all he could to facilitate the repairs and replacements. When Ed saw us coming towards him, I on this tall gentleman's arm and my husband carrying the guitar, he stopped in his tracks and said, "When did you take up guitar playing?"

"I didn't," was my husband's reply. "It belongs to this gentleman. Mr. Sandburg, this is our friend Eddie Ziegner."

Ed nearly dropped both bottles. Both Carl and Ed stood there with their mouths hanging open. Sandburg's amazement was at the booze. We had not gone far when he could stand it no longer. "May I ask to what do you owe your good fortune in the gift of a bottle of Jack Daniels?" So we explained the furnace ordeal and he understood perfectly. Later that evening, Sandburg was to enjoy those gifts—he knocked off that Jack Daniels with us and a few other friends. Eventually when I visited Carl Sandburg at Connemara, he suggested I not bring up "the gift" in front of his wife.

Probably the most important reason for the success of his visit with us was the fact that I did not advertise his coming to us. No one but his agent and his family knew. That was the key to the spontaneity of the visit and the disarming encounters enjoyed by all who happened into our house. And when calls came in from New York and Chicago, he would not take them. We were to instruct everyone that he would take no calls until after his lecture and he would be unavailable "until the day after tomorrow."

I doubt that anyone who hasn't been to a Sandburg lecture could have any idea how much energy went into his preparation. He wrote, he practiced, he read the newspapers and learned what he needed to know about the locale in which he was performing. When you understand that he was very conscientious about how he "went over" with his audience, you can understand how all of that preparation and the delivery itself was totally consuming for him. He was spent when he walked off the stage. Exhausted, mentally and physically, and, remember, in his late seventies. Then, though it seemed to some to be grandstanding, after an hour or so of resting, he would emerge regenerated and ready for some refreshment and good conversation. His schedule, which reversed night and day, had to be this way. You create when you feel creative. Time has no meaning in the creative process.

Leon W. Russell wrote a news report of the lecture in Indianapolis. It gives you an idea that Carl Sandburg didn't just get up on stage and ad lib. Nor did he pull just any old song out of his songbag. His performance was polished to the good, barn-siding-like finish that made him so appealing. Here is what Russell had to say:

> *Carl Sandburg set one foot on a chair, swung his guitar into place, and recalled the rich heritage of American folk music for an enthralled audience of 1,500 last night in Caleb Mills Hall.*
>
> *The 78-year-old poet, historian and Lincoln biographer sang with the unpretentious simplicity of a grandfather entertaining his admiring progeny.*
>
> *Like a grandfather, he had just given wise advice to young people, distilled from the richness of a life of scholarship and authorship that has placed him firmly in the top rank of American literary figures.*
>
> *The audience chuckled in appreciation as he explained that he spoke only to the young. "I'll let the old folks go to hell in their own way," he elaborated.*
>
> *He counseled young people to find time to be alone. "Loneliness will help young people," he said. "They need the value of creative solitude."*
>
> *"All our advancements have been the result of solitude and loneliness and prayer by certain men, who knew how to use solitude."*
>
> *Freedom of discussion and inquiry should be kept open, Sandburg said.*
>
> *He condemned the "danger of doing what everyone is doing, and the fear of not saying what everyone is saying" by those who fall back upon "the influence of unworthy authority."*

All writers love to read their reviews. Ours were very good.

The Managing Editor of *The News*, Wendell Phillippi, lived behind us, and I lied to him to get him over so I wouldn't have to tell him who was at our house. So Sandburg met people that interested him, including two W.W. II veterans whom I later arranged to have stop by. He was quite humbled by some of the stories and very happy to hear all of it. He asked the questions. He also met a lawyer friend who had been in on the liberation at Auschwitz and with whom he had a lengthy conversation. He was very moved by this encounter.

When I mention little kindnesses and his appreciation of them, I mean with everyone.

The big leg of lamb dinner was planned for the night of his lecture. The menu was organized so there would be leftovers that might come in handy. It was a good dinner. It served us well—for two days plus a train ride!

My cleaning lady, Delia, sometimes helped me out when I was in a pinch. That evening when she was serving dinner, just as she got to Sandburg, I said, "This is our guest, Mr. Carl Sandburg." And to him, "This is Delia, who really bailed me out here by cooking and baby sitting." She was poised and he was duly appreciative.

When we left the dinner table that night he said to me, "I like the way you did that. Introduced us nice and natural." Kind of like the way, later, he would take the violet I picked at Connemara and stick it in my shirt front. "The violet just matches the color of your skirt. I like that."

Mrs. Sandburg later told me that he had described his visit in detail, and so I was satisfied that our house was the right place for him to be at the right time. It was going to be a very long time before I got the answers to why our visit had a certain intensity that I could not, at the time, fathom.

My husband's panic about not knowing enough about Lincoln was time wasted. Carl Sandburg was not at our house for a seminar on Abraham Lincoln! He was there for a place to stay that felt comfortable and companionable. He seemed thrilled to hold the baby, to tell stories and sing, using our house and friends for background. His feet were tired. He was tired. So good; take off the shoes, shed the coat, put the feet up and just roll with us.

Only one hitch in this tale, and God forbid he ever knew this. The first night he was with us we stayed up very late talking. When we all went up to bed I realized I had forgotten one thing. Carl had our room and the two children had our old room, and the baby was in the other room, and *we* had no room. Lord help us!

Yes, we slept on the floor at the foot of the beds of the two older children. When they awoke to see their parents on the floor they were mildly confused. That was remedied the second night by two couches in the den!

But Carl Sandburg did not count rooms. Only his own which, thankfully, he found warm and comfortably quilted. He asked for nothing special. He noticed books in the den and the paintings on the walls. Interested—not critical.

Too soon, our visit was over and it was time to leave for the station. That was when my little boy came back to the door and called out to him, "Mr. Sandbogue,(*sic*) I wish you were my grandfather."

As we went toward the car, Sandburg looked back at Billy and said, "Did you hear what he said? Why that makes a fella almost want to cry." And he brushed his hand across his face. He later told Edward Steichen about this. Much later, I would find out from his daughter, Helga, why his sensitivity to us as a family was so marked during that visit.

On the way to the station he wanted to know when we were planning our trip to Florida. Told, he asked if we would come to Flat Rock on our way back. He would like to give us some of the books from his personal library before the books got packed for the trip to Champaign, Illinois. "You have been so kind to me," he said. "I would like to do this for you."

I could understand my little boy's remark upon parting with his new friend.

NAMES
by Carl Sandburg

There is only one horse on the earth
and his name is All Horses.
There is only one bird in the air
and his name is All Wings.
There is only one fish in the sea
and his name is All Fins.
There is only one man in the world
and his name is All Men.
There is only one woman in the world
and her name is All Women.
There is only one child in the world
and her name is All Children.
There is only one Maker in the world
and His children cover the earth
and they are named All God's Children.

(and, added by me after the visit.)

P.S. There is only one grandfather
and his name is All Grandfathers.

The third Sandburg segment, also in 1956, happened when we stopped by Connemara on our way back from Florida and spent a day and an evening with the entire family (save Helga). And that was given increased meaning by Edward Steichen there—having just returned from a European tour with his *Family of Man* exhibition. He was at Connemara to "visit and rest up some." Of course that was the very best of best because we walked into a cross section of love that may never be equalled . . .

Steichen and his sister, (Sandburg's wife) Lillian Paula Sandburg. Sandburg and Steichen were at their very height of admiration for each other. Daughters Margaret and Janet Sandburg were so happy to see their Uncle Steichen, and his fondness for them shone all the while. At the same time, this intimate reunion of the Sandburgs and their beloved Steichen was shared with my husband Bill Zaring and me in such a way that we never felt like outsiders in the least.

Our host walked from the house as we first arrived; the Sandburg image of the unpressed suit, string tie and white hair in his eyes was replaced by baggy brown pants and a gray wool lumberjack shirt. A fatigue hat was pulled down over his sunglasses. The hat was a "Home Front" fixture given him by Admiral Nimitz.

Sandburg welcomed us warmly, "Well, I see you made it all right." Then he invited us to step aside a moment before we proceeded any further. He wanted us to know about his daughter, Janet. Janet was the victim of an accident many years before. When she was in high school she had been struck by a car in front of her school and had had irreparable damage from a skull injury. She still suffered from severe headaches, but he said, "She is a good little farmer and a big help to her mother." I was about to meet a very engaging, lovable child of middle age who was also to become my friend and pen pal.

As we proceeded to the house, we met another daughter, Margaret. She joined us in our walk and I began to see that she was a really conscientious helper and serious thinker. Sandburg said she was his "right hand man" in keeping his files straight, and all in her head. Margaret, too, had been ill as a child. She had suffered from epilepsy and had only in recent years been given some relief with the aid of new drugs. Two very serious problems to reconcile forevermore.

Margaret was a true bibliophile. Carl Sandburg never had his library catalogued, saying he knew where everything was. He meant that Margaret knew unerringly where everything was. Janet helped her mother raise the kids, that is, the baby goats she bred, her prize-winning animals. Margaret helped her father mind the books. So Janet was "kids" and Margaret was "books."

On this particular day, Margaret's main job was in the interest of getting their good friend, Adlai Stevenson, elected President of the United States. They were a busy and happy working family. They read together, talked together, laughed together and loved together . . . closely knit. And even though the years had been a struggle, as Sandburg said, "Well, I been eatin' regular."

Due to the years of medical bills for both daughters, there had been more fame than financial gain. Things were easing up, though; they had weathered a lot and they had all lived through the hard years. Now what both the Sandburgs wanted was security for the future of Janet and Margaret. Helga, the youngest daughter, had published three books by then and has published one since. She also painted oil portraits. She is now the wife of Dr. George Crile of the Crile Clinic in Cleveland and has a son and daughter who are grown. They were "Swipes and Skabootch" (John Carl and Paula) to Grandpa—who was "Buppong" to them.

Mrs. Sandburg was the last to meet us. Here was another surprise. It occurred to me that I had never heard very much about her, although Mr. Sandburg called her from our house and spoke of her often. Behind this man quietly stood a magnificent vision of sweetness, gentleness, efficiency, intelligence, and talent, who, I believe, was indeed the most important person in their lives. Paula Sandburg (Lillian Paula Sandburg, sometimes referred to as Lillian) was a lovely shadow of peace. She had stood by the little group through heartbreaking times and made them what they became, a source of joy and goodness to each other and other people. When we met, she said, "You were very nice to come. Carl told me how kind you were to him in Indianapolis."

She apologized for the papers stacked in the study; everything was covered including the file cabinets. Carl said to me, "She is my bookkeeper, my tax man and my secretary. She keeps track of all of the business for me." Of course some of the busy look was due to her own goat breeding business.

Mrs. Sandburg was one of the country's foremost goat breeders. Her goat herds were made up of beautiful, refined animals who had come from Switzerland, Africa, and South America. There are speculations as to why Mrs. Sandburg turned to goat raising, engaging in it for a long time and very successfully. Maybe it was for essential diet reasons or maybe because daughter Helga had said she wanted to be a farmer and asked for a cow—a goat being a compromise. Logically it was because she was a genius in the field of genetics who was in demand as a lecturer and an advisor in several agricultural colleges throughout the Country. She, too, might have been a writer; she had, after all, been a teacher. She was enormously bright, speaking several languages, and she held a Phi Beta Kappa key. In spite of all of this, she kept a low profile.

Perhaps she was wise to stay behind the scenes and let her genius shine through others. She had no part in the public life of her husband, preferring to remain at home. The only time she ever shared in any excitement was when she went to Chicago for Carl Sandburg's 75th birthday celebration in the Blackstone Hotel.

Harry Golden, their neighbor, who was a well known newspaperman, editor and author, described her as "beautiful in a Grecian sense, her clothes, her hair, everything about her being graceful and simple." And publisher Alfred Harcourt said, "She is a remarkable combination of scholar, business executive and old fashioned housekeeper. She works harder than most women can imagine, working with her hands as well as her brain, and in spite of labor through the years, she has managed to keep her tea rose complexion which makes her one of the loveliest women to look at."

She was a beauty—defying description when I saw her and probably always. She had an ethereal gaze, a look of peace and tranquility. The price for that peaceful gaze was probably high, but she was left with an inner glow that shown like a golden light.

During that day at Connemara, I witnessed Mrs. Sandburg and her ultimate patience and noble gentleness with all around her. Though her duties consumed much of her time and energy, she took each segment of her daily life in stride with a sweetness and tenderness which were touching, as if the word "stress" was unknown to her.

And she had so many details to deal with. Her own mind was an entity in itself. I am sure her husband was amazed at her wisdom and her prowess in the field of "management," . . . juggling monumental tasks with apparent ease. Sandburg once said to me, "Both Steichen and his sister, whom I married, have minds definitely superior to mine in several areas."

The Sandburg house was Spartan in appearance. The big living room with plain, white walls was furnished with just the necessities for comfort, the grand piano having become a mountain of manuscripts and books and letters, as did most everything else in the room. Mrs. Sandburg explained that everything we saw was being sorted out for the van that would take all this famous literary memorabilia to the library at the University of Illinois. The many bookcases from floor to ceiling all over the house were now being emptied and there were boxes everywhere.

I have a clipping of an Associated Press news story dated June 17th, 1956. The headline reads, "U. of Illinois Gets Tons Of Carl Sandburg Books." The story continues:

> *The University of Illinois has received more than four tons of books, manuscripts, pictures and other materials, the first shipment of Carl Sandburg's private library. The Illinois-born*

poet-historian's library was bought by the school with a $30,000 gift from the University of Illinois Foundation. Two-thirds of Sandburg's material is being used by him at his Flat Rock (N.C.) home and will be shipped to Illinois later.

The 150-case shipment contained manuscripts of all of Sandburg's works as well as typescripts and proofs with the author's personal corrections. Considerable Lincoln material, which will be integrated with the university's other Lincoln collections, also was sent.

Still to come is Sandburg's extensive collection of contemporary poetry, his correspondence files and numerous other items.

Dr. David D. Henry, university president, said the Sandburg collection "is a rich source for scholarly study in contemporary literature and will greatly enhance the university's work in this field. It will also be a continuing memorial to one of America's most prominent citizens and one of the best-known interpreters of American life.

A measly $30,000? I couldn't believe it then and I can't believe it now. But, the melee of papers, clippings and snapshots piled in that room eventually became the treasure trove left behind to attract his biographer Penelope Niven.

We returned to his study. Mr. Sandburg was about to present us with keepsakes of his personal library at Connemara. He put on his green eye-shade and took the books off to a corner and wrote a special inscription for each designated book. Later, my youngest child was to look at *Rootabaga Stories* and ask, "Who was Uncle Carl?" My daughter, Cathy, lifts the heavy saga *Remembrance Rock* and reads, "To Billy, Kathy and Gaye, with love and kisses from their far off uncle, Connemara Farm, Flat Rock, North Carolina, 1956." My son regards *Homefront Memo*, a war book, and reads "Luck stars be over you, with love."

We continued our tour of Connemara. Big Glassy is a huge, round, extraordinary rock on the Connemara property. Rivulets of water stream down its surface giving it its name. Here was solitude and here was where Carl Sandburg often went to write. I wonder if it was here that he wrote "There is such a thing as creative solitude—A certain kind of loneliness out of which have risen the works of the creative spirits of the past. They were not afraid of being alone, they had learned how to use their loneliness."

Over near the rim of the rock there was a man sound asleep, surely, I thought, some weary traveler or hobo with his hat pulled down over his eyes. Sandburg ignored this scene. Finally, I asked, "Do tramps stray clear up here?"

"Shhh," he admonished. "That is the Great Steichen. He just came in from Europe. He has taken *Family of Man* all over the Continent and he is bushed. He came here to stay and rest for a few days. You will meet him later at dinner. Come along." (Assertive, protective.)

The *Family of Man* was a collection of 508 pictures of the human race, all colors and strata of man. It was the first time in a collection the sequence of the birth of a baby was published—from the laboring mother to the child's arrival in the delivery room. I suppose today this could be ordinary for children to see, but for many in that day it had an element of real mystery and showed the miracle that birth will always be. I owe Carl Sandburg my thanks for help in explaining to my children that vital and inevitable time-worn question. He had given us a copy of *Family of Man* and told the children it contained a beautiful story and they must read the pictures. The preface to the book was done by Sandburg . . . and most all of the photographs Sandburg used in his own books were done by Steichen. He, in fact, drew the title from his description of the world which was the *Family of Man*. This term came to him when, early in his research on Lincoln, he came to realize that Lincoln believed that all men everywhere are a family.

Edward Steichen, as I have said, was Paula Sandburg's brother and Carl's best friend in all respects. Steichen is to photography what Sandburg was to literature, and it would not be fair to dwell on the author and leave Steichen out of the picture.

To explain their meaning to each other is to quote Sandburg . . . "I have known Edward Steichen now for fifty-three years. There can be no such thing as measuring the depth of his influence on my life . . . . He has been rated by good authorities as the world's greatest photographer. For those who wish to read of his life through the year 1929, I can refer them to a book written by me titled *Steichen the Photographer*. I could make a list of scores of photographs by Steichen, each and every one a poem, a document or a vivid high moment. Often when a news photographer is shooting me, I ask him, "Do you realize that you are photographing America's first biographer of a photographer?" Sometimes I myself smile and add, "If you can say distinctly 'biographer of a photographer,' you are definitely sober."

And in another letter . . . "When I am naming important teachers and personal forces in my life, I must name Steichen and his sister. They have been a faculty of many professors in several fields whether the fine arts, genetics or healthy and wholesome mysticism. No man was ever more lucky in a brother-in-law. When I look at his brilliant record in two World Wars, his depth of love and devotion to his country added to his immense performances in the field of photography and the fine arts, he definitely had a kind of majesty in my book."

And what did Steichen think of *his* brother-in-law? At the 75th birthday celebration in Chicago, Steichen was called on for a few words. He said, among other remarks, "On the day that God made Carl, he didn't do anything else that day."

During the Second World War, War Correspondent Lt. Commander Edward Steichen, aged 62, went into the Navy as a photographer. He felt compelled to mingle with servicemen, as did Sandburg (a situation Sandburg describes in *Homefront Memo*).

I should pause here to bring in an interesting *Indianapolis News* connection. Bob Doeppers, *The News* photographer, and Steichen worked on the same project during World War II. They were shooting and editing the film "Fighting Lady" about the Enterprise during the Battle of Midway and other South Sea skirmishes.

Bob Doeppers was impressed by the strength and professionalism of Steichen.

> Ed was a taskmaster but easy to work for and a great personality. I imagine his work overseeing the Government project during the '30s in the Dust Bowl taught him how to handle subordinates. As an enlisted man I never became that close to him—but I developed a great respect for his integrity and knowledge. He developed his plan for the day—made all hands aware of it and what he expected them to accomplish. I never heard him put anyone down and we all strived to do his bidding. I wish I had known him as a civilian.

Working together only seemed to cement the strong affection and admiration Sandburg felt for Steichen. Together they had produced *The Road to Victory!*, which was a procession of murals depicting the nation at war, displayed at the Museum of Modern Art in New York. Carl Sandburg wrote the text and Commander Steichen selected the photographs and directed the project. These two men had a powerful bond which seemed to be felt whether they were separated or together. And the strongest part of the bond was their shared admiration for the brilliant diamond, Lillian Paula Sandburg.

One of the murals shows a whole wall of mountains and next to it three studies of elderly American Indian men, and between the two in large print the text read, "In the Beginning There was Virgin Land and America was Promises—and the Buffalo by the thousands pawed the great plains—and the Redman gave over to an endless tide of white men in endless numbers with a land hunger and no end to the land they wanted. Over the Eastern Seaboard through Appalachia moved this human tide of pioneers and home seekers—out among the spreading arteries of the Mississippi Waterway System—out to the Rockies and beyond to the long sunsets of the West Coast."

And here before me was the great man Steichen, creator of some of the finest photographic work ever done in America, asleep on a rock, under a hat. This was a picture that sadly was never snapped!

On we went, though, with the tour winding its way through the pine-needled paths, past a fallen down tree or a caved-in outbuilding or a run-down slave cottage. You might want to say, "Why don't you fix this place up some?" There were some twenty buildings on it. The answer is, Carl Sandburg liked it natural.

"Now, take that fallen tree hanging over that path. Those roots will rot and go back to Mother Earth and that's where they came from in the first place." And the tree roots seem to be symbolic of his earthy wisdom and philosophy of life and death.

T.K. Whipple, in writing of this author said, "The best term that I can find for Sandburg is that of Psalmist. His feeling for the sky, the ocean, the wind, for all the more grandiose aspects of nature, for vastness of time and space is like that of the psalms."

As we continued to walk the Connemara acreage, we came upon a pastoral scene, a peaceful group of goats lying around a large old tree. There were beautiful Nubian goats with tan and white coats, long ears with the lighter colors broken by shades of brown. They were beautiful and haughty. Others were the Toggenburg Swiss goats with their splendid looking, light beige coats. Then there was another distinctly black and white breed, the famous goats of Paula Sandburg.

If Carl's section of Connemara was gradually going back to the earth, this part was up-to-date, modern and unbelievably clean and tidy. Feed-racks made of redwood with blue roof tops stood high off the ground. Connemara goats never ate anything off of the ground—they were royalty!

Even the salt licks were on sticks and stuck in the ground around the barnyard. The reddish barn was clean and newly painted, and these animals seemed to be aware that they were special. They furnished all of the dairy products at Connemara and for a nearby dairy as well. Sandburg seemed very pleased and very proud of the goat herd and explained, "Goats have many virtues . . . intelligence, friendliness, and frugality. Moreover, they provide the family table with milk, butter, cheese and meat . . ." Paula Sandburg bred goats for high milk production. Paula also bred for looks and beauty, as well just to generally perfect a fine breed of animal.

We saw the famous "Brocade," who was the award-winning triumph of Paula Sandburg's efforts. She has been photographed for beauty and for her production—she achieved the highest milk production ever.

Exciting as all this was, there was a limit to one day and we could feel it coming. The cooling rays of the sun spoke of dinner time. The dinner table that evening was a bounty of food that was, with the exception of baked ham, provided entirely from the farm. I sat next to Janet, still in her blue jeans and plaid shirt. She had fed the new kids and had finished her job in the basement room which was meticulously kept for the formulas and equipment for the newborn babies. She was bubbling with news for her uncle Ed, who was by now refreshed and dressed in Navy fatigue pants and white oxford cloth shirt with rolled sleeves. Margaret, looking very much like her father, spoke seriously and seldom.

It was hard to focus attention on any one person, as the importance of Steichen, the intelligence of Paula Sandburg and the obvious happiness of Sandburg with his lot in life, permeated the room. The thing that was awesome was the presence of so many geniuses at once—each so well known in his or her own field and so stimulating to listen to. Not often is my tongue tied and never did my mind feel so minuscule. It was my cue to be a quiet observer. The way Mrs. Sandburg easily handled everyone's questions and the excitement of the reunion with her brother while still making the guests feel welcome and part of the group . . . well, this was yet another talent.

I will never forget the dinner that night. Besides the baked ham, we had boiled potatoes bathed in goat's butter, fresh broccoli covered with a sauce made from goat's milk and butter, another vegetable with goat's butter, and bread and goat's butter. And to drink? A tall glass of goat's milk. It was a fairly concentrated indoctrination. I decided later that the taste of goat's milk is as pleasant as cow's milk and slightly sweeter.

We could tell that Steichen and Sandburg had a favorite game they liked to play at the table. They played with words, and everything had a double meaning or deep subtle wit or was a three dimensional pun. It was mental sparring for the quick-witted, fun-loving alert mind. "Forgive us our press passes" is typical of the puns they loved.

The cook was setting up chairs in the study. The meal was nearly over. She asked how many wanted coffee. In a moment we were each served our own individual thermos bottle of coffee. Then Janet said, "It is almost time, Daddy." And suddenly we were all moving to another room. "Take your coffee with you," Mrs. Sandburg said. The chairs were lined against the wall and we took our places; it looked serious, like a meeting was about to begin. Sandburg turned on the T.V. set and said, "Do you people get Douglas Edwards? We never miss the seven o'clock news."*

We watched the news and drank our coffee, each at our own leisure. When dinner was over, our day was over! Sandburg took his guitar and sang a few verses. Janet came in to say good night. She asked for my address and said she would write to me. Margaret said she was going upstairs to read.

Mrs. Sandburg was talking to her brother about her prize Nubian, Brocade. We collected our books. We said good-bye and thanks to all for a profoundly full and special day. Carl walked us to the drive; I kissed the rough cheek good-bye and we took our leave of Connemara. As we drove toward the road, I with my prized books clutched in my hands, I looked back and there was the big Swede waving his Nimitz cap to us. This was the man who might have been a big time baseball player had he not stepped on a broken pop bottle and ruined his foot, who probably was a carbon copy of Lincoln in his early thirst for reading and learning by the light of the fire. The man who was a softie for the people, the prairie, the fighting men, the mountains, the fireborn, the height of the sky, the luck of the stars, the newspapermen, the dish-washers, the hags and bums, the smoke and the smog and the clear mountain air; the man who was *The People, Yes*, was fading out of sight.

I was limp with the greatness of the day and the humanness of the great. If I recovered from being awestruck, I promised surely someday to get my impressions down in written form and share them.

After this time spent with his family in his home, we kept in touch. In 1957 a package came in the mail. It was a copy of *The Sandburg Range*, compliments of the author, sent by Harcourt Brace, Publisher. *The*

---

*Douglas Edwards died in 1991 at the age of 73. He was one of the most notable of all the news commentators and his list of achievements is long indeed.

Sandburg Range is a bedside book, covering Sandburg's "everything." It is still beside me wherever I go.

It was in the later 1950s and early 1960s that I felt Carl Sandburg was hitting his stride in all areas. He went to California where George Stevens needed his expertise producing "The Greatest Story Ever Told." He was on TV. He was in Washington, a darling of the Kennedy and Johnson era, in a period that I thought he probably relished. Later I asked him if he was "going Hollywood?"

"No!" was his reply.

I think maybe Hollywood was going Sandburg.

Then my own life took a nose dive, and I was going through what grieved him so in Helga's life. A divorce. Black days. I never told him. In that period I got back into writing as a special correspondent and I carried my press pass with pride. It gave me power and a sense of confidence.

During the summer of 1961 I spent a month in California. In August of that summer I phoned him and tried to get from La Jolla to Los Angeles to see him at the Bel Air Hotel. But with my two girls in tow it didn't work out. So we settled for a long telephone conversation, and I told him I would write about his Hollywood days for *The Indianapolis News*, which I did.

There was only one flaw in our California conversation. When I suggested meeting him at Disneyland, thinking he would really enjoy it, he grew quiet. No, he would *not* like to meet me there. Mr. Walt Disney did not happen to be one of his favorite persons. He did not elaborate and I dropped it with him. Then I wondered why? I couldn't imagine. It always bothered me. When I began this book I wrote George Stevens, Jr. to find out if he might have the answer. His father had been the producer of "The Greatest Story Ever Told." His answer follows:

Dear Mrs. Failey:

I never discussed Walt Disney with Carl Sandburg and all that would occur to me was that Carl was so interested in the many dimensions of humanity that he might well have had very little interest in cartoon figures.

Carl worked on the screenplay of "The Greatest Story Ever Told" with my father. Dad had great appreciation for Carl's poetry and his writings, especially Remembrance Rock. *He found Carl's collaboration nourishing.*

With warm regards.

*Sincerely
George Stevens, Jr.*

The following article was the result of our telephone conversation that day in California.

> *Hollywood, Cal.—A visit with Carl Sandburg, who is in Hollywood as adviser to George Stevens on the production of "The Greatest Story Ever Told," always is interesting.*
>
> *He has been in Hollywood for more than a year and will be there until the picture is finished.*
>
> *The author now is 84 years old and his memory is matched by his mental agility. Has he gone Hollywood?*
>
> *It would seem not. Sandburg has, for years, worn a silk ascot-type scarf around his neck, accompanied by a white wool sweater which is punctuated with moth holes. This is his morning working, reading and writing costume.*
>
> *But he appears to me to fit the concept of the Hollywood director with the beret and the megaphone shouting "Cut!" from the seat of a deck chair. (I would love to have seen him on the set in his canvas chair with "Carl Sandburg" lettered on the back panel. Knowing him, I can see a sparkle—a new, distinct kind of self-esteem in those eyes. Ah, Hollywood!)*
>
> *When asked how he happened to change his mind about the movie industry, he explained that only one man—George Stevens—could have gotten him to Hollywood. He considers Stevens one of the great directors of our era.*
>
> *How does he work, when does he write and how does he keep up the pace at his age?*
>
> *He takes no calls before noon. He keeps his visits short. He disciplines his time to fit his schedule. At the moment, he is reading a manuscript for a book that he has been asked to preface. "You can't write a preface if you don't read the manuscript," he said. "And it takes me two days to read 150,000 words." He also said he can't begin a new week unless all the previous week's work is done by Sunday night.*
>
> *The most surprising thing was his contempt for Disneyland. He has not been there and does not plan to go. His reasons seem to be purely personal. My parting words were, "Don't you dare go*

back home without seeing Disneyland." And he laughed. But he didn't go.

Another article, written during Sandburg's Hollywood years by Wendell Phillippi and printed in *The Indianapolis News* on April 14th, 1961, follows:

> *Carl Sandburg rewrote some history last night.*
> *He said Abraham Lincoln didn't write the Gettysburg Address on the back of an envelope. In fact, he said Lincoln didn't carry envelopes with him.*
> *On "CBS Reports" (Channel 8, WISH-TV) Sandburg said the Gettysburg Address was the greatest short speech in history with vast implication in every sentence.*
> *He said the editor of the* Chicago Times *called the speech "terrible" at the time but he was later found to be of unsound mind.*
>
> *Sandburg compared the brevity of President Kennedy's inaugural speech with the Gettysburg document and added that Mr. Kennedy's State of the Union message was practical and showed the writer had the capacity of a good historian.*
> *Other Sandburg comments from an interview by Howard K. Smith of "CBS News":*
>
> *"The Civil War should be studied, not celebrated."*
> *"Lee ended up in Gettysburg because he was confident a victorious invasion of the North would lead to the capture of Philadelphia, Baltimore and Washington. This would mean European support for the South."*
> *"Meade trailed Lee and 'Gettysburg just happened.'"*
> *Agrees with historian Gen. Fuller that "Grant's victory at Vicksburg was far more important than Meade's at Gettysburg."*
> *"Churchill, in calling the Civil War America's noblest struggle, has forgotten about the War of Independence."*
> *"If Stonewall Jackson had been in command of Pickett's charge the outcome would have been different."*
> *"Meade was good but not a great general."*
> *"The Civil War would have been shortened without a doubt if Lee had accepted Lincoln's request to be C-in-C of the North."*

"*The North had shovelry; the south chivalry.*"
"*Remarks by Eisenhower and Montgomery that the Civil War generals didn't know what they were doing and should have been sacked at Gettysburg were without merit.*"

Wendell Phillipi finished:

The drama and presentation of the [last evening's TV] film proves television is coming of age. The cold, barren and windy setting dramatized the torments of a battlefield. The actual wind blowing Sandburg's scarf was much more inspiring than a studio fan blowing an American flag in the early era of TV attempts at patriotism.

It did seem a little wrong to have an 84-year-old man walking over a battlefield and spending an hour in the cold, bareheaded most of the time. But that's Carl Sandburg. His love for Lincoln, Grant and the American soldier have sent him more miles to explore, exploit, and write about than any modern general or doughfoot.

When Sandburg was in Hollywood he changed his whole style. He began wearing suits and ties, or suits with turtleneck sweaters. For dress occasions he put on light gray suits with dark shirts, looking a little Hollywood in fact.

George Stevens had insisted on having Sandburg with him as technical advisor because he was a great student of the Bible. He said, "Carl Sandburg knows as much about the Bible and can interpret as beautifully as anyone I know and I need him."

I heard he was living in Marilyn Monroe's dressing room, which he called Marilyn Monroe's undressing room. He later was given a less spectacular dressing room. He slept in a fifty-dollar-a-day suite at the Bel Air Hotel in Beverly Hills, and he told them it was too fancy for him, asking to be moved to something less elegant where he could feel more at home. They moved him to a twenty-five-dollar-a-day hotel room.

In April, 1991, I took a walk around the lovely grounds of the Bel Air to see if I could catch a feeling of the past there, of Sandburg there . . . yes.

Sandburg liked some of the movie people, and the star of "The Greatest Story Ever Told" happened to be Elizabeth Taylor, who played the part of Mary Magdalene in this Bible story. By and large, he liked the people who were real, who were of foreign extraction, for instance. He always liked Kim Novak. He met her parents—he found them kind and earthy peasant-type immigrants whose daughter had made good. They were proud of her and she helped them out financially. Kim Novak should have known Carl Sandburg. He would have understood her. He would have told her he appreciated her talent, her work, her background.

I thought Sandburg did not care for Marilyn Monroe, but I understand later he became a good friend of hers. She even wrote poems and shared them with him.

I believe this was the only period of his life in the public eye where Carl Sandburg "lived it up," enjoying even at his advanced stage of life success and notoriety. He was mingling with glamorous people, adding movie people to the list of celebrity friends. These were the days when he counted as friends some of the best writers in America: Ernest Hemingway, Robert Frost, Archibald McLeish and so on.

During that period, he wrote the following letter to his friend Harry Golden (Golden was a newspaper man and a neighbor of the Sandburgs):

> At the annual meeting of the Friars last January, at a dinner honoring Gary Cooper, I made a five minute speech saying at the end, "I believe we are correct in saying that Gary Cooper is the most beloved illiterate to appear in American history." Then I turned and walked three steps to Gary Cooper and kissed him on the forehead, the first time I have ever done such a thing. Gary, who at one time studied cartooning, went to work on a message and passed it on down to where I sat next to Audrey Hepburn. I enclose it for you howsoever you may wish to use it. But, for Christ's sake, don't lose it . . .
>
> Do I recall your saying that J.F. Kennedy recited "Cool Tombs" or did he merely mention that he was familiar with it? I had a nice letter from him acknowledging warm appreciation of a two volume deluxe Remembrance Rock I sent him. In my inscription in Rem Rock I wrote, "I am one of the many who register to your Inaugural Address as an American Classic." He closed his letter, "I have been an admirer of yours for many years and therefore I am extremely pleased to have this inscribed book."

I think Norman Corwin answered a question I had about that period when he said that Sandburg got awfully tired during the Hollywood days. But what a glorious time he must have had.

And then in that next year I remarried and took on two more children to raise . . . once again my Sandburg lights went out. In that late-sixties time frame I was invited to join the Indianapolis Woman's Club and, of course, my first paper (and my best) would be about Carl Sandburg.

However, back in the Fall of 1961, when Carl Sandburg was 83, I wrote to Sandburg and asked him if I could possibly meet him either at Connemara, in Chicago, or wherever might be convenient to interview him and go over some notes and some ideas for an article on Connemara Farm.

My husband and I had taken some color slides of the farm and had some marvelous pictures of the goats and the countryside, color pictures of the mountains and the trees and some very good photographs of Mr. Sandburg. I also had two or three pictures of Margaret and Janet, but none of Mrs. Sandburg. I thought that if we could have an interview I could use some of the pictures and make a layout. I had first approached *The Indianapolis News*, but Wendell Phillippi, the Managing Editor said, "Well, this needs wider exposure than it's going to get in our local paper. Why don't you contact a big magazine or get *The New York Times Magazine* section or some such thing to do this?" He was very interested in it and promised he would do anything he could to help me. My point was that Connemara should be recorded. I knew that Edward R. Murrow had been there, but not very many people had spent a whole day or had a meal there or had met Steichen at Sandburg's house. The following is Sandburg's answer to my suggestion that we get together for an interview:

Dear Mary Jane,

Your letter to Bel Air was forwarded here. The weeks across October and November are all uncertain at present. I expect, however, to be with the George Stevens unit for several months. I may be out there in October or it may be November before I rejoin the unit. This is the situation. Next week I go with the CBS Television crew for five days in Illinois in places having to do with Lincoln. October 25th I give a 19 minute address at the Library of Congress dedicating a Civil War Centennial Exhibition. October 26th I give a recital in the New State Department Auditorium. After that God only knows whither I wend. It was not easy going to do a Preface for a book on President Kennedy's speeches and messages to Congress from the Inaugural through the Session of Congress. I am not herein doing a chapter of autobiography but merely letting you know that in this particular Autumn I am not among the unemployed. You are gracious to know and we will see what gives.

*Affectionately Yours,
Carl Sandburg*

This was the last letter I received from Sandburg, showing how he was spending the last few years of his life and how productive those years were. And it proves that he could never retire. He rejoined Stevens and continued working harder than ever, thinking, I suppose, that he would get home to Connemara, but being kept from it by the delays in the movie schedule. "The Greatest Story Ever Told" could not get produced or directed without the Bible expert, Sandburg. So he kept on working.

He had written to Paula saying, "I guess I won't get home in November but I hope by the end of February I will be back to Connemara to stay and then we will take our walks together—holding hands," which was one of their favorite occupations.

People were always getting (they still do) Sandburg mixed up with Robert Frost, the great poet from New England who is not unlike Sandburg. Robert Frost did for New England what Sandburg did for Chicago, the Midwest, and the Prairie. I love a story about the two of them together. Frost once invited Sandburg to come to his house for dinner where he was cooking steaks on the terrace. He put the steaks on the grill and Sandburg did not come downstairs. He still didn't come downstairs, and when the steaks were over-done another poet who was a guest, Archibald McLeish said, "What in the hell is Sandburg doing up there, trying to comb his hair out of his eyes?" Where upon Robert Frost said, "Nope, he's trying to comb his hair into his eyes!"

By 1963 Carl Sandburg was back at Connemara to stay—at last. As he said, "To every man, be he who may, comes a last happiness and a last day." He had written twenty-three books and had gone back a century to relive and write the story of Abraham Lincoln and the war years. He had given the sum total of everything he had written or learned or done to *Remembrance Rock* in 1067 pages.

What happened to me between 1961, after our last letters were exchanged, and 1967, when Carl Sandburg died, I can't explain exactly, but I failed to maintain contact with him. I ran into a whole new can of worms (second marriage) and I started working the twenty-four-hour shift. With my proclivity for taking on more than I could handle, I was in the fire more than out of it. The two sets of children Skip Failey and I had put together when we married were quickly moving into their teen years in sets of two. During those years I was getting educated to the world of teenagers and their various escapades or activities and my time was consumed. My world became hopelessly tangled up with motorcycles and noise and driving permits and braces and doctors and dancing school and parties and bonfires. But it was also pleasantly filled with the fun of a cheerleader daughter and all the activity that position brought. And there was the sheer pleasure of a little girl who was still sweet and uncomplicated and loved animals. It is an understatement to say my life was fragmented.

Before I was able to see Carl Sandburg again he became ill, and my only links to the family became Janet's notes at Christmas. Then came the news that he was gone.

I was crushed to think that the great genius was dead. Why had I let those kids keep me from doing things I wanted to do? It was I who dropped the ball and burned the bridges with my "far off uncle," and it made me very sad. My little friend Janet had lost her father, Margaret had lost her intellectual mentor and companion, and Paula Sandburg was left to care for all these loved ones without the presence of her beloved Great One. And my dear, sporadic friendship was over.

Typically, when someone famous dies, a local news staffer remembers that this person visited their town some time or other. The person with the memory usually gets sent to the "morgue" to look up the occasion and see what was documented during the visit. Then phone calls are made to those who were involved to verify the information and ask what is remembered that might be of interest.

When Carl Sandburg died I was called, and I remembered it all!

But how did the press know that Carl Sandburg had died? Who gave that out? How does it work? Today the press can bury you while you are still able to watch the TV news. Sammy Davis, Jr. could easily have heard about his impending demise and his doctor's remarks to the media. My heart ached for the man. I believe he and his family were done a terrible injustice. It's a prime peeve of mine with the media that they rush in like ghouls or vultures to peer over deathbed scenes. Everyone, after all, dies the same way eventually—rich or poor, celebrity or street person, any color—they stop breathing. Let it happen in ultimate privacy, not hoopla.

It was a different scenario when Carl Sandburg lay in his bed next to a big sunny bay window in his wife's room. The nurses and Lillian Paula Sandburg waited quietly nearby. And when the end came "peacefully," no one did anything for a spell. Then someone realized the world had to know that one of its greatest writers had passed away.

Joe Wershba of CBS had long been Carl's very good friend. Wershba was an early producer for "Sixty Minutes," and had been on Edward R. Morrow's, "See It Now," staff.

Not knowing how to release the information to the press, on her brother's advice Paula called Wershba in New York and asked if he would see to it. So it was Joe who released the news to the press. It was the proper and private manner in which this all unfolded that impressed me. His passing was treated in the same natural way that he had lived his life. There were no trumpets blowing.

The pond below the house at Connemara lay undisturbed. Big Glassy still sent its little shiny water ribbons down its sides. Sandburg's place for solitude and thinking remained. The goats were down at the barn doing what they always did, undisturbed.

Pretty soon, back at the house, some activity began. The phone started to ring. But basically, it was an unsensational and clean way of handling the inevitable event.

It was left to *The Indianapolis Star* to say it in the most eloquently lyrical way for those of us in the Hoosier State:

> *Carl Sandburg, poet of America, breathed out his soul into the air and sky of the continent he loved at the height of its summer glory, and left behind, for us and those who will follow, his many mighty visions.*

Then it came time for Paula Sandburg to consider the reality of the new situation, and she was right on target. The house would have to go . . . the future of the girls had to be considered. They all had loved Connemara, its music and its mountains, all two hundred and forty-seven acres of it—for twenty-two years. However, to be practical, the house would have to go, and another house replace their "love home."

Carl Sandburg's ashes were buried beneath Remembrance Rock in Galesburg, Illinois, the town of his birth. Mrs. Sandburg sold the house to the Parks and Recreation Department of the Federal Government. It became an historic monument.

A lovely red brick colonial home was purchased in Asheville, really perfect for them. Paula put it all together, knowing that Janet and Margaret would be settled and happy there. She lived with her daughters until February 18, 1977, when she died at the age of 94. Her ashes joined her husband's under the great rock in Illinois. A wonderful companion had been hired to manage the Asheville house where the two "girls" lived on alone, and all was complete with the addition of a golden retriever for Janet and a third floor library/study for Margaret.

How would I know they were happy with the new house? My friend Janet wrote the following to me in 1969. Knowing Janet had spent her life taking care of many little kids (baby goats), it was a great relief to get her cheerful letter.

11,18,69

DEAR MRS. FAILEY,

> IT IS CLOUDY AND COOL OUT.
> HOW IS THE WEATHER IN INDIANAPOLIS?
> WE ARE LIVING IN ASHEVILLE. I LIKE ASHEVILLE VERY MUCH.
> OUR HOUSE HAS 3 FLOORS.
> THE 3rd FLOOR HAS 4 ROOMS.
> 2. THERE ARE TWO GUEST BEDROOMS.
> THERE IS A BIG STUDY FOR MARGARET.
> THERE IS A BATHROOM, THE BATHROOM HAS A TILE FLOOR. THE REST OF THE ROOMS ON THE 2nd FLOOR ARE THE FOLLOWING.
> MY BEDROOM, MOTHER'S BEDROOM, MARGARET'S BEDROOM. MY BEDROOM IS THE ONLY BEDROOM ON THE 2nd FLOOR THAT HAS FOUR WINDOWS. I HAVE A RCA COLORED TV. THERE IS A COLORED RCA TV IN THE DEN.
>
> 3 THE ROOMS ON THE 1st FLOOR ARE THE FOLLOWING. SUN PORCH, LIVING ROOM, DINING ROOM, PANTRY, KITCHEN, DEN AND POWDER ROOM. WE HAVE A PATIO. YOU CAN GET ON THE PATIO FROM THE SUN PORCH OR THE DEN. YOU CAN GET TO THE PATIO FROM THE OUTSIDE.
>
> THE DOGWOOD HERE HAS LOTS OF BERRIES. WE HAVE TWO APPLE TREES ON OUR PLACE.
>
> 4. THERE IS A HEMLOCK HEDGE IN FRONT OF OUR HOUSE NEAR THE ROAD.

>   THERE IS A SHOPPING CENTER NOT FAR FROM
> OUR HOUSE.
>   IN THE SHOPPING CENTER THERE IS A BEAUTY
> SHOP WHERE I GET MY HAIR WASHED AND SET.
>   I THINK OF YOU QUITE OFTEN
>   WRITE SOON.
>
>   LOADS OF LOVE, JANET
>
>   P.S. WHAT IS ZIPS CODE NUMBER?

Another dry spell in my Sandburg saga began, and all my notes were put away. Life went on busily and not without sadness. Then lo and behold, the letter that started this chapter, and my memories arrived! I met by chance a wonderful and bright new penny—Penny Niven.

We made an appointment and were immediate friends. Her book on Carl Sandburg has inspired this book! She has been my burning torch and prod, she who never knew Carl Sandburg personally, and I, who did, now have a beautifully flowering, caring, friendship. She rekindled my friendship with Margaret and Janet, and through sharing these friendships with all these wonderful Sandburg people, Penny and I formed deep ties.

There were, of course, other letters after the first one:

> CARL SANDBURG ORAL HISTORY PROJECT
>   *September 15, 1985*
> Dear Majie Failey:
>
>   *I was delighted to have your good letter, and I look forward so much to meeting you and talking about Sandburg and a number of other interests I sense we have in common! By now you have had a wonderful journey, and I hope to hear about that, too!*
>
>   *I am sending this note to Michigan and to Indianapolis, to welcome you home and to urge you to let me know when the travel dust is settled enough so that I may come to Indianapolis and take you out to lunch.*
>
>   *I will enjoy telling you about my work (my postman calls me the Carl Sandburg Lady, and my daughter cautions her friends not to get me started on the subject of Sandburg!) and about the progress of the biography. What an adventure this has been! I do wish that, like you, I had known Carl Sandburg in his lifetime.*

I hope you will share your Sandburg paper with me. I might have some ideas about some outlets for it, in fact. I am so interested in hearing about your visit to Flat Rock, your impressions of the family and of Uncle Ed Steichen, and your perceptions of Sandburg's Hollywood sojourn. I can hardly wait for you to get home!

My schedule is flexible, and when you have settled into the fall rhythm, let me know what is good for you. I can drive over to see you on short notice, and almost any time. I am writing at home these days, so the 966-1666 number is the one to try first, should you wish to call. I hear from Peter and his nice secretary Leslie that you are a special person indeed. I can tell in your writing. I look forward to our visit!

Cordially,

Penny McJunkin

In the winter of 1985-1986, I went to Richmond, the Earlham Campus, and did, in fact, meet Penny. And like Sandburg's, her friendship, too, is addictive. She became very important to me. And I was enormously sorry she did not know the poet, for he would have gone "nearly silly" over her!

She finished her own biography on Carl Sandburg, and though it may have cost her dearly, it is her calling.

Jennifer McJunkin was barely a teenager when she realized that her mother Penny was getting more and more absorbed in the life of a poet named Carl Sandburg. Not that that wasn't all right; her mother had done a lot of reading and a lot of research in preparation for her favorite teaching subject, Nineteenth Century American Literature.

But Penny was going beyond the limits of "normal." She was devouring Sandburg information. Exasperation finally caused Jennifer to tell someone, "My Mom is obsessed by this dead guy." And so she was.

However, obsession was not the original goal. She did not know in the beginning that people who get involved with Carl Sandburg get hooked. But it's true! Ask Harry Golden, his outlander, writer friend, who wrote tons of papers on Sandburg. Ask his friends Robert Frost, Archibald MacLeish and all the others who were his contemporaries. Ask Ernest Hemingway. (If you could, of course. This whole marvelous generation is gone!) Hemingway's wife, Mary, was Society Editor for the *Chicago Daily News,* and she loved Carl. Everybody loved him, including the CBS crew who met him at his farm and produced "See It Now." Anyone who had the Sandburg experience could tell you, meet Carl Sandburg and you've had it. You're hooked. Give up. Love him and he loves you back. This guy *was* addictive.

Penny didn't cover her eyes and jump into her Carl Sandburg biography work. It happened like most love affairs do, gradually.

Penny has always had a way of falling into something she hadn't counted on. Good and bad. Radar she has—for people to whom she is sensitive. By the time I met Penny, she was deeply engrossed in her book, *Carl Sandburg: A Biography*. Never in a million blue moons could I have forged ahead, obstacle after stumbling block, as she did.

How did Penny get involved with this Sandburg stuff and take on this giant task of writing a Sandburg biography? A large volume of over a thousand pages is not just any little book. How did this all start? Her letterhead reads, "The Carl Sandburg Oral History Project." That was the beginning.

She wasn't particularly interested in Carl Sandburg at the outset. She never thought to go to Connemara. Then one day in the summer of 1970 her mother-in-law, who lived in the vicinity, asked Penny to go with her to see the Sandburg home. Penny went as a favor to see the site, which was being run by the National Park Service as a national monument.

When she went through the house at Connemara, she was struck by all the papers that were just lying around the house mildewing and being eaten by mice—the same papers I had seen in 1956, which were supposed to go to the University of Illinois. When Penny told me her tale I agreed, something was very amiss here.

I remembered myself going through the house again soon after that time and seeing what I thought was the old Nimitz cap on the piano or table. I asked one of the rangers about it and he didn't know what it symbolized or where it came from. Furthermore, if I could positively identify it, they would be happy to know about it. I wondered and pondered and worried about why the place looked as though they had all just walked out and left it. (Now, it is supposed to look like that.)

But Penny also thought about this. It must have bothered her sorely that all of these valuable papers were unattended and disorganized. It was *then* that she offered to help go through and sort the material. And then the National Park Service and the University of Illinois hired her to take care of the papers, which had not been organized. I presume this whole house was full of papers and manuscripts and bits of papers and pieces of scratch that had to be sorted; at any rate, it turned into a bottomless pit of a job. Penny rescued them all. This was long before Penny ever dreamed of the idea of a biography.

After getting substantially involved in her Sandburg Project, Penny ran into troubled waters back in Richmond, Indiana. The course of her marriage was entering "turmoil stage." In order to sort things out she began to yearn for the peace and solitude of the Blue Ridge Mountains. If she could be there, in the country that Sandburg had loved, she might find answers. She might find the peace that hard work in this setting could bring.

So Penny began to work on the papers. Doing that brought her a whole new identity and a new set of challenges and goals. It brought her no solution to her own problem, however. Gradually the whole scenario in Richmond began to disintegrate. It was during this period that I made plans to visit Penny. We spent a weekend together in Hendersonville, N.C. in 1987. Hendersonville is near Flat Rock, which is convenient to Connemara, as well as to Asheville, where Margaret and Janet Sandburg lived. That weekend Penny had a real plum of an idea—to re-introduce me to Margaret and Janet.

I took a plane from Indianapolis to Asheville where Penny met me and took me directly to Margaret and Janet Sandburg's house. On the trip from the airport I found that after thirty years I had no sense of time passing. I pick up in my mind where I leave off with people, anyway, and my characters don't age. I don't age in my mind's eye—I can't see my own wrinkles or what the years have meted out to me. Maybe it's that way for everybody.

So Janet Sandburg was going to be the same pleasant teenaged daughter and the "pen pal forever" friend I had left back at Connemara in 1956. She would be the bubbly "nursery maid" to all the goat kids, her enthusiasm boundless. Her tragic car accident in high school had spared her one of the things most of the rest of us have to combat aging.

She would always be *l'esprit de printemps* to me. The breath of spring that she seemed back in 1958. Instant friends. Would I like to see her room? she had asked. Of course. Would I like to see her senior yearbook? Sure. Would I write to her? Yes, I would.

How descriptive she had been in the letter describing their new home. And how much her training on the farm and the long walks at Connemara had awakened her to the beauties of nature and the harbingers of Spring! I was enchanted by this woodland elf. And I could depend on her letters to keep me in touch with the family. No matter where her father was, she had been writing to me and she was telling me what *she* wanted me to know.

Janet, I thought as I drove up to the house with Penny, you should know that you brought me much joy.

I wondered if the spell was still working. Penny had just enough time to bring me up to date and give me some details of the situation so I could adjust to the new scenario.

The three-story, red brick house looked good to me. It was surrounded by a lovely yard guarded by thick hemlock trees. Across the street was a nice green park and the street was well shaded in summer. And there were sure to be snapdragons, daisies, gladioli and all the favorite flowers, as well as vegetables out back, in the garden. Paula had been a superb gardener. The girls, especially Helga, had always been planting and growing oriented. Gardening was a shared interest for all of Carl Sandburg's family.

We sauntered up the walk to the front door. Almost before the bell rang, Margaret and Janet were at the door. Bommer, the happy golden retriever, banged his tail against the foyer wall. Penny did the "Look who's here act," and I walked straight over to Janet. "Better not hug her," I thought, and offered my hand. There was an aloof and puzzled look on her face. "Janet, do you remember me? Majie?" It was years ago, and if my mind's eye saw me as unchanged, she must not have. She looked at me blankly ... the expression moving toward wild look and confusion. She took her eyes away a moment and then said, "No."

Someone had opened my time capsule and let us both out.

Almost immediately Janet went for the dog leash and said, "It's time to take Bommer for a walk." And out they went. I was crushed. But what did I expect after all these years? It had been, maybe, ten or more Christmas letters ago since I had heard from Janet.

I wondered what kind of luck I would have with Margaret, who had no reason to remember me. When I visited Connemara, Janet had taken up a lot of my conversation time while Margaret was intently working on letters for her father. She was also very engrossed in Adlai Stevenson, who was then running for President of the United States.

I remember that the entire Sandburg family was firmly convinced that Stevenson should be elected. They went to great lengths to help the Illinois Democrat along the road to victory. His presidency, however, was not in the cards and that was a great disappointment to the Sandburgs.

During my visit those many years ago, Margaret was not very well, tiring easily and resting some each day. Her main-line communication to her dad was very strong at that time, and she struck me as serious, studious, and very winning. I liked her. She had just seemed remote and preoccupied.

Well, Margaret did vaguely remember me and was very pleasant. We chatted, and I noticed that every so often Margaret placed an affectionate pat on Janet's shoulder. There was clearly a bond of love between them and a quiet protective eye that followed Janet.

Since neither lady could drive, they were blessed by beautiful and caring, dark-skinned Lee, who looked after them. When I say beautiful, I mean it. Lee emanated happiness and love, and her kitchen was the perfect place to cozy into. I sensed a stability there that I know helps the deceased Sandburgs rest in peace all the way from Remembrance Rock to the Luck Stars in the heavens. So Margaret was very warm, though not loquacious.

And Penny was obviously the love and light of their life. She was so kind to them, and they were just like little girls who could hardly contain their excitement when she was around. She had become an integral part of the Asheville household. She went to the house at least once a week just to visit and to check on things, doing work with Margaret and checking on their health if necessary. Whatever seemed to be needed Penny was there to oblige. She was "absorbed" by all of them.

Right at that time, without even projecting into the future, the thought struck me, "What would they do if Penny went someplace besides North Carolina?" That thought kept growing. Then it was shoved back by a trip to the third floor to see the Sandburg study which was Margaret's workplace, a cozy room with bookshelves on all the walls. It was very nice and inspiring; not chic, but not Connemara either.

And the books. Lord, I can't imagine any more books than were in that room. Not Penny's papers and books, not the Sandburg's living room walls of books, not Carl's study walled in with books. Margaret Sandburg's walls looked like her Father's walls—only organized. And Penny's office had looked like that as well. I thought I had seen all the Sandburg books at Connemara—Sandburg books and papers seemed to be coming out of a "word popper." He was prolific beyond my comprehension!

Margaret herself had changed. In place of the workday slacks and old shirt worn at Connemara, like Papa's, she had on a dress and hose and gave a more decisive appearance than I had seen before. She had indeed taken her place as the head of the house. Intellectually speaking, she was now an author in her own right. She worked every day on papers and letters that became books or articles. Margaret, among other things, has edited and compiled a book entitled *The Poet and The Dream Girl*. It is a collection of her parents' love letters. While some of the earliest letters are missing, Margaret found more than enough to fill a very good "read."

In one of the letters Paula wrote to Carl, "Before you came into my life, the power to love didn't have a chance to grow in me. I had more love already than I could use, than I could find a worthy object for . . . and now! Now I have YOU TO LOVE."

Margaret had to deal with big blank spaces. Letters not dated—letters not found—letters without reference. But from her sanctuary, Margaret manages to deal with such problems.

By now, it should occur to you that this is a very prolific family of letters and books. And you ain't seen *nothin'* yet!

Before Penny and I left that day, Janet came into the front hall and pointed upstairs to where her room was, stating, "I got the biggest room in the house. Do you want to see it?"

Well, thank goodness for that. It wasn't all gone after all.

Even while we visited that weekend, Penny was in the process of dreaming another Sandburg dream. If she could get all of the Sandburg friends, co-workers and family together—and acquaint all of them with each other as individuals, wouldn't that inspire a rebirth of Sandburg?

In the beginning of Penny's task most of these people were just names in a pile of old papers. Penny had no idea who they were. Norman Corwin lived in California. Joe Wershba was in New York. And Lucy Kroll lived in New York.

After my visit with Penny in Hendersonville, I went on to visit another friend, Barbara Laird, who had also moved to the mountains. She was the hostess in Washington who provided "the visit" for the PD's, her girlhood chums, of whom I was one.

Penny deposited me, literally, into Barbara's car at the specified meeting place, and she and Barbara met and made plans to meet again. Her last words to me were, "I'll let you know about the Symposium. It will be in October of 1988." The seeds were there, and they grew. And our Miss Penelope was wide eyed with success under a sky ablaze with Luck Stars.

So in October, 1988, true to her dreams, Penny Niven provided Sandburg friends and enthusiasts with a very moving and motivating experience in Flat Rock, N.C. She entitled the symposium "Poetry and Politics."

When Penny had taken on the project of sorting the Connemara papers, as I have said, she had run across repeated names in the piles of papers and old files. She had written letters to them all, tons and tons of letters. Many of them attended her symposium. Sandburg, even after death, still held a magnetism for them.

Joe Wershba was the man who had announced Carl Sandburg's death to the public, and his importance to the Sandburg family was strong. Joe had been with CBS for years, and he was with Edward R. Murrow when the crew went to Connemara to film a visit with Carl Sandburg at his home on Murrow's program, "See It Now." Joe and Carl became very close friends and the families of both were very important to each other. More than once the Wershbas and their two children had stayed the night in the home. Joe does an amazingly accurate impersonation of Carl Sandburg's voice. It haunted me when I met him, because his voice was a dead ringer for that of our "far off uncle."

Norman Corwin was another name in the file. Hollywood producer, author, director, sometimes controversial personality, he had himself written and produced "The World of Carl Sandburg," starring Bette Davis. The passing of time found Norman and Penny spending many hours and exchanging many letters on the "project."

And then another name in the file—a certain Lucy Kroll. Now who was that? The answer was that she was Carl Sandburg's agent. Her many hours spent at the farm were golden and priceless. Who could have been more thrilled to see the Sandburg works in good hands? In time Lucy would prove to give her best energy and support to Penny in her work. And there couldn't be a more loveable person to have as Penny's overseeing angel. For meeting Lucy Kroll I owe Penny another fine gift. (She, like Penny, has provided motivating nudges for the completion of this book. When I told her about the title I was considering, she said, "I like the title. Now get going!")

And so, it was a natural cluster of pearls that Penny was able to string together for the symposium, a perfect assemblage of people from Carl Sandburg's productive years. They were able to produce sweet nostalgia for those years as well as give the historical and economic background of his works. The event was amply supported by the Department of Literature and Language at the University of North Carolina at Asheville, which was a beautiful campus setting, lending itself to the subject.

It was Luck Stars all the way and the sky went high and wide and blue. The leaves were exploding with autumn color, the sun warm and friendly. The scene was set to perfection, providing a deep feeling of the presence of Carl Sandburg.

Those who came to speak or to listen or to be any part of the program were involved in a very emotional experience.

Penny's dream of the symposium was perfect and it did three things. When the cast of characters came together, they did indeed bring Sandburg to life. Penny may not have known him personally, though that was only because of timing and fate, but when this event was over, she herself seemed to know the poet better than we did. She was very close to really knowing him . . . as close as you can get. When you finish a biography of a man as great and colorful as Carl Sandburg, you are nine-tenths of the way to a personal relationship. Before three days were over, I began to think she was jesting about not having been personally acquainted. And the fact that she could get the main people in his career together gave her extended credibility.

The other thing this symposium did was give all of us the chance to renew and relive what each of us had done at one time or another with him. And it gave Margaret and Helga (the daughter I had never met but about whom I knew he had very deep feelings), a chance to give their input to all these associates and friends. Penny gathered the entire crew together at the same time, on his turf, to celebrate Carl Sandburg's life, friendship, and never-ending love of the land and its people.

Carl Sandburg's relatives included his three daughters, his granddaughter, Paula, who wrote a lovely book about Connemara, *My Connemara*, her two young children who were as well-behaved as any two could be, and a very proud Helga, the daughter, the mother and the grandmother. The full family circle was there and it was a pleasure for everyone involved. Penny had assembled a Sandburg spectrum.

The title for the event was "The Carl Sandburg Symposium: Poetry and Politics." It began on Friday, October 21, 1988, with Professor Xian-Zhong Meng, a visiting scholar at the University of Illinois, giving a talk on, "Carl Sandburg's Popularity in China." It was a topic I hadn't considered. Professor Meng was hungry for everything he might learn here. We sat together a lot and got acquainted, and in that time and in his speech I could see he was formulating a plan about Sandburg and China. The Chinese professor seemed to have a mission. Eventually he wanted to write his own book. Meng presented Margaret Sandburg with a beautiful Chinese scroll which he had had friends in China make for him to give her, black and white with some pink and lavender etched in it.

Next to speak was Margaret Sandburg, and her topic was "Oriental Influences in Carl Sandburg's Work." This was long, scholarly and intellectual. That morning I sat with Margaret, so I knew she was nervous and that she had worked hard on this. And I hoped that I could provide her with a little soothing listening to make what was obviously an ordeal a little easier. It seemed to be very tiring for her to speak.

That afternoon the program continued. The next speaker was Helga! At long last, Helga Sandburg, the missing link in my saga. The night before, there was a very nice dinner party in a club in Asheville, where Helga and I had met briefly. The moment I met her I knew she was electric, with golden hair pulled back into a kind of bun and a young face that was alive with enthusiasm. Her smile was warm and she seemed to enjoy the whole evening.

She was very gracious. There were a zillion questions I wished I could have asked her. The title of Helga's talk was, "My Father and the People." It was a very good, first-hand view of the poet, direct, telling and witty. I hoped to get to know her sometime during the weekend. Since then she has published a wonderful book, *Where Love Begins*, about her father and the family and her own life.

Next on the program was Joe Wershba, an early producer of CBS News' program "Sixty Minutes." His subject was "Carl Sandburg the Journalist." The minute he spoke we knew that he was a "pro." And it wasn't long before we could all understand why Wershba and Sandburg were such good friends. As I mentioned previously, Wershba had also been with Edward R. Murrow and had been a staff member when CBS went to Connemara to film the home and family of Sandburg. He was to be a very colorful addition to this group, the tie that bound all the participants together. He could *be* Carl Sandburg.

In the evening there was yet another lecture. This time it was Norman Corwin, author, director, producer and the author of *The World of Carl Sandburg*. He was a fascinating man who represented the part of Sandburg's world that came later, in California, with the movie industry, and Corwin's symposium audience was spellbound at hearing him describe that world. There would be more, but not until tomorrow. We were all aware of the power and the glory of the poet and were thirsty for more the next day.

And the next day, October 22, proved to be even more poignant. It was all at the Flat Rock Playhouse, across the road and below the big white house on the hill. On stage was Sandburg's empty chair, with his lap robe draped across the back and his guitar beside it. It would turn into one of the most golden warm October days of the fall, and all of the Sandburg friends and family would end the next day bound forever by their love of the poet.

The whole day unfolded with CBS cameras in the background at Flat Rock as Charles Kuralt's crew was busy filming the whole program. There were cameras and crews and long cords and lights to battle, but it was all part of the scene, and the next Sunday would prove it was all worth it. Hooray for CBS and "Sunday Morning!"

In the morning Professor William Sabo, political scientist from the University of North Carolina spoke. Title: "Political Issues in Sandburg's Times," a good background that made understanding some of the writings of that era easier. Those were hard times, and often misunderstood times.

Robert Morgan, a poet and English professor from Cornell University gave us "Political Themes in Sandburg's Poetry." He made a big hit by starting his talk with a speculation from two laboring friends. One asked the other, "How much do you s'pose they pay him fer one o' them pomes?"

The Morning Star was Penny Niven, our Sandburg biographer who tied it all together with, "Linking the Life and the Work." The cameras were on Penny, standing on stage in her bright red suit, her blue eyes sparkling with love for her poet Carl Sandburg. And all her relatives glowing with pride at having her as part of their family of "the man." Her soft southern voice did not disguise the depth of her feelings, nor the hundreds of hours she had spent to bring him back to all of us.

The afternoon gathering took place at the Playhouse . . . from the song program done by the Sandburg Folksingers to a special production by the Flat Rock Playhouse, "The World of Carl Sandburg."

The main course and the biggest feast of the entire program was the panel discussion: "Poetry and Politics, Sandburg Style and the Writer's Role Today." This was made up of the delicious renderings of Norman Corwin, Helga Sandburg, Robert Morgan, Joe Wershba, and Penelope Niven—all moderated by Shirley Wershba, Joe's wife.

Shirley's statement, "When you were Carl Sandburg's friend, he adopted you and you adopted him." This, of course, was the essence of it all. We were all adoptees. It went high and wide, that stage show, with Joe Wershba doing his perfect imitation of the Sandburg voice and Helga giving her father to us, personally.

Professor Morgan gave us the background, and Norman Corwin, the producer, fascinated us with the stories of Sandburg on his turf, Hollywood. And of course here again was Penny threading and weaving them all together into one colorful tapestry of Sandburg's world. Norman Corwin had the most wonderful delivery (I am sure he has performed Shakespeare). Norman must have brought it all in focus for Professor Meng, who sat with me during this performance. After the panel was through, Mr. Meng stood up, as if in a trance. He then turned to me and said, "Ah now, at last, I understand the poet Mr. Carl Sandburg." Bravo Norman! You opened up the Sandburg stars to China.

I looked back at the stage once more. There was the empty chair with the wool shawl laid across the back and a guitar leaning against the leg.

The symposium was over. We were tired but so full of Sandburg's world that we were running around asking the principles to autograph a Sandburg book, written by Harry Golden, with a new preface by Penny, which we had all purchased that day. Each and every one of us was grateful to belong to the same society. I was grateful that the night before at Margaret's house in Asheville, I had been able to speak with Helga about her sister Janet. I told her about my day, long ago, at Connemara and how I had related to Janet. Besides, I had brought with me a large photo of Janet, very adept and happy, gently feeding a baby kid with a bottle while another one stood behind and looked on. She was competent help to her mother. I think this photograph was taken during the period of the "Rift," when Helga and her father were distanced by misunderstandings and hurt feelings over Helga's divorce. Helga's caring and interest were understandable. In the background of that picture was her father, standing behind the gate, quietly observing the procedure.

I had to write later to Helga and ask her about the "Rift." She explained:

20 October 89

Dear Majie Failey:

I have your letter of 11 October, which is a delight. . . . 1956 was the time of the Rift, and every now and then I hear of someone whose children "healed and comforted" my father during those days. Thank you.

You do know, as you sound like a "strong" woman, that I would not have lived any of my life differently. I believe in sorrow and difficulties and tears along with the rest because without that, how do you really understand joy?

Thank you for the Ann Arbor review. And keep in touch. Best. . . .

Helga Sandburg

So, after my contacts at the symposium and the correspondence with Helga, I finally understood the real significance Carl Sandburg attached to the visit so long ago at our house. We had been "home" for just a short while to a man with a deeply aching heart.

We all went back to Connemara where a little group of ladies had prepared delicious hors d'oeuvres to serve with wine and punch, inviting the public, too. Interested public! And then there were tours of the home. Penny was busy hostessing and after awhile, things cooled down and the crowd thinned.

Then Norman Corwin, the Wershbas, Professor Meng, Lucy Kroll and I took the tour together. This was hard. Lucy, who had been such an integral part of the farm when she was there working with Sandburg, found it very emotional and stopped short. Joe Wershba got behind Sandburg's desk and imitated the poet in the wonderful rolling thunder or gentle lamb voice and really spooked me. He stood up and looked at the pictures on the wall. "Who is that man?" he asked. "That is Steichen," I said, proud that I knew something he didn't know. A goat, heavily laden with milk was also among the photos. "Brocade," I said. "The prize of Paula's goat herd."

Finally, daylight was giving way to darkness and we were all getting tired and ready to go back to Asheville. It had been a wonderful uplifting weekend, thanks to Penny Niven.

After the symposium I mailed Helga Sandburg some of the photos I had taken back in 1956 while visiting Connemara. She sent me a nice thank-you note which included a line which sums up the weekend.

"The symposium weekend was a symphony—with everything being repeated and the melody going on . . . ."

The symposium was fuel for the fire. It brought it all together. Remember, all this was organized and executed while Penny was working on her Sandburg biography. She was going to find out that publishing is not a piece of cake. There were interruptions, delays, harassments, and unforseen problems, but finally another star was born in the person of Penny.

Penelope Niven published the sum total of the years of toil and trouble and heartbreak and came up with a book that gives the poet back to us, his "Family of Man." It was the result of foraging through countless manuscripts, unpublished works, and scraps of paper which looked worthless—yet contained priceless words. Pencil stubs in ashtrays and cigar butts and old hats and crates of old papers were just a typical everyday look in the house that was Carl's look alone. Mice were chewing on these priceless bits of literature at its American best. There were only ghosts there now in the place, and Penny had to dig and dig, and paste and paste and think and think and guess and wander back and forth. A tremendous job. I can't believe what she ferreted out to accomplish this book.

"Organize" is a very inadequate word for this job—it was far more than organize. When I refer to heartbreak, this is what I mean—it would be hard for anyone to have to call it quits on a marriage, go through a divorce and face raising a daughter alone while writing a book. But the power and strength of Carl Sandburg's words gave her the stamina to push on and on . . . and on.

And she did. She made phone calls to identify writers of letters she found to the poet; she made countless trips to meet and later to know people in Carl's life. She became an integral part of the household of Margaret and Janet Sandburg. And then she became a part of the whole family, where she will remain.

In August of 1991 Penny's book was published. It thrills me to read the reviews as they appear, and to find that all of those years of bone-hard work have come to fruition and that there will be a golden harvest of Carl Sandburg appreciation across the nation.

September 27, 1991

Penelope Niven
Preston Villa
Dallas, Texas

My Dear Penny:

This is in answer to your letter of August 1, 1985. You asked me if we could meet and I would share some of my Carl Sandburg memories and stories with you. You gotta be kidding!

Look what you've done.

You've finished the book. Yippyiokyaye . . . Hot dog and Halleluya! Enclosed you will find a picture of you at Borders Book Store sitting at a large table wading through stacks of thick books with a pensive portrait of my far off uncle on the cover. The words "Carl Sandburg—A Biography," at the top . . . "Penelope Niven" across the bottom. Autographing, signing, speaking and charming the socks off all those people who were there to meet you.

You did it. You did it. And not one bad review—only raves for its excellence, and gratitude to you for bringing back to all of us the wisdom and the values and the life story of the poet Sandburg, whose heart beats with yours and mine and the Family of Man. And for giving us fields of golden wheat, the prairie, the mountains and fog and skyscrapers and Chicago and the acres *and acres of stars and blue skies . . . and at a time when we all need your gift of Sandburg desperately.*

*All love,
Majie*

The totally grace-filled experience at the symposium and Penny's magnificent biography, which brought Carl back to us all, had warmed my heart. Most of all, I realized that the people at the symposium had valued Carl Sandburg as a friend, and it was in that way that I choose to remember him. I wanted to think about what that meant.

In his book entitled *Carl Sandburg*, Harry Golden, Sandburg's neighbor, had a paragraph headed "Some things we buy, some not."

He wrote:

> *A friendship with Carl Sandburg is like no other friendship. It involves more than mere pride of fellowship with a great literary figure.*
>
> *Friendship with Carl Sandburg is a complete thing. It is so complete that at every stage of the relationship you feel helpless because he gives so much more than he receives. He throws his whole personality and loyalty into it. Certainly there is nothing you can give Carl . . . . He sends you books, he responds to requests for encouragement or endorsement, and if you are his friend, it means that everybody associated with you, your family, your publisher, editors, your friends, associates, and even your employees, none of whom he knows or has ever seen, are his friends too, taken in one fell swoop.*

I beg to differ with one of Golden's lines. He said "There was nothing you could give Carl" and so Golden would find himself constantly at the receiving end. I know what he meant, but there is something else that must be said.

You could brush his coat shoulders off before his lecture and you could straighten his limp black tie. He would smile appreciatively, grateful for your caring. He was grateful for the simplest touch. At our house, "How about you and me going into the kitchen and we'll see about a sandwich from that leg o' lamb. That's good stuff. How about an apple? Are there any of those good homemade cookies left? Let's get a couple of those apples and

I'll have myself a meal. Got any little paper bags? Say, this is eatin'. Now I won't have to go into the diner for dinner."

So why was he so happy with a brown paper bag and a "lump?" Well, maybe that gave him back his hobo days for just a while. Those days weren't all bad. A lot of good words came out of those nomad days. And a thoughtful hostess would give him the gift of privacy and rest after a performance.

As a matter of fact I often reflect back to Union City, Indiana, where we first met at the home of the Keck family. Stella Keck was easily one of two people who influenced my lifestyle and taught me the responsibility of being a good hostess. She saw that everybody met at the reception for Carl Sandburg after his lecture. While he rested, everyone who didn't know each other was introduced. That included me, the roommate who knew very few there.

When Sandburg reappeared, she introduced him to everyone and saw to it that Carl had a tiny briefing about each one. That immediately gave him a starting point. He was seldom at a loss for words, and that was at the essence of his friendship and graciousness.

I also observed that Stella Keck never left out a guest. By the time an evening was over, she had had a personal word with every one of her guests and they were identified fully. This is not an easy job for some, and I learned from Stella the meaning of the phrase gracious hostess.

You could mean something to Carl Sandburg by just being sensitive to his needs. During his visit with us in Indianapolis I brought out a lap robe and tucked it around his knees as the house cooled with the night. He nodded and leaned up toward me and said, "You are very kind to me."

It is important to bring up our children to care about the needs of others. Kindness, consideration, respect, graciousness—and especially friendship. Those are all good words.

Gifts to Carl Sandburg were likely as not intangible. The caring was the gift.

Connemara, home of Carl Sandburg and his family in 1956. Paint peeling, large and airy rooms, no curtains, and a hunk of tobacco hanging on the front porch—all typical of the poet.

In the lovely Blue Ridge Mountains of North Carolina, Connemara drifted easily into Mother Nature's way of "letting things be."

Carl notes "that violet in your shirt, it matches your skirt exactly." We were touring the farm, and he is wearing his Admiral Nimitz fatigue cap.

The goat farm. Mrs. Sandburg had a unique operation of genetically perfected herds. Brocade was one of her prize-winning producers.

Terms of endearment. My far-off uncle says, "See how that goat takes to you?" I had a salt-lick in my hand. That did it.

Penelope Niven at the book signing for her *Carl Sandburg: A Biography* in Indianapolis. The reviews were raves.

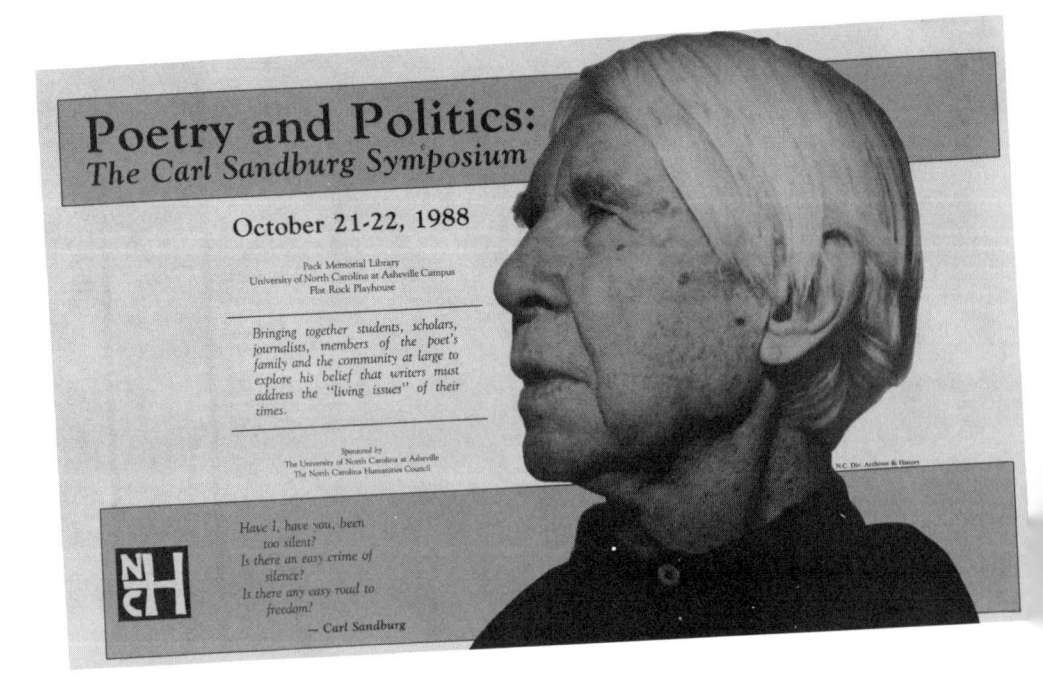

Poetry and Politics:
The Carl Sandburg Symposium

October 21-22, 1988

Pack Memorial Library
University of North Carolina at Asheville Campus
Flat Rock Playhouse

Bringing together students, scholars, journalists, members of the poet's family and the community at large to explore his belief that writers must address the "living issues" of their times.

Sponsored by
The University of North Carolina at Asheville
The North Carolina Humanities Council

Have I, have you, been
too silent?
Is there an easy crime of
silence?
Is there any easy road to
freedom?
— Carl Sandburg

Penny Niven gathered all the people Sandburg had worked with and his family and friends. The Symposium brought Sandburg back for those of us who had known him, and brought him forward to those who hadn't.

7

THE WEDDING

And now I need to go back in my own life, to the time when I last spoke with Carl Sandburg.

In August of 1961 I was happily ensconced in a cabana at the La Jolla Beach and Tennis Club with my two little girls while their brother, my son, was at Camp Charlevoix in Northern Michigan. I was divorced.

My dear friend and far off uncle, Carl Sandburg, was, as I have said, at that time in Beverly Hills, enjoying the perils of the limelight shared by celebrities, advising George Stevens in "The Greatest Story Ever Told."

I had called Sandburg and suggested we meet at Disneyland. He had suggested the Bel Air Hotel, where he was living at the time. I pushed Disney. He balked. Something was not going right here. However, his plans for his Hollywood sojourn were duly reported by me in a column I sent to *The Indianapolis News*. He meant business about Disney. It took me half a lifetime to figure it all out. He didn't care for Disney's approach. It wasn't his style—at least that was my guess.

And, on the other foot, I was dealing with Dr. Seuss, whose real name was Theodore Geisel. I called the doctor for an interview and got the royal boot from whoever took that call. I decided right there that he could put his own cat in his own hat. So that summer, and that August in particular, we were not batting a hundred on the world's most celebrated entertainment for children. I vowed to think about this! Then we all trooped back to Indiana after a very happy and sun-filled month. We left our favorite, far off uncle Carl, without seeing him again.

One year later, August of 1962, was an entirely different scenario. Carl Sandburg was not in my thoughts, and I was reading Dr. Seuss to my youngest, having forgotten my grudge. I forgot everything. I was getting married again! It was enough to make me confused about my own name, which was, actually going to change to Failey. I was marrying Skip, my old friend from high school days and member of the Farragut Society, that small group of infamous "angels."

With my proclivity for taking on more than I could handle, and my tendency to try to please everyone, I was soon in over my head, contemplating a fork in the road that would lead to trouble. I was about to create my own sit-com . . . with no pay. He had two children; I had three. They would soon be "ours."

That summer five trusting children went away to summer camp and they all came home to the wedding plans of their respective parents. It was impetuous to do a whirlwind, end-of-summer wedding on the spur of the moment, but it all sounded so convenient and sort of romantic. The bridegroom's family had a summer cottage in Harbor Springs, Michigan—the beautiful Sandland. It could be the focal point and the meeting place for everyone involved. My sister and her husband and their four children were vacationing at nearby Walloon Lake, having come all the way from Long Island. The question was, could we get married there and then and accommodate all of our relatives and all the children and all of their cousins? It was going to be difficult; one child was in New Mexico, and the other four were in Northern Michigan.

My mother helped by flying northward with the New Mexico camper, and meeting a plane full of arriving relatives . . . thus getting them all to the northwood nuptials on time.

In late August it was decided by the mother-in-law-to-be that our wedding should be in the little summertime Episcopal Church (St. John's) with the reception held at the cottage. All we had to do was find a hotel that could accommodate us all, and the rest of the problems would take care of themselves . . . getting all the children gathered in from their respective camps, as well as coaxing and guiding other relatives to pre-arranged resting places in Northern Michigan.

It was soon apparent to me that I was drowning, but I was too proud to call the whole thing off or postpone it till a better time and a better place, like—say, *home!*

Skip was a widower with two young sons, who would be added to my own family—a son and two daughters. The children were not strangers to each other and they were so close in ages that the four of them could not have been borne by the same woman. Only the youngest would escape what became a homefront battleground. At the same time, she would be left out of a lot of action and experience some lonely times.

That didn't occur to me on the shores of Lake Michigan in 1962. What occurred to me was that I had to arrange for a spontaneous wedding, get five kids back from camp and a bunch of relatives together, try to make everything fit nicely, and get to the church on time. My mind did not project beyond the present crisis, luckily.

There was no room for friends; it had to be family only (and my roommate and friend forever, Margaret, from Union City).

The wedding went as scheduled, and it was lovely, some way. We never found the time, though, to plan a honeymoon, much less go on one! Our best man had arranged for rooms, for a few days, in a nice resort, not far away.

This proved to be a rotten idea. When we tried to leave after our luncheon reception, three of our children were hanging on to the fenders of our car crying, "Mommy, please don't go. Take us with you. Don't leave us here with Nana. When will you be back?" Sobs and tears. And then GUILT. Why hadn't we just waited until fall? Because that would mess up their starting school and, logically, by then we should all be under the same roof with a semblance of order. "Should" and "logic" got me nowhere.

And the honeymoon? We were upstaged by a cat. Maybe it was a throwback from my bad attitude about Dr. Seuss—I do know that it was a punishment beyond belief. After living through the traumatic logistics of this wedding, and leaving a trail of brokenhearted children behind, we were alone at last.

Settling down to a bottle of champagne and a rehash of the whole affair, we were interrupted by a meaningful, whining, meow! Oh no! Not a black cat! Not tonight! But oh, yes. This cat sat on our window sill and gave us a long line of eerie moans. No amount of coaxing or bad cat names would intimidate this feline intruder. Finally we looked at each other, then back at the cat and said, in unison, "Here, have some champagne! Now get lost, begone!" After a splashy snootful of the stuff, the wailing subsided. Ah, that was over.

Alone at last . . . After an hour or so the cat was back. I stared at it in anger. There had been a sign that said, "Absolutely no pets." I had seen the sign with my own eyes when we registered. So we called the management. They didn't respond. When it became apparent that this damned cat was not going to shut up, we took steps—serious ones.

The bridegroom got out of bed, took a pillow case with him, and marched out the door in his pajamas. This was followed by the sound of a car. The cat and the man got as far as the security gate, where they were stopped by a guard. A meow issued forth—from the darkness of the front seat. "Oh, you got Mrs. Courtney's cat, eh?"

"This cat is going for a ride," said the new man in my life.

"Don't blame you at all sir, it happens all the time." After a long ride through the Northern Michigan hill country, the irate new husband returned. The gate man saluted and said, "Have a good evening, sir." It was near dawn.

"By the way," asked my absentee husband, "just who in the hell is Mrs. Courtney?"

"Oh, she owns this place," was the reply. So endeth the first day of the so-called and ill-fated honeymoon. And how about day two?

The second day of the honeymoon my husband opened the trunk of the car and I discovered the golf clubs were also on the honeymoon. I didn't play golf! Which meant that golf had been planned, but not with me!

On the third day after the cat spat and the golf outing, which was a nice day for four ladies to visit for eighteen holes while their husbands played the eighteen, I began to get edgy. I worried about the children. Where were they and who was really taking care of them? I was worrying if they were worrying about me. (They should have.) And that was the day I said, "Let's go home."

That was a wonderful idea. We would go back first thing in the morning. After a wonderful dinner with friends who seemed to surround us, I looked forward to packing up and going back and then going to bed. A good night's sleep would fix everything. Not on your life!

About 3 a.m. there were shrieking, howling, yowling, awful cat noises, the sounds of revenge. It pierced the neighborhood. We were the neighborhood. Why was it that no one else turned in a complaint? Or could it have been that we were right next to Mrs. Courtney? Well, we left bright and early in the morning. The honeymoon was officially over—a cat-astrophe.

A week later, everyone returned to their respective homes, and the wedding was neatly stacked in the photographer's file cabinet. We headed home for Indianapolis at last, thank God! But there was a persistent gnawing in my stomach. It wouldn't go away. I was beginning to be aware of what I'd bitten off.

In my naiveté, I assumed the new family would be happy as seven clams. Wrong! And I had neglected to check birthdays, or I would have figured out just after the first one became a teenager, three more would become teenagers soon after, without a breather. The two oldest boys, one of his and one of mine, were eleven months apart. My oldest daughter and the younger step-son were only three months apart. My youngest, Gaye, would be tortured for years as the youngest.

A college friend of mine from Washington decided I should provide Fred Silverman, the "sit-com" king, with some new and refreshing material. All I had to do was punch out what was happening at our house, which was constant, nerve-wracking crisis, and he could have great plots for his shows. I thought it was a lot less amusing than she did.

Anyway, by the time we were settled in the Fall, just in time for the new term, I realized I had five children in five different schools. Dear God, do you realize that meant five different PTA meetings and five "back to school" nights? Multiply everything about school five times . . . transportation, routines, personalities, meetings. It did not take me far into October to discover that my husband hated, and always had, all schools in any form. He had no intention of ever listening to another teacher. Not his children's nor mine.

We soon found out that our house was not going to do for this group. Too small. They weren't going to share. Not rooms, not friends, not clothes, not anything. And then we discovered that between us we owned four houses and not one of them was big enough for this bunch. And so we started our new life of adjustments with four albatrosses around our necks and a swarm of realtors surrounding us. "Think! Why don't you *think?*" cried my mother.

As soon as we had arrived back in Indianapolis I started working the twenty-four-hour shift. Apparently, our house was the only possible place in town for a rock band to practice. But, as I have said, it was also pleasantly filled with the fun of a cheerleader daughter and all the activity that those pom-pom days meant. It was not all castor oil, but it was not all roses and lollipops either.

Schools were an ongoing source of anxiety. The boys were at home, away at school, home again. In again, out again, and I became the team water-boy, always running trying to catch up with the players with a towel hanging out of my back pocket and water sloshing out of my pail. One little mistake in the morning in our household could ricochet into a major catastrophe by dinner time. And if seven of us sat down to a roast, potatoes and gravy dinner, I would mentally plan tomorrow's supper right then. It would be baked hash with the leftovers, with salad and dessert. That would do it. The next day I would go to the fridge to start on my plan and when I opened the door—*There Was No Roast!* There would be no hash. Teenaged, late-night snacks took that roast right down to the bone. It was in this period that my language habits changed . . . a lot of words were shortened to four letters.

Also, at this time I was asked to become a member of the Woman's Club. Very flattering indeed. I said NO! Flattered but battered. I couldn't take on another burden.

I was really tempted. The Indianapolis Woman's Club was a fine institution indeed. It has already had its one-hundredth birthday—I knew because my mother-in-law was a past president.

The programs were never boring and they were always preceded by a very luscious luncheon fare, with flowers and fanfare for the guests who were giving their papers that day. It was against the rules to ever give a paper that had been published. After the presentation to this very selective group, "you could publish." I finally got the point across that since I had married the son of one of the pillars of the group and had taken on the thankless task of raising her grandsons, I could not possibly join this group. I barely had time to brush my teeth. That was acceptable, they said, if I would reconsider at a time when there was a little slack in my rope. If there had been slack in my rope I would have wound it around any one of several necks. I later succumbed, of course, and read the Sandburg paper, as I've told.

I began to seriously consider converting my daily nightmares to money by writing those "sit-com" skits. The material just kept coming. Like the night we were called home from a dinner party because some kid had driven our tractor mower into the pool. We had found the big-enough-house all right, but actually all it was going to do was bring on my nervous breakdown sooner. But then I couldn't have a nervous breakdown. I didn't have time!

Sometimes I thought longingly of the beautiful days in college—on the college board at Wasson's, or especially at Pine Manor in Wellesley, MA. I pictured myself at the French House, being served breakfast in bed before classes. There my only task was to pull down those grades and perform my simple duties, blissfully unaware of the firestorms ahead for me!

Every time I planned to allow myself the luxury of a nervous breakdown and the rest home, something else would happen. Like the day the priest called me from the school. One of the children's five schools was a parochial school. My children and I were Episcopalians, my husband was an atheist, and his children were Catholics. My husband was good at avoiding issues, so I held the hot potato to my ear as the priest said, "There is something that would make me very happy."

"What is that, Father?" asked I.

He answered, "It would make me so happy to see all of your nice new family come to our Catholic Church."

I got over that eventually. Don't try to convert an Episcopalian to a Catholic. Not my family! I felt hostile, yet I thought I might have to change my mind, because one lovely post-Easter week-day, I saw Father arriving with a carload of Easter lilies. Peace at any price. A few days old, but it's the thought. "Hello, Father," I said peaceably.

The priest smiled, wanly. "Say, I was wondering if you could keep these lilies in your greenhouse and take care of them for me so we can use them again next year."

Next year the little boy in the parochial school was transferred to public school!

It was all of this that separated me from accomplishing all of the list of "things to do while you are still alive." It cut me off from communicating with the Sandburgs (except Janet). Her letters were, bless her heart, the one thing I could count on to keep in touch. Those years of being run over by teenagers, schools, in-laws, friends, running a big house . . . trying to be Mrs. Perfect, had all caused me to start losing my identity.

Working at being a good step-mother made me forget sometimes that I was also a mother, not the wicked step-mother but MOM. There were times when I neglected my own children in favor of step-children. That's when I really started to lose ground. I really feel that if I had taken time to even read from any Sandburg book, it would have restored some of my perspective. When you try too hard you usually fall on deaf ears or callous egos. I finally gave up, saying, "What the hell," and lived for the good moments, which did occur.

For the first time in our lives, we began to travel. As wedding gifts, both of our fathers had given us money, which we put in the bank to accrue interest. About three years after that, one of my close Dana Hall friends and her husband had moved to Holland, so the husband could become the head of ESSO Nederlands. We were invited to visit them in the Hague, and it was a wonderful way to go to Europe for the first time. We had a week of tours and trips and excursions, from the windmill country to the gorgeous tulip gardens to the Delft china factory. We had a boat trip on the North Sea and then went on to Germany and the Rhine River castle trip, then finally to Paris for ten glorious days before we flew home to our waiting brood.

In 1976 we went to London to meet friends and then on to Italy, where my cousins had a lovely farm house with vineyards and olive groves and Afghan dogs, which they showed all over Europe.

These trips were about ten years apart; most of the time in Indianapolis, though, we were tied to the home. Our summer vacations were spent in Harbor Springs, and those, too, were happy days. I grew affectionately attached to my in-laws, B. Failey and Mary Parrott Failey, the girl of the wistful look in the Victorian wedding dress. My grandfather died in 1943 and then my father in 1964, so these new relatives added meaning to my life. In 1971 both of my parents-in law died within six months of each other—a tough emotional loss.

From the beginning, our house had become a place to entertain, which we did, enjoying it a good deal. Almost as soon as we moved into the new house, we began planning for my new in-laws fifticth wedding anniversary party. It was to be simple, with only very dear friends invited, Ruth and Eli Lilly among them. Busy as he was, still involved in the active management of the business, Eli Lilly still kept up with the fond past—he had his group of old school chums to the lake every summer. Old friends are best.

A little later, at Christmas, a letter from Eli in response to a small gift spoke of his loyalty and goodness to those he cherished:

Dear Faileys:

Your ever present kindess in the shape of cookies and pecans was most heartily received and appreciated. The name Failey, which occurs in my memories very frequently, always rings a very pleasant carillon of bells and will do so as long as my memories are above ground. My thanks and best wishes to the third and fourth generations of the Failey family.

Cordially,
Eli Lilly

But back to the lovely party, with candelabra burning bright, gardenias here and there, a lovely cake iced with spun gold sugar, the champagne flowing and a surprise that would really make that party swing!

The front door chimes rang throughout the house, then in walked Mary Failey's sister Josephine Parrott Wallace of Southport, Connecticut (whose Wallace connections I've mentioned earlier). She was a vision in gold—from head to toe. She had even sprayed her hair gold. It was the hit of the party. The society editors never got wind of the party. Success!

Skip and Kurt Vonnegut, two old Shortridgers from the heyday, began to take up their friendship again. Kurt and Skip always have and still do call each other "Sport."

By this time Kurt had gone to Cape Cod and married a girl named Jane Cox, who was one of my Tudor Hall classmates. I really loved Jane, who was smart, as bubbly as a glass of champagne and just as nutty as I am. She was supportive and proud of K.V. We all had some wonderful times in those years before success came charging in and saved their hides and changed their lives. At that time, their lives were as full of kids as ours were, and both Jane and Kurt gave their housefull equal time and concern. There were some dandy episodes, and I'll mention how they became the stuff of Vonnegut writing later.

One of the good times we went to Barnstable, where the Vonneguts lived. Kurt took us out for a picnic on his new Boston Whaler, which he'd bought with the $3,000 he'd received as a literary award. We ended up happily shelling on the beach at low tide. I have kept one of those shells to remember the time, for an ashtray for Skip.

Kurt Vonnegut is one of the people I love. If he weren't a "far out" writer and thinker, possessed of gifts of humor and insight far beyond the average person's, I don't know how he would have survived all of the trauma he has encountered. He does not bellyache about any of it! His humor carries him, covering up the hurts if and when they appear.

I feel totally safe and secure with K.V. If others offer their own critiques of his work in this provincial piece of America's heartland we live in, I say FORGIVE 'em and go on. I feel the strength of Kurt's fairness in judging people, and the class he shows when he accepts backstabs with grace and humor. But if I were not such a lady, you know what I'd say to his critics—don't push me.

Here are some of the letters back to us.

West Barnstable
Massachusetts

March 6, 1965

Dear Sport & Majie:

Here is awfully good news for you both: Woofy and I will be moving in with you on the evening of Wednesday, March 31, in order that I may make my television obligations on the following day. Does Jerry Smith own the TV station? Is there more than one?

We will continue to stay with you on Thursday and Friday as well. On Saturday I shall fly to New York, where I am loved and well-known, and Aunt Jane will move in with her folks for a day or two. We have no special diet requirements. It would be nice to have a Princess extension phone in our room.

You say your children are mixed up. This is because you haven't brought God into your home. I will explain this in more detail when we see you.

*In Christ,
Kurt*

Yes, the Vonneguts were coming, and I thought it might be fun to have a party for them. I wrote them about this—and asked who they would like to see. Answer:

> West Barnstable
> Massachusetts

Dear Majie:

Sweetheart, I don't know many people out there any more. I'm not too bloody popular around here, as far as that goes. I am touched that you and Sport would want to give a party for us, and here are some names. If some of the people are mortal enemies of yours, they are probably mortal enemies of mine, too, so don't invite them.

Mr. & Mrs. Benjamin D. Hitz?
Mr. & Mrs. Gordon Englehart?
Mr. & Mrs. Richard Vonnegut?
Mr. & Mrs. John Rauch, Jr.?
Dr. Robert Failey?
Mr. & Mrs. James Failey?
Mr. & Mrs. George Jeffrey?*
Mr. & Mrs. William Wildhack?*
Mr. & Mrs. Noble Dean?
Mr. & Mrs. John Dean?

Keep it small. Don't invite these people. They are just people I've heard of.

Cheer up. We will bring you a swell present of some kind.

Love,

Grace
Metalious

P.S. Invite anybody you want. We expect to charm one and all, and, if the opportunity arises, to settle some old scores.

It's probably time to talk about Kurt's comment "I'm not too bloody popular out there." It was true. Kurt had found his world—his writing one—in the East, and the East is—well, it's different. He had tried to keep up with Indianapolis generally, but he was often misunderstood. Here's an example. The Indiana State Library wrote him asking him to donate his books. He wrote a very nice explanation of why that shouldn't happen: that he felt his works were worthy of being purchased and that was how he wrote them, and that he valued them more than to give them away. That made the library mad, when they should have really realized he was right.

People often wanted him to M.C. their events, or show up as the celebrity guest, and when he couldn't do it, or felt he might be being used as the "big name person," they felt he was slighting his home state. All that must have hurt him; Kurt is a sensitive soul. Still, he kept trying and in 1965 was coming back to visit us and see some of the old group.

When the Vonneguts arrived, Kurt took one look at our "cottage," hit the dinner chimes in the hall which were impressive, left by former owners, and said, "Christ, this looks like Flanner and Buchanan Mortuary, Downtown Branch."

Then their youngest daughter, Nan, and our youngest, Gaye, took off and were not seen for the rest of the day. Later they returned, after having spent the afternoon telling each other how much they hated their parents. Kurt and Jane had made Nanny leave her cat behind, and seeing our cat Frisky just poured salt on the wounds.

When they went home, we missed them, we loved them. Kurt sent this letter back.

April 12, 1965

Dear Sport & Mary Jane:

That was neat, staying with you. How much nicer it is to stay with old friends in Indianapolis, instead of in a motel where the manager knocks every two hours and asks if you're through.

We were a smash in Indianapolis, and we killed 'em in New York City, too. Jules Ffeiffer and Marc Connelly were among the guests, and we were mentioned favorably in Variety. If anybody wanted to stop us, I tell you frankly I don't think he could do it. There is something about Hoosiers with forward motion.

I have worried some about the record I got for Gay (Gail?). Anyway, it is pretty deep music, and is probably over her head. Jimmy Smith's "Battle Hymn of the Republic" is to me what Beethoven's Fifth was to my old man. Have you heard it? And I've worried too about our not having told you all we know about handling teenagers. There were loopholes in our instructions, because time was so short, and you could do everything we told you and still fail. Do feel free to write about specific problems as they arise.

About the crease Englehart put in the midnight blue Corvair: Avis did not notice it. I thought of all the forms I would have to fill out if I confessed, and decided to brazen it through. If Englehart would feel good about confessing, the airport is the place for him to do it.

Thank you for sending out my fan mail. One was from Gloria Feld. Anybody remember her? The other was from a guy who sells portable boxing rings. He lost his eyesight and got it back, and he wants somebody to make a movie about it. A lot would depend on whether he was optimistic or not when blind. Cheerfulness is everything.

About the T-bird, Mary Jane: I slaver for it. There remain two questions to clear up: how I could pick it up, and how I could pay for it. These should be settled late in June, say. I should have some money late in June. The reasonable deal, it seems to me, would be for me to buy it at its bluebook value, and sell it back to you at its bluebook value at some fixed time in the future. If you went on owning it, you would be sharing liability with some very rough kids.

Much love to you all. Remember us in particular to Frisky.

K&J

Well, about the T-bird. He had admired it, effusively, but somehow I did not take him seriously. I sold the blue T-Bird! To this day he remembers that car. Finally I did tell Kurt, "The day after I sold it, the transmission fell out. Now what kind of a friend would that have been?"

We went to Broadway for an opening night.

Happy Birthday Wanda June was done off-Broadway in the sixties. The play was inspired by my father; it starred Kevin McCarthy.

Now, and ever, I was a PD, and my heart would always belong to Shortridge High School. In 1968, Richard Nixon was elected President of the United States. He appointed Melvin Laird to his cabinet as Secretary of Defense. Not only did we know Mel as the Congressman from Wisconsin, we also knew him first-hand as the husband of one of *us*. We all had been following the career of the ascending congressman through the eyes of Barbara's family and from the media due to the fact that we were in that period of history that many would like to forget. Marches were very popular as a method of demonstrating distaste by rebellious youth for government policy, the war in Vietnam, discrimination against minority groups, pollution and grievances in general.

Over lunch at one of the famous PD gatherings, which included all of us, we decided that we should have a PD march on Washington . . . more especially the Melvin Lairds. Some nerve! Oh please! Why not! Just a friendly little march!

The plans went into motion and by some great stroke of luck and the good Lord willing, eight of us arrived in Washington, D.C. on April 20, 1971. The week that followed will never be forgotten by any of us. Barbara, our hostess and our leader was followed for five days by eight lady ducks who quacked with glee as they initiated a new kind of march. Methinks we did "protest" too much! Or too long.

I wrote of our visit to my dear, aging aunt, Jodie Wallace, wife of the grandson of General Lew Wallace, and got this typically Jodie letter back:

Dear Majie:

>*Your letter is a delight and arrived at the most appropriate moment—when hearing about the gay side of life was the tonic I most needed. One of my breathless emphysema attacks hit me and the doctor said, "Horsepittle for you, Dear." So Billy [her son] and I hopped into an ambulance with an oxygen cocktail shaker handy, and I spent three days in the Bridgeport Chateau of Horror getting my bronchial tubes rejuvenated and being the "Emergency*

patient who is so bad it is almost funny." When Maggie [her daughter] talks about it she adds flourishes that make it glitter.

I loved Washington when I lived there fifty years ago. Our beautiful first house, 1010 Sixteenth Street, has an office address beside the front but looks the same, and I feel that other children and their nursemaids are taken from the park to the White House kitchen for hot chocolate and whip cream by the cop on the beat—as of those days.

Love,
Jodie

We did so many things every tourist does in Washington, but a touch above, the F.B.I. and the Mint and the White House, they were all taken in by wide-eyed and fascinated PDs.

Of all the places we went, I was probably going to remember the Ford Theater. It was a lasting tribute to two men—Abraham Lincoln and Carl Sandburg. Newly refurbished, the theater still was alive with the horror of that night in 1865. When the Lincoln box was pointed out and the story of the infamous night was told, I imagined I could see the figure of Carl Sandburg leaning over to speak to the president, his shock of white hair flipping into his eyes so that he had to throw his head back to see. He said something to Mr. Lincoln. The President nodded and they both faded away. I was taken back to 1959. On February 12 Carl Sandburg had addressed Congress, and he spoke of the terrible time of Lincoln's death.

In the time of the April Lilacs in the year 1865, a man in the city of Washington trusted a guard to watch at the door, and the guard was careless, left the door, and the man was shot, lingered a night, passed away, was laid in a box, and carried North and West a thousand miles; bells sobbed; cities wore crepe; people stood with hats off as the railroad burial car came past at midnight, dawn or noon.

That awful moment was painfully alive for me as I stood in that box.

And then we went across the street to the little house where Lincoln lay on a simple bed and died. At the same joint session of Congress, Sandburg, then 81 years of age, commemorated the 150th anniversary of Lincoln's birthday. The power of his words then are forever lasting.

> *Not often in the story of mankind does a man arrive on earth who is as hard as a rock and soft as drifting fog, who holds in his head and mind the paradox of terrible storm and peace unspeakable and perfect.*

I suppose as Sandburg never got Lincoln out of his soul, so will I never really be rid of Sandburg. Of course the fascinated PDs could not quite figure out why I stood in front of President Lincoln's box for so long—totally mesmerized, in a world of my own. Washington affected us all differently. But we were all affected forever.

We were on a constant high from morning till night. I don't remember nap times but there surely were some. Dormitory life all over again, and young again! All we needed were the beer jackets and Tommy Dorsey records. But Dorsey is gone, long gone.

I think it is worthwhile to note that as we head full bore into the nineties this same little group of PDs survives. We are still here and in reasonably good health. We do not all live in the same city, which sometimes results in enormous long distance phone bills. We still occasionally get together and have long conversations "over lunch" which invariably end in an explosion of nostalgia.

Surprisingly, we always get around to talking about "the boys." Hah. Some still argue over who took whom to what dance and what they wore. At least three of us had dates with Kurt Vonnegut (I didn't. He was too tall. I was too short!) There are pictures in our scrap books to settle any controversy. To this day Kurt keeps amazing track of all of us.

Sadly, some of us had reversals in our lives; financial, emotional, and personal losses. Some of us have found that as wonderful and as educated and qualified as we all thought we were, we are no longer sought after as we once were. And when forced to find employment, we are not even wanted. We are perhaps only still beautiful to each other! It is still an unwritten rule that our parents established for us as teen-aged high school girls: we stay on track and try to do our best, respect the rules and respect each other. This helps us as we approach senility! Our network is our life line.

Note: Barbara Laird passed away January 9, 1992. Not the first to break our chain, but the first to "walk into the sunset."

In 1978 my mother died, and Kurt send a comforting and solicitous note.

THE WEDDING

Dearest Mary Jane:

Gee, I really pity you, losing a darling mother like that. And yes—I'll tell Jane, and she'll be so sorry, too.

When I think back to the Great Depression, I remember the gloomy satisfaction the Indianapolis Germans took in the collapse of the world. And I remember how startling and nourishing it was to talk to your mother, who found life so amusing, and who was sure intelligent women in that city in those days were as rare as lighthouses in McMurdo Sound.

That was rude of me not to tell you that my trip to Maxinkuckee was off. You were so generously responsive when I told you I was going there. I chickened out. Mary Jo's son-in-law told me I was right not to go, that all the outboards would have broken my heart.

Much love, as always, to you and Skip, the only real pals I've got out there.

Kurt

Kurt came into town in the 1980s. I took him and his daughter, five-year-old Lily to see the Children's Museum. She joined other kids in climbing all over a big black marble cat that was near the main entrance, establishing instant friendship with her fellow climbers. I pointed to an area a little to the north of the big entryway, called the Allen Clowes Garden Gallery. This nice area contained a bridge, a pond, animals and fish that are indigenous to Indiana. Across the walkway was a huge dinosaur the size of a boxcar. What a place for kids to wander!

"I think it is so neat," Kurt mused half aloud, "that the Clowes family has given so much to Indianapolis when they were not from here." He was referring to the fact Dr. G.H.A. Clowes was called from Canada to Indianapolis by Eli Lilly and Company. Dr. Clowes had researched insulin, and Eli Lilly and Company became the major drug firm that produced this life-saver for diabetics. The company's marketing of insulin provided a bonanza for the city and state, because the name Clowes (pronounced "Clews") became synonymous with philanthropy—the arts and theatre and symphony and colleges and schools and churches have all reaped the rewards of Clowes generosity. And Clowes, and the Lilly family and Foundation prove again what I said early in this book—that "society" at its best meant people who have received well and generously given back, building their community.

Kurt knew what that was all about, and I think it was swell of him to put that little thought out into the group around the Children's Museum.

Then there was Kurt's sixtieth birthday party in 1983. By this time Jane and Kurt were no longer married, and the Big Apple was home to Kurt and new wife Jill Krementz. Jill spent a year preparing for a totally wonderful party at Michael's Pub in New York. She had a book created and bound in red, with messages from all of his friends everywhere.

We all gathered, hoping that Kurt would be surprised. As we mingled before the "grand entrance," I noticed the variety of people at the party—all the Vonnegut relatives who were able to come, including brother Bernard, Kurt's wonderful best friend from the war Bernard O'Hare (of *Slaughterhouse Five* fame), bound to Kurt through all the suffering they endured, and famous friends, too.

Before THE APPEARANCE Kitty Carlisle Hart, who is as charming and smart as she appears on TV, Norman Mailer and his wife Norris, Gary Trudeau, John Updike and Martha, Kevin McCarthy and Marsha Mason from the play and others—all of these mingled with the assorted Adams and Vonnegut children, waiting.

Jill, with her shining black hair and Oscar de la Renta black silk short dress, shone with joy as Kurt finally made his grand entrance—Surprise! We were proud of ourselves for not spilling the beans. Though Kurt looked handsome and gracious in his tux, and though the whole party was spectacular and filled with memorable people, there was above all a warm, family feeling to the event.

The next day family and close friends gathered at the Vonnegut's four-story Brownstone for juice, coffee, and rolls. Vonnegut children and all the other children, spilled out of the house and into the courtyard in back. Our hearts were very full when we boarded our plane for Indianapolis. I was glad Kurt was living in New York City, which he called Skyscraper National Park.

And so, on to the Class Reunion (1940–1990). Fifty years!

My phone rang, first thing in the morning, June, 1990. It was a beautiful, sweet-smelling, budding, seventy-five degree, perfect summer morning.

"Hello?"

"Majie, this is Kurt Vonnegut." Sounding serious.

"Good morning, Kurt Vonnegut," I cooed, counting the roses that had bloomed overnight.

THE WEDDING

"I'm not coming."

"What do you mean not coming? I was just putting rose buds in your room."

"No, no, I can't come. I'm sick as hell."

"Kurt, you're kidding me. This is a joke." This was no joke. I listened. I wilted. Kurt was ill, pumped full of antibiotics—the first person we knew to be victimized by the stupid little black tick that carried Lyme Disease. This was no TV commercial.

Kurt, who spends his summers in the Hamptons, Long Island, is an accomplished gardener. He has a knack for placing pots of impatiens around his patio better than anyone else. He is so practical that he plants daisies, snapdragons and phlox on one side of a picket fence, and vegetables on the other. His yard is beautifully lush and green. Apparently, as he was leaning over in his garden, a tiny black tick found its way onto his back. Named for Lyme, Connecticut, this disease descended on Kurt via some little bug carried by deer and mice. It knocked him flat. Large doses of antibiotics are the only solution for this devilish ailment and without that medication, a person's entire nervous system can collapse.

And so, it was no joke. A little red circle with a dot in the middle was the culprit's telltale sign.

Our friend, our buddy, could not make it back for our 50th Shortridge High School Reunion. We had a special table arranged with his friends. He was going to speak, because he was famous now, the author of *Slaughterhouse Five, God Bless You, Mr. Rosewater,* and recently *Hocus Pocus* and *Fates Worse Than Death.*

We had even been able to put a lid on interviews and talk shows, so we could be normal old friends together. Very kindly, the press promised not to swoop down like vultures. Kurt had said, "This is my high school reunion and I want to see everybody and we are going to have fun." He was excited. We were all excited . . . But now, we were all sick for Kurt. This great time in our lives bombed out because of a terrible little black bug. It was as if a school bell rang out through the halls and collected us all in a common bond of disappointment and feeling for our classmate.

We had wonderful people in our class, successful and talented. Kurt, of course, was deservedly the most famous and we are all very proud of him. Moreover, he has been a spokesman for most of our children, who think he is especially cool!

Kurt was to be the program on Saturday. We'd proceeded without him, assembling in Caleb Mills Hall, where we had all sat so long ago listening to Mr. Hadley talk of high achievement and endless opportunity and pride in your work. Caleb Mills was a man who said, "A disciplined mind and a cultivated heart are elements of power." Good thoughts! He also was the first professor at Wabash College and the founder of the public schools in Indiana. We proceeded on in our own way with the program, revised to fit the new circumstances.

Our classmate and M.C., Victor Jose, wrote to Kurt after the reunion, "I'm sure all of us wish we could bottle up some of the atmosphere and excitement and emotion we all experienced." And added, "Almost a rebirth or re-creation of earlier life." Well said. That was accurate and true in my case. Well, there are other schools in the world but none exactly like Shortridge High School. It has been said by countless others.

It was good that high school was so wonderful and it was good that many of us did not know that our "last convertible" ride would be in that June of 1940. Some of our goodbyes were goodbyes forever.

In that far-away time, how would Kurt have known that in just a few short years he would leave Cornell University and become a private, first-class, with the 106th Infantry and spend time in a boxcar and be tortured by Nazi soldiers? And would he have ever imagined the beautiful city of Dresden being bombed by a firestorm?

Or how would I envision that I'd hear about President F.D. Roosevelt's sudden death, while I was sitting in a reporting class?

That reunion day just reaffirmed what I already knew. My high school days, the high school days of that entire generation had truly been happy days.

Still, we had muddled through in a pretty impressive and reassuring way. Possibly it was because we emphasized the simple, accentuated the positive, as Johnny Mercer used to sing. We did not grow up thinking about F.D.R. Our parents reminisced about boring things like the WPA and soup kitchens, but we dreamed of that sweet music of Glen Miller and dancing and dates and about being popular. How many dates and how many dances!

Could life have been any better or simpler then? Shortridge High School stood for excellence and boundless opportunity in an America where the dream was still fresh. It had a wonderful faculty that everyone respected and as a rule it was backed by caring parents who knew what was going on. We all lived in friendly neighborhoods, and we walked to school if possible and walked home. No bussing was needed. Parents drove from distances too far to walk. We had sidewalks for walking and our parents didn't spend endless hours in the car hyping us up with too many activities. When we were off the track, they told us so. And we listened.

We went where our interests took us with a few forced things like dancing school and music lessons and the orthodontist. We all knew everyone. And after dates (or for dinner or lunches) a nice man named Walter Eaton offered the best restaurant on the Northside. He also knew where most of the kids were, who their parents were, and where they were going.

Life was sweet and uncomplicated. We felt solid and secure in these days before STDs and AIDS and experimenting with drugs. If things were not great at home, tomorrow was another day at school and usually that was good. We did what our parents wanted us to do and we didn't talk back. I think the word was respect. There were none of today's hostilities. There was affluence but there was not the worship of money that we see today, the oceans of fancy, expensive cars we see in high school parking lots, the "Shop till you drop" obsession in shopping malls. After all, our parents were just coming out from under the terrible blow of the Great Depression. We were taught to be frugal and to save—not to spend.

You paid in cash and did not casually pop out a plastic card at the drop of a hat. Needs were distinguished from wants. Rich kids and poor kids were friends. There were few blacks, but those who were in school were friends, too, and we did not have the racial problems.

Values . . . yes, there were values and quality. But in people, not in supermarkets. I think we should take a good strong look again at the values of responsibility with money (personal and national), friendship uncomplicated by over-sophistication, parental respect and home entertaining. And time for prayer and reading and communication in the homes, too.

The Class of 1940 went out of the hallowed halls and into the debacle of a long, painfully long, World War II. And so our age group quickly had to give up peace and contentment and adapt to war and then survival. We had to learn to give up . . . period! And try to put something back, too. Add unselfish service to your list of values.

Again, it was good that high school was so wonderful—a lot of the time. But in comparison to life as it was about to become, it was "happy days."

We would see.

And about the most serious thought for the day was the admonition as we left school for vacations:

    1. Read a good book.
    2. Make a new friend.
    3. Do a good deed.

Still good today, and always.

The 1962 wedding of William H.C. Failey and Mary Jane Alford Zaring at St. John's Episcopal Church, a charming little summer church that closes after Labor Day.

How the PD Club had fared in the seventies, after they had found out what life was all about. They are holding a photo from 1938—a vision of their former selves.

Mrs. Farquhar's Kindergarten seventy-odd years later, with spouses. Front row, left to right: Ruth Allison Lilly, Eli Lilly, Nora Taggart Chambers, D. Laurance Chambers, Ina Hollweg Vonnegut, Lydia Latham Breunig; Second row, left to right: Mary Parrott Failey, William G. Sullivan, Anton Vonnegut, Florence Latham, Robert B. Failey, Mary Gladding Johnson, Theresa Pierce Krull; Third row, left to right: Nicholas H. Noyes, Ruth Pratt Bobbs, Marguerite Lilly Noyes, Ruth Carey Haines, Sylvester (Bud) Johnson, Leroy Breunig.

Courtesy of Lilly Archives

Kurt Vonnegut and Skip Failey with the author. The two dune buddies of yore still call each other "sport." Something is funny here.

Kurt after his keynote speech for Wordstruck, a new step in attention to literacy sponsored by the Indiana Council for the Humanities.

In my kitchen, November, 1991. We were always in the kitchen. Kurt has finished Wordstruck and can relax.

Just like Booth Tarkington—a frustrated cartoonist. Pretty good, too!

8

WENDELL CRANE PHILLIPPI

When I discussed *The Indianapolis News*, I left out one of the first-class persons there, especially to me, not only then but as the years rolled along and into this later period in my life. Wendell C. Phillippi was one of those men who had been away in the war and who, as soon as he was home, came straight back to *The News* still wearing his uniform. Wendell came home a hero, with a chest full of decorations and a wealth of dramatic war stories, and he began making a real contribution to *The News* from the moment he arrived.

He had a colorful military career and has, by circumstance and ill fate, been more maligned than any of my newspaper friends. It is important to give Wendell a special focus because he, more than anyone, has lived what I am saying about the Press and the changes it has undergone.

When Wendell came home from the war and came back to *The News*, he was on the State Desk. As Society Editor, I had to be sure that all out-of-town and around-the-state weddings were included on the page. Wendell was often the one who brought the information to me to write for the page. Sometimes we had so many weddings to write that we got plain harassed. On one of those days Wendell came back to the society desk with one too many to write and I refused to accept it. He walked away muttering, "Oh all right, I'll do it myself."

That was the last time that ever happened because, soon after, he moved up to City Desk and he never asked me to write anything again. He *told* me! And up and up he went until he was Managing Editor of *The News*. Of all the staff members that I loved, Wendell is way up there near the top.

When the young, traveled, war-weary vets came back, they were ready for a change in the news format. Dull stories were out. Old "line 'em up and shoot 'em" pictures were out. The page makeup took on a more exciting look, and dull headlines were out, being replaced by bigger, more modern-looking type faces. Relentless, one-column heads disappeared. Wendell played an important part in these changes.

You have to understand just how professional Wendell Phillippi was as a newspaperman, and just how honored he was as he continued his "second" career in the military, to understand just what the media did to him much later, in the case of Vice-President J. Danforth Quayle.

Wendell's wartime service record went something like this. When he went into the Army he served in the U.S. First Infantry, 6th Division. In 1942 he entered Officers Training School. Following graduation, he joined the 36th (Texas) National Guard Division.

He served in campaigns in Italy, France and Germany. Far from being just any draftee, he covered himself with glory. He received the Silver Star, Bronze Stars, and Arrowheads for invasions at Salerno and at Frejus-San Raphael, France. Translated this means seven campaigns and two invasions. You could say Wendell took to the military!

And as if the war wasn't enough, he then joined the Reserves for fifteen years and rose to the rank of Major General in command of the 38th Indiana National Guard Division.

During the Korean War he went on active duty at Fort Benning, Georgia, and in October of 1962 Wendell was in Washington at the Pentagon awaiting activation orders for the 38th Indiana National Guard during the Cuban crisis. Then the Russians backed down in the face of the American blockade and removed the missile sites.

Being a military man did not preclude Wendell Phillippi's being an innovative and productive member of his home community. He stands for so many things that are moral and good and Christian. Wendell was a true newspaper man with the ideals of honest and dedicated journalism. He loved his work and it spilled into his life as an involved, community-conscious man.

Wendell Phillippi exploded into this world on July Fourth, and he has been something of a firecracker ever since. Wendell's homespun humor and practicality speak of a small town childhood. His father was the local funeral director. Before Wendell retired he asked all of his staff members to write their own obituaries. "I thought, if you wanted a decent obituary, you should write it yourself." Good idea! He was especially proud of being the first editor from an Indiana newspaper to be president of the Associated Press Managing Editors Association.

On *The News* Wendell adopted a cartoon figure named Herman Hoglebogle, originally drawn at Broad Ripple High School by Tom Johnson, to dress up photographs and make points for civic improvements. Herman scorned exposed garbage, fell into chuck holes all over town and gave the rather staid old *News* a new crusader, and a safety "caution" light to school children.

While working on the City Desk, Wendell designed the north-south one way street pattern which was eventually adopted by the city. He also pushed for the construction of the Civic Auditorium. And there were many other civic activities and organizations that he either promoted, served, or started. I say he wasn't born, he was fired out of a cannon.

Wendell surely was shot into public prominence in 1988.

Hoosier Dan Quayle had been nominated for the vice-presidency of the United States, unexpectedly, by candidate George Bush. The press, with its usual fanatical "probia" was digging like a bunch of bulldozers into every nook and cranny of Hoosierdom to find dirt. There is no other way to describe the process.

One thing that was questioned over the week or two after Quayle accepted the nomination was his war record. He had been in the National Guard. Some bright reporter decided he was a "draft dodger." The trail eventually led to Wendell Phillippi, who commanded the Guard during the Viet Nam War. Had he "pulled strings" to get Dan Quayle relieved of active duty and into the Guard? Wendell was badgered at home, beseiged for answers, not believed when he gave them, treated rudely in the process and hanged by implication. Many reporters, playing judge and jury, decided that Dan Quayle had done it all—whatever it was that the reporters said, and that Wendell Phillippi was close behind him. Guilty on all counts, though we don't know what they are.

In October, 1982, at an Associated Press Managing Editors meeting, this retired National Guard Major General and former distinguished Managing Editor of *The Indianapolis News*, was allowed to "explain." It was his day to report what happened when Vice President Dan Quayle joined the National Guard. The press pushed it all onto Wendell's plate and made him feel he had a national obligation to explain that he did not pull strings to get Quayle in the National Guard. It also put him on the defensive for the military outfit.

This was less than fair, but Wendell turned the hot seat into a bully pulpit—using the opportunity to sum up all the flaws in the national press that day and, like many other news media pros to whom time has given wisdom and courage and a sense of decency, he gave them a piece of his well seasoned mind.

His speech to the Associated Press Managing Editors clearly describes the fiasco; the excesses and nightmares that I, too, believe are peculiar to the power of the press. So spoke Wendell Crane Phillippi in his own defense against media misdemeanors:

> *For better or worse, my title is "Media Misfire." I am here as a defendant, I guess, after I have been tried in a kangaroo court by some of you in the media. Your attention has been flattering, but not rewarding. I come with some credentials. I served on the Freedom of Information Committee for the APME (Associated Press Managing Editors) before some of you ever got out of college. I was in the trenches fighting for the Freedom of Information Act of 1966. And I have been associated with an AP member paper for more than fifty years . . . all of which goes back to college days when Kent Cooper, the great founder of AP (Associated Press), allowed his university newspaper to belong to the AP.*
>
> *I have also served on ASNE Freedom of Information (FOI) committees and in 1969, the year of Quayle's enlistment, I wrote the following line in my military-FOI report, published in the 1970 yearbook. "It was a year when the American public realized we were in a winless war in Vietnam, despite what our military and civilian leaders had been saying for several years."*
>
> *So I'm no novice in this business. I have been on both sides of the fence in things military and the media.*
>
> *I can tell you one thing: My friends and acquaintances have been having a field day with me, saying: Wendell, you're on the other side of the fence now. You now know how it feels to be belittled, maligned, misquoted and harassed. The barbs are not disguised. Unfortunately many of them are very bitter when they say that. And I'm bitter as I talk about the so-called Quayle-Phillippi enlistment affair. Bitter because I was misquoted around the world from one little reporting, editing mistake and have been called everything from a nuke lover to Danny Boy, squealer,*

turncoat, dirty Democrat and on and on. Our arrogance at times is more glaring from the outside looking in than from the inside looking out.

But I'm an optimist. I don't mind being harassed—I'm one of you, and I'm used to it. Brown County humorist Abe Martin always said, "An optimist is a feller that digs dandelions out of his yard."

It was no secret that I had made a phone call about Quayle's enlistment. My family, friends and business acquaintances knew all about it. I was warned that if I talked, I would be crucified. I did, and I was crucified. I never thought of uttering "No comment."

But imagine my surprise when I learned what a great enterprise had been done when it came out as an exposé . . . It was reported that I made a multitude of calls. I said I made one call to one person. I said Quayle was probably a good man with a college degree. It came out that I highly recommended Quayle for the Guard and intervened and got him a coveted position. I even became a friend of Quayle's family, and then a good friend and then a close personal friend. And then I found out we talked about his chances of going to Vietnam—if the Guard would likely be called up. If so, would he have to go to Vietnam? It was all news to me . . .

The fact is that I am not a friend of the Quayle family. I worked for the Pulliams. [Dan Quayle's uncle]. I resent the closeness charge to people who think socially, politically and economically opposite of me. I want to make sure you understand that I resent guilt by association or have any affinity for the John Birch society.

Interviewers repeated the same questions, worded differently, over and over . . . apparently when answers were uninteresting, a more flamboyant or newsworthy connotation was substituted.

Many of your reporters listened to me and complained: "There's no story here" and then called the office and returned with more questions.

It may come as a surprise to you that I did not have a multitude of friends to contact in the National Guard.

Generals, like editors, pick up a lot of enemies on the way. But I plead guilty to making a call for a multitude of men to join the National Guard because I think it is the greatest backup force *for our regulars in America. I made calls for rich men, poor men, black men and white men. I must confess to you that, over the years, I also got calls wanting to know how you could "get out of this chicken shit-outfit."*

To tell you the truth, Dan Quayle probably had a greater risk of seeing combat with an Indiana National Guard unit in 1969 than Ronald Reagan did as a producer-captain in the Army Air Force in World War II while he was making training films in Hollywood because General Westmoreland wanted the entire National Guard of America mobilized in the Vietnam War."

*   *   *   *

I have always followed three rules on accuracy:
First, be accurate.
Second, be accurate.
Third, if you can't be accurate, be consistent. Well, by God, you followed my third rule and you were consistently inaccurate.

*   *   *   *

The great Associated Press chain of accuracy broke on August 18, 1988. AP picked up a member paper's story that said I made a "multitude of calls for Senator Quayle." That member paper called me four times and I said I made one call to one person but over the years had made a multitude of calls for other people. The AP reporter later confirmed to me that I told him one call to one person.

Reporters demanded over and over to know the name of the person I called. I refused because I wanted to make sure my memory was correct. Actually he was in Canada fishing, and I could not contact him, but a reporter did by using the false ploy by radio that there was a family emergency. He went by boat to the mainland—frightened—and returned the radio call. Is that kind of subterfuge professional?

When I learned a few hours later that I was being misquoted, I immediately called long distance to ask for corrections from the AP and others. The AP correction had an error in it when it said I called Guard officials. I also found out for the first time that I had highly recommended Quayle for a Guard slot. I complained about the correction without results. Finally, two weeks later, I got a, quote, "clarification" in my own newspaper on the front page. The publisher in a letter on September 7th called it a correction. Three weeks later AP made a second correction but omitted one story I had mentioned which moved out of Washington the day following the correction and still contained the error of "calls." Some of you wrote your own stories from wire services—how could I correct that? There is something flawed in our correction systems.

I wonder how many of your libraries have a correction flagged on the stories in your files? I never saw the AP correction in print.

· One error or lie, repeated over and over, as Senator Joe McCarthy found out in the 1950s, can come to be accepted as the truth.

Mike Davies, one of our past presidents, did call me to get the facts straight and my side of the story. He pointed out that even after the correction, his paper was using calls instead of one call to one person.

I have clippings from front page stories and editorials from all over the nation saying I made calls. There was no way of stopping the flood. If I had it to do over again, I would spend more of my time talking to television and radio. While they can cut you off, they can't change your words.

* * * *

The media left me with the opinion that they did not give a damn if the National Guard survived or not.

You refused to use my small, four-graph statement pointing out the role of the Guard militia in our history and citing the 38th Division's near call-up in 1962 during the Cuban crisis.

* * * *

Humor was a little hard to come by during the Quayle brouhaha. . . . We did not laugh when a reporter asked my wife, Barbara, how much money I got for getting Quayle into the Guard.

I was not amused by all of the page one headlines indicating I had done something unethical, if not illegal, day after day.

After so long though, I was beginning to feel as though I had done something wrong. Especially when I picked up a paper after I had thought the fiasco was about to die down, only to read: "Adding fuel to the fire was the admission (you might as well read that confession) by a former executive of The Indianapolis News which is owned by Quayle's relatives, that he had recommended Quayle be recruited into the Guard.

*   *   *   *

I kept my sanity by remembering what Abe Martin said: "Laugh an' the world laughs with you, weep an' it keeps on laughin'!"

*   *   *   *

The media does invade privacy. When the phone rings every fifteen seconds after the previous call, there isn't much time for the luxuries of life—such as eating, drinking, and sleeping. I am happy to announce that I did not get any calls on the night of August 18–19 from 1:00 a.m. to 3:00 a.m.

Your buzzsaw reporting did raise these questions: How much are editors responsible for the "pushiness" of their reporters? Are reporters afraid for their jobs if they don't get the story you want?

*   *   *   *

Do the media have any built-in restraints when they explode into a private citizen's life?

Can facts be ascertained with one question rather than the same question worded differently ten times in hopes of a change or slip of the tongue?

*   *   *   *

Ours is an honorable profession. Please keep it that way . . . and fight for freedom with fairness every day. But exaggeration is not playing in Peoria today, folks. Let's not follow the pattern of the National Enquirer, Pat Robertson or the European rags. Instill in your editors and reporters a new sense of decency and common courtesy which many of them do not have in the pursuit of a Pulitzer Prize.

When you go home will you make sure your library correction system says I made one call to one person for J. Danforth Quayle?

And when I go to the great beyond, just remember an old friend of mine on The New York Times wrote in jest the lead of my obit many years ago. It reads: "The general, who grew beautiful peace roses, died today." Please don't make it read: "The general, *who made the telephone call to get Vice President Dan Quayle into the National Guard, died today."*

* * * *

I hope you have learned two lessons from my experience: Remember, a story you pick up may have been wrong to begin with so double, triple check.

And remind yourself every day that the correction may never catch up with the first day's headline error—so be careful.

Hugh Sidney in 1987 gave us a challenge when he wrote: "Journalists were originally created to enlighten, not to threaten, to inform, not to perform, to know, not to show."

Wendell's case is only one example of trashing by implication, of journalism by innuendo and falsehood. The Thomas/Hill hearings in the autumn of 1991 was another example of "dirt dishing." The senators insulted the U.S. by "trashing" the facts and by making the allegations pure sleaze.

It is the height of irony that Wendell Phillippi, an excellent newspaperman in a variety of top capacities, who took *The Indianapolis News* through several years of highly ethical journalism, should be the victim of sleazy, irresponsible journalism at the national level.

On the other hand, his experience with the press was a perfect vehicle to force the media to take a closer look at its purposes, practices and assumptions. In a way, typical of Wendell, he was very efficient. If he had been able to choose his cross of controversy, he couldn't have chosen a more likely one to open up some useful dialogue about the two establishments closest to his heart. A little housecleaning, you might say.

When Wendell returned from World War II, you could say he never took his uniform off. Wendell's editorial room style was crisp, explosive, bossy at times, but above all, he was fair and a stickler for accuracy—a militaristic journalist.

His neighbors, who knew and loved him, always chuckled at the way he walked and talked and thought the military. He took our ribbing gracefully and always brought us roses from his garden.

Recently General Phillippi had a license plate made that has PURPLE HEART with the emblem on it. He is pleased to advise that, while traveling, it gives him great pleasure to be saluted by passing military motorists, past, present and future! And I salute you, Wendell, for your courage and honesty.

Anyone who was in World War II will be glad to know that "This General" has a fine book, *Dear Ike*, to his credit. It is his own account, as seen through the eyes of a combat soldier, of the historic land battles in North Africa and Europe.

"General Phillippi's book is must reading for all those 'dogfaces' who struggled through mud, rain and snow and incurred enemy fire and land mines all across Europe, but who were never exposed to a grand strategy except taking the next bunker, hill or town." (Indiana Adjutant General Alfred H. Ahner. *The Indianapolis News*, October 22, 1991.) Therein lies the tragedy and the truth of that war.

Wendell C. Phillippi today. Managing Editor of *The News* for many years, author of a World War II book *Dear Ike*, and General Phillippi till "Death do Us part."

9

WAR AND OTHER LATE NIGHT MUSINGS

It is two-thirty in the morning and I am acutely aware of snoring which gets louder from two-thirty to four-thirty. That is precisely the time of day that I get very articulate, and the words in my vocabulary bank flow freely and easily. At ten-thirty in the morning my mind is blank, and I can't even think of a synonym for tired. This gives me only two hours a day for heavy creativity—and they are in the dark.

That means that I have to give up my warm bed and move all the pillows that support the various aching joints (aging is for the Japanese, they revere it!) and force my feet to the floor and point them in the direction of the room with the typewriter. For this prolific time of the wee, small hours I am grateful. It is very quiet. I can think. I can write now.

When I sit down to write, it is as if the shadows of all the great writers I have been privileged to know are behind my typewriter. Never far from my mind is Carl Sandburg, and the inspiration he gave me personally, and the nation in general. Also in my mind are those excellent craftsmen and artists in the newspaper world at *The News*, where I learned not only to put together a story, but also to become a member of the human race. You have to earn the right to be a team player on a newspaper staff, and in the case of *The News* in those days, it was because you upheld standards, perhaps more unstated than stated, more than anything else.

Typesetting ink must be indelible for life. If it isn't, why do you suppose this one-time Society Editor turns to the Woman's Page as soon as she picks up the paper, before even turning back to the front page to read about the President having Thanksgiving dinner in the desert with troops at war?

When Desert Storm was in progress, in full fire, we were totally consumed by journalists and reporters' views of reality. Flags were waving! Kuwait had to be saved. Bombs were arcing to earth as we were at the dinner table, shuddering—and asking people to pass the butter.

I, like most others, didn't think we would actually be in a war. We totally mishandled the war in Vietnam, and we treated our men like lepers when they returned, having really won nothing in a war that was not our war in the first place. There were not many military names that I remember from that foray.

I had a son-in-law in the Vietnam war, and he was blown off his ship by a gun turret explosion that killed three of his comrades before his eyes. That is now and forever a bad dream, along with hearing and sight defects that cannot be repaired! He got no hero's welcome when he returned home. Oddly, I cannot remember the press coverage of the war, except that it brought the killing and horror into our living rooms. Some of it was of the old mold—to tell the story straight and leave opinion and coloration out. But too much was politically motivated and distorted, and this was the beginning of "probia," the political cast to writing we see in coverage of wars today.

Newsweek reported a quip from a student at Oklahoma University early in the Persian Gulf war that pretty well wrapped up the whole story. "I'm gonna pop some popcorn and watch the war." We didn't even go to the grocery store we were so mesmerized by the conflict. We were like a bunch of dolphins at Sea World being fed fish.

The American people, though, do want heroes, and they got them in the Gulf War. In that swift, intense campaign, General Norman Swartzkopf became a symbol of American strength and toughness that no one would care to tangle with, a symbol of the general and all soldiers too. He had confidence in what he was doing, and he was compassionate toward his soldiers of all colors, all creeds. He made us feel protected and safe.

The media cultivated that picture, but it was a picture of what we wanted and what was pretty. The way that TV tells world news is highly personal, with people staring out telling us face to face what we should think. In this way, it is much more pleasing than the impersonal newspaper accounting of the same news. We have to applaud the coverage because it is so interesting—and so far away. Keep it far from our living rooms. War is war, and war is hell and we don't want any of it. We don't want our fathers, sons and grandsons going into it—and wait a minute, now it's daughters too.

In spite of the high-interest reporting, I don't ever remember the press being so maligned and so criticized for reporting and mis-reporting as they were during this short war. Taken as a whole, those criticisms were justified, it seems to me. There was no reason for the press to spend so much time repeating the same news releases over and over. Then there was so much inaccurate reporting. We were listening to the war stories and we were being fed the wrong facts and the enemy was privy to all of it on CNN. What really was the war? What we seemed to see was the greatest fiction since Peyton Place. The press in some ways fought that war, both TV and print news journalists.

I kept asking myself what Sandburg would have done if he had been a writer covering the Gulf War. What would Kurt Vonnegut have written if he had had a correspondent's assignment? Or Fremont Power or Herb Kenney? Reportorial quality has changed.

New technologies have come, of course. The old hunt and peck system, well known to editorial writers ... who needs it? Word processors and screens and automatic corrections have made obsolete the old craft of the black pencil, the jar of glue and stack of tan newswriter's paper. And newspapers have to respond to the "news magazine" format—TV has forced them to do investigative journalism, to feature glitzy people and to tell what they have to say in short style. "Entertainment and lifestyle" are the big emphases in a fast-moving, buy-it-all culture.

Still, there will always be a newspaper. Eugene S. Pulliam, publisher of *The News* and *The Star,* recently defined his own view of the place of print journalism in the twenty-first century in an article for *The News.*

"The printed word is here to stay," Mr. Pulliam said. He sees more visual interest in newspapers of the future, and an emphasis on local news.

Newspapers, Mr. Pulliam said, have a special mission for the public interest. "I think newspapers will continue to be the only sizeable check on government," he said. He saw a better educated public, more in-depth stories and the chance for good investigative reporting. Newspaper journalism isn't now dead, nor will it be!

Perhaps in the future there will be higher quality investigative reporting, as Mr. Pulliam says, but from what I see now, there is still a long way to go. Today there is less space for quality journalism, more newsmongering and, to my mind, fewer ethics.

So let me answer the question: what would the great writers I've talked about in this book be doing if they were reporters today? They'd be doing what they've always done as writers—telling the truth. Here is some advice I think reporters today should look at today, based on the writing of the "greats" of the heyday.

1. Tell the truth and not your own opinion. Don't grind political axes. Don't backscratch. Let the editorial page give us opinion designed to shape our thinking. Don't compromise when the truth needs to be said no matter whom it offends, be it the juvenile center abuses or the need for one-way streets or who called whom about the National Guard.

2. Stop digging dirt just to "get the story." Dan Quayle and Wendell Phillippi became the story themselves, their honest denials merely adding flame to the fires of cynical, story-crazy reporters. If you want to dig dirt, go get a bulldozer driver's job. It pays $45 an hour. (My God, that is my entire week's salary on *The News* in 1945!)

3. Give us good, positive reports about people who are succeeding, stories about the human heart, the greatness and sometimes sad times of the human spirit. Uplift us a little, raise our spirits, make our day. Choose interesting material, not political intrigue and slime and deviation.

Yes, there are good stories written, but they do not get chosen by news editors. Some of the best stories, the human interest ones, get chucked into the wastebasket, or in our day and age, not picked up from the computer printouts—passed over so we can read about every detail in the lives of Donald Trump and Mike Tyson.

The man who decides what comes off the wire services (or computer banks) is a man of great power, and thus was it ever so. At the birth of the Dionne quintuplets in the early thirties, the Wire Editor at *The News* took the story off the wire, shrugged his shoulders and gave it two paragraphs on a back page. Not interested. The other papers grabbed it and put it on the front page. A first in history! The Wire Editor, dumb cluck, did not think this was news, explaining lamely to his boss that the story was in the circular file. "Well, get it the hell out of there and put it on the front of

Section Two." Too late. The other papers got the first break, and the people who read *The News* that day missed a darn good story.

4. Don't overlook humor. We all need a laugh now and then. There was a very funny story that didn't get any further than the east coast. It is about a senior citizen who was driving around a shopping mall parking lot in the pouring rain in her Mercedes trying to find a parking place. After driving around for some time she spotted a slot and headed for it. As she did this a young man in a Porsche pulled right in front of her and took the parking place. He jumped out of the car, waved to her and said, "That's what happens when you're young and agile, lady."

He walked on and the lady stepped on the gas and ploughed right into the back of the little sports car. As he ran toward his car, the lady called to him out of her window, "And that's what happens when you are old and rich!!!"

I ask you, would anyone with a sense of humor pitch a story like that?

5. Most of all, help us learn about the other people on this planet we share. Give us stories about people. Mass media can have a tremendous role in uniting us as people on one planet, in helping us know what being human is about.

Listen:

> *The people is Every man, everybody.*
> *Everybody is you and me and all the others.*
> *What everybody says is what we all say*
> *And what is it we say?...*
> *Listen. . . .* from *The People, Yes.*

In 1989 the whole world belonged to little Jessica, who fell into the well. The whole world became brothers when the whales got trapped. We all cried when the third whale was lost. And the whole world raged over the oil spill in Alaska. These stories got more coverage than politics and crime for just a day or a week. They belonged in our hearts. We cared about the urgency of the crises as though we were the principles.

And then Ryan White's story came to grab us all once more. We followed his troubles after catching AIDS from a blood transfusion, in being denied school in Kokomo through fear and ignorance, in transferring to Cicero, where he was accepted. We admired him as he became the number-one spokesman for AIDS while still fighting the disease.

Riley Hospital for children at Indiana University was plugged into Ryan's plight, for that is where he spent his last illness. Bill Shaw, a correspondent for *People Magazine* wrote a most moving story.

We all kept a vigil, all the world over—while he lay dying. He was a valiant little prince. When Ryan White did succumb to AIDS, he brought out the very best in the whole country. He taught such a lesson to us all, and the biggest celebrities joined hands with the richest and the poorest in a grief that was almost inconsolable. This boy brought out the best and the "real" in everyone, commendably in this instance. Grief can reduce one to bare-bone, gut-felt reaction. And the reaction was good, done in love.

Love helps us bear grief, and the media was genuine in portraying all of this through real tears. We should always revere the lesson Ryan White taught us about tolerance and prejudice and ignorance. All of us. Forgive us our press passes if anyone ever forgets this saintly youth who was just trying to be a normal kid.

Why are people so bigoted that they would torture a sick kid by ostracizing him—and later, worst of all, desecrate his grave? It could only be ignorance, and reading these stories taught us all, all over America, that we should not let Ryan's tragedy be repeated.

The Reverend Bud Probasco presided at the funeral. "Ryan had been called for a purpose," he said, then went on, "I think God is communicating to us through Ryan to give us understanding and compassion and empathy. He has changed the way the world views people with AIDS." And his mother, Jeanne, just before he died, said, "You're gonna do good for everybody who is sick. It's a shame it has to be you." Elton John, who sang at Ryan's funeral, had said of Ryan's family, "They inspire me, they uplift me. They've given me more than I could ever return. Such strength and courage, such dignity and such decency."

The world ached. The whole country mourned. Every person turning on the TV had something every hour about Ryan White.

As happens, of course, we go on after the big hurt begins to subside. I still think, though, that we go on as better people.

6. Eliminate vendetta journalism, made of political innuendo, dirt-dealing and name-calling. In the fall of 1990 I turned to the Phil Donahue Show during a Dan Quayle segment. I watched, appalled as the Vice President of the United States was mocked, shown in a made-to-order press version which attempted to paint him as a master of malapropisms, fumbles and clutzy comments. It didn't work. Dan Quayle came off looking clean-cut, handsome and normal in spite of the job some reporters who probably have crooked teeth and halitosis tried to do on him. As a former member of

the working press, I resent the attitude that makes ridicule a writing tool, and put-downs a habit. To all those who brand George Bush a "wimp" and wrap up thirty years of public service in one phrase, I say, "Take a hike." To all who capsulize Dan Quayle's whole career with a story on how he is a "nerd," I say, "Take thirty." The years of these men have done us proud and restored our credibility. We thank them for that.

7. If, indeed, journalism is a craft, then I plead for better apprentices and more discipline and polishing of the art of wordsmanship. Just as we were proud in Indiana that we had a Booth Tarkington and a Meredith Nicholson, today we can be even prouder that we have a Kurt Vonnegut. Stories of Kurt's like *Slaughterhouse Five* and *Galapagos* have placed him, rightly, among a handful of America's top writers for perception, prophetic vision and handling of the English language.

Kurt, you are a member of the "Fireborn" club. It takes a lifetime to qualify for membership and you have passed.

> *Luck is a star*
> *Money is a plaything.*
> *Time is a story teller.*
> *The sky goes high, big.*
> *The sky goes wide and blue.*
> *And the fireborn—they go far—*
> *Being at home in the fire.*
>
> Carl Sandburg

Although Kurt suffered mightily from his ordeal as a prisoner of war, he never asked for special treatment, and that is one of the reasons he is one of my heroes. Instead of allowing his ordeal to destroy his life, he chuckled over the fact that he lived!

Kurt Vonnegut today is a storehouse of outrageous humor for the young and for those no longer so young. As this is written, he is challenging the president of Indiana University, Purdue University, Indianapolis to produce a better name than IUPUI. He suggests Hoagy Carmichael University!

The young might not know that Kurt has taken more than one man's share of tragedy and trauma and turned it into the most delicious repast of the printed word. His long, lanky frame houses what he has always had, a lot of Good Stuff.

Kurt is also a hero because, though he never aired it, he was obliged to go above and beyond the call of duty as a person—as a son, a father and as a brother. While suffering sharp hunger pains, he endured yet another tragedy that called for as much strength as trying to outwit the Germans. His second challenge came when he was a young writer, trying to make ends meet while writing, by being a volunteer fireman, by selling Saab automobiles and teaching and doing anything else to help provide for two little girls and a son. A storm was brewing. The storm that blew trauma and heartbreak into this family of five, with his wife having to bear the brunt, was bringing his four orphaned nephews into their family. Alice, Kurt's beautiful sister, died of cancer, leaving four young sons, one barely toddling. The day before her death, her husband, Jim, was killed in a train wreck. The commuter train he was riding jumped the tracks over an open drawbridge and went into the Newark River, killing everyone on board. He was on his way to see Alice in the hospital. Kurt reached her side and realized that his sister knew about the accident, quite by accident. She whispered her last request to him, "Please keep the boys together."

So Jane and Kurt did just that, except for the youngest, who was to fill a giant gaping hole in the lives of childless cousins who wanted, above all else, to take him and raise him as their own, and who were stable and financially able. Although it was a hard wrench and broke a promise, it was best . . . and so home at the Vonneguts was a family of six children and a kettle of fish that was to simmer for years on a very hot stove.

I would dedicate everything I ever write to Jane and Kurt for having no choice in a matter that would affect eight lives forever and would test every vestige of their endurance. It was way beyond the meaning of fair that Jane, too, lost her life to cancer, just as it seemed the battle of the children was won. However, she left her legacy by writing her story just before she died.

Angels Without Wings is a story of valor and triumph. Who knows who won or who lost or if they did? Kurt was a gentlemen who kept his word to his sister and who fought the wages of the Vietnam war through these children. And Jane was Lady Jane who tried her best to keep drugs and mayhem out of their lives. There were losses and there were gains. The end result is that six adults are alive and well, having survived their own private wars.

Kurt continues to write, superbly, for the good of us all, and he continues to enrich the lives of his old crowd from Indianapolis with genuine friendship, even though it has been a few years since he was pushed into his locker at Shortridge High School by the football heroes. It's been a while!

Times change, certainly they do.

We are on a space ship headed for the year 2000. We are on interstate 1990s, driving way over the speed limit, hell-bent on finding the Exit 2000. We are half scared of where that road leads and half exhilarated over where we think we know it leads, and wondering if we can do anything about any of it. All of us are choking on the fumes from the heavy traffic, as cars push us out of the passing lane so they can go faster. My son the farmer has shown me the idea of a really clean earth. His love of rolling fields, his fight to keep the countryside clean have taught me, too.

We reach for a drink of water, knowing that we are wallowing in a luxury that is an endangered resource. We can't see the mountains for the smog from our cities. We call it "freeway" pollution. Everybody is coughing, wheezing, whining, complaining, rushing, angry and hostile. Those who aren't angry are trying to keep their personal oasis safe and a secret from the madding crowd. They say on the highway one must be a defensive driver. They also say in New York City you have to be a belligerent driver. *I hate that!*

I would rather think of walking up that long hill in the Blue Ridge Mountains in Flat Rock, North Carolina, to a place called Connemara Farm. My trips back to Connemara, both in reality and in dreams, have been the balm and serenity which bring the chaotic present into some sort of perspective. Each of us, I know, has his Connemara, his spiritual oasis. It just seems harder to find it, to find time to get to it.

Our children have children and they are way ahead of their grandparents in the high tech world. Kids in kindergarten are using computers. My granddaughter has taken her word processor to Indiana University. I didn't even own a typewriter my freshman year.

Those of us in the over-fifty generation are in a bind. Should we throw our hearts over the jump and develop the new technical skills? Learn about their world or ignore it and hope it goes away? No. We will have to learn how to cope as best we can because the world has gone too far and we can't get off until our "stop" is called. And there is so much more coming. A hurricane and a Russian coup in the same twenty-four hours?

As we prepare to enter the future, I think we need to look at values from other days. We need to see what the contributions of the real "first families" of the past brought to our society—not to wallow in mindless nostalgia, but to have a choice, an option, in a world where the values don't seem to be working.

And we need to look at the great prophet-poets of our country, people like Sandburg, who keep asking the same questions we haven't answered, but some day, surely, must answer. What about hunger? What about pain? What about opportunity? What about hope? What about prejudice? What about trees and birds and babies? What about belonging to the Family of Man? Why have terror and crime and drugs and sick humor and deviation become the style and even the norm now?

The box I would most like to see destroyed is the T.V. How often do you consider the amount of grief this four-corner baby is causing us as a world? Do our children need terror and destruction and evil as role models? If I could make any difference at all to my grandchildren's world, I would destroy the violence on the box that is so ubiquitous, so universal, that it can fit in a car or cover the wall.

Frank Lloyd Wright described the "Destruction of the Box," and his description is a related truth, although it is a different kind of box. He meant if you live in a box you are confined by four walls. You can't see out unless you make windows. But if you knock down the walls and open the sides of the box and cut out the corners, you can see the sun and the sky and the earth all around you. In other words, *in the world of the architect, you do away with confinement and open up your vistas with light and sight.* They do this with the use of glass, and I am sure a lot of other ways not known by me, and I believe the media at its best could break down the walls of the world for us all.

If you are a young newspaper writer, reporter or columnist, just remember: Newspapers are not tabloids. Journalism is a craft. Honesty is sometimes painful, but don't compromise. Don't alter the facts. It is hard enough to distinguish fact from fiction.

And especially if you are young, remember this: Some of the best writing came from your grandparents and your parents' colleagues. Remember, too, that there are no age limits for writers. Young, middle age, golden age and old age are all contributors to our culture. And it isn't just in writing—it's in ideals that work in living, day to day.

From now until the year 2000 let there be a return to real reporting and ethics of all sorts. Make journalism a proud word. Keep the dirty newsprint from coming off on our hands and forgive us our press passes!! It's a matter of quality. Let's look for quality journalism, and quality living and a quality earth. Let's clean up our act! The pollution of the mind is related to the pollution of the earth.

Not long ago I came across a poem.

Earth Not All Poetry To One Nine Year Old Girl.

I am the ill Earth.
People have cut down the trees,
which are my lungs.
They have polluted the air,
which is my brain.
They have polluted the streams,
which are my blood vessels.
They have polluted the oceans,
which are the chambers of my heart.
My wrath has gotten gigantic.
My wrath is hurricanes and tornados.
I am the ill Earth.
If people trash me,
I will die, and so will they.
                    Misha Mayr, El Paso

I am so sure that Carl Sandburg would have acknowledged this child's poem that I can imagine him at his desk, reading it and then calling to whoever was nearest to him. "Say, will you look at this, written by a nine-year-old girl who has a feel for what it's all about." He was able to communicate such a deep feeling for God's gifts to man. And here we are blowing it all away.

Indianapolis-born architect Nathaniel Owings, of that great generation that built Indianapolis society in the best terms, made some pertinent observations along these lines.

> *I feel we may have risen to a crest in over-expansion in the industrial revolution, and are going back to a grassroots natural approach.*
>
> *I love the black earth of the Midwest. I got into architecture from Indianapolis. I went to Europe after World War I as a Boy Scout (rising to Eagle Scout soon after) representing Indianapolis, and when I saw those old cathedrals I was so moved I told my mother I was going to become an architect.*

His 1972 book, *The Spaces in Between,* ("It's my biography, really," as he says) speaks of the legacy of architecture.

Our legacy is to have a better place to work, a better place to live. We are supposed to improve conditions where a person lives and works. Our legacy has to be for our grandchildren to have cleaner places to live, get them back to the earth, get them back into their gardens. I hope our profession is concerned with use of land. Everybody can build a building, but we should do it without destroying land, do it so people have better air, more open space, clean water.

God has given us the earth, and the prophets—artists and poets of all ages, colors and creeds—have given us a vision of life. Let's look to them and learn. This plea for the nineties and the twenty-first century comes most vehemently from the mouths of our children, who are not as complacent as we are. As for me, I will listen. God help them and be gracious to them, for it is growing late.

Eugene S. Pulliam of *The Indianapolis News,* who earned the wide respect he has among news people the hard way—as a working print journalist.

Names

There is only one horse on the earth
and his name is All Horses.
There is only one bird in the air
and his name is All Wings.
There is only one fish in the sea
and his name is All Fins.
There is only one man in the world
and his name is All Men.
There is only one woman in the world
and her name is All Women.
There is only one child in the world
and the child's name is All Children.
There is only one Maker in the world
and His children cover the earth
and they are named All God's Children.

Connemara Farm
Flat Rock, N.C.
December 25
1 9 5 3

Carl Sandburg

There is only one grandfather
and his name is All Grandfathers

A Carl Sandburg classic, for all times—with one addition after his visit to us.